HACK'S 191

HACK'S 191

Hack Wilson and His Incredible 1930 Season

BILL CHASTAIN

LYONS PRESS
Guilford, Connecticut
An imprint of Globe Pequot Press

To buy books in quantity for corporate use
or incentives, call **(800) 962-0973**
or e-mail **premiums@GlobePequot.com.**

Lyons Press is an imprint of Globe Pequot Press.

Text design: Sheryl Kober
Layout artist: Justin Marciano
Project editor: Kristen Mellitt

Library of Congress Cataloging-in-Publication Data is available on file.

ISBN 978-0-7627-6963-6

Printed in the United States of America

10 9 8 7 6 5 4 3 2 1

To John Kuenster
Thanks for the beginning.

Contents

FOREWORD

When I think of Chicago, fun comes to mind—great town, great fans. If you are a Cubs fan, you never change. You'll be a Cubs fan for life. That's the case now, and it's been the case for as long as I can remember.

There is no greater city in the United States to be a fan favorite, and Hack Wilson became as big a fan favorite as that city has ever known. After he had 191 RBIs, he owned the city—anybody with 191 RBIs ought to own the city.

A lot of people might think I'm old enough to remember Wilson's playing days—I'm not. I did read some about that historic season, and I heard people talking about it during my playing career and in the days since I quit playing and went on to managing and coaching. I wish I could have seen some of it, because Chicago is particularly fun when you're winning, but I didn't quite get there. Driving in 191 runs—are you kidding me?

I wasn't around for the 1930 season, so Bill Chastain's *Hack's 191* is a great way to go back to the days of Al Capone, Prohibition, the Windy City, Rogers Hornsby, Joe McCarthy, and Hack Wilson himself to find out what happened during that historic year.

Wrigley Field was the perfect setting for Wilson to establish his record. It is baseball heaven, simple as that; that's some ballpark. The place has two different personalities. You can play there on consecutive days and the experience can be like playing in two different parks. When the wind blows in you can't hit a ball out of there. And when the wind blows out, you hit a fly ball that should be an out and the wind will blow the thing into the seats. That's the way the park was. I managed there and I can remember looking out over the center field fence, and I lived there on Waveland Avenue. Every morning I would take a look at which way the flag was blowing, in or out, and that's the way you'd figure out how to play the game that day. You might play the infield in with the wind blowing in during the first inning. You could win or get beat 1–0. Other days you just hope you can keep getting the ball up in the air so you can outscore the other team.

Driving in runs is a big part of playing winning baseball. First thing you need is guys to get on base, and the Cubs had those guys in 1930. Then you need a guy like Wilson, who actually seemed to hit better with runners aboard. A lot of the current baseball experts contend that you either hit or you don't with runners on base. I don't believe that. Great hitters rise to the occasion when the game is on the line. Wilson had to be great to come through in the clutch as much as he did and the players in front of him had to be great, too.

I've always wondered why the RBI record did not receive more attention. Why isn't Wilson's record talked about like the home run record? You could ask a hundred people and only a few might know Hack Wilson had the RBI record. Ask that same group about the home run record and they would all know. That's sad since RBIs are so meaningful; a season where you get 191 RBIs—and in a 154-game season—that's just unheard of. Except it shouldn't be.

Hack Wilson is a tragic figure for the way his career and life ended. But he'll forever remain a baseball icon, and I doubt his record will ever be broken.

—DON ZIMMER, JULY 28, 2010

CHAPTER ONE

Sunny Boy

HACK WILSON STUCK OUT LIKE A PIT BULL IN A POODLE SHOW. Standing 5'6", 195 pounds, this freak of a man wore size 6 shoes and an 18 collar on his shirts. Thick muscles in his shoulders and neck embodied the sweat and toil from his days swinging a hammer in the shipyards and working in various steel mills. Yet tiny hands prevented him from using a regular bat, so the handles he used were quarter-size in diameter. Violent collisions with the baseball often occurred when he whipped his bat through the strike zone.

New York had Babe Ruth. Chicago had Hack Wilson.

Wilson lived large and the city with broad shoulders embraced him. How could Chicago not love Wilson? He stood as an Everyman in a Cubs uniform and someone who, according to Bill Veeck Jr., would give anyone the shirt off his back.

"Literally and figuratively, I saw him do it more than once," said Veeck, whose father Bill Veeck Sr. worked as the Cubs general manager. "He'd wear gaudy shirts and those floral ties—let's call them lurid. And he loved checked suits.

"Hack was a saloon man. It was Prohibition, and they called them speakeasies and other things, but it was all the same. Wherever we went, he'd draw a crowd around him. With Hack, guys would always come up and ask for something to remember him by, and he'd peel off his shirt—for the simple reason he could always put his jacket back on and still feel respectable."

Wielding a bat he called "Big Bertha"—a 40-ounce, thin-handled number with a large barrel—Wilson clubbed his way through the National League in 1929. At the end of the season, he had a .345 batting average, 39 home runs, and 159 RBIs, which were good for a free beer on any barstool in any speakeasy in Chicago. By virtue of Wilson's slugging and that of the others in the lineup, the Cubs waltzed to the World Series, capturing the National League pennant by a 10 1/2-game margin over second-place Pittsburgh. The city of Chicago loved the Cubs and could not get enough of their team.

Few cities in the United States felt the boom of the 1920s like Chicago.

Stock prices soared during the decade. Take the examples of American Can, AT&T, and RCA. In March of 1928, American Can sold for 77, AT&T 179 1/2, and RCA 94 1/2. By September 3, 1929, American Can had risen to 181 7/8, AT&T stood at 335 5/8, and RCA 505.

Such gains empowered a city like Chicago, which thrived as the population center of the Midwest, boasting nearly three million residents. Like other cities in the country, Chicago lived with Prohibition, also known as the Noble Experiment, which followed the ratification of the 18th Amendment on January 16, 1919, and was put into place on January 16, 1920, in response to considerable pressure from the temperance movement. Prohibition banned the sale, manufacture, and transportation of alcohol for consumption. Never did one law get so ignored by the masses. You could outlaw many things and the general population would obey. But where alcohol was concerned, those who liked to drink continued to do so regardless of the law. Quelling the gusto of a thirsty nation by law could only go so far, spawning a public demand for alcohol and places where alcohol could be consumed. Since law prohibited such a practice, businessmen on the other side of the law answered the other half

2

of the basic economic function of supply and demand. Prohibition agents worked for the federal government to try to slow down the supply, raiding distilleries and speakeasies whenever possible, only the battle to be waged was too large. Breweries and distilleries were easy to build and operate underground, and Chicago had more than its share of these illegal operations, which were run by gangsters. None of the gangsters was bigger than Al Capone, who ruled the Chicago roost to make sure Windy City citizens could get a drink.

Capone, though capable of brute force, had risen through the ranks by perfecting the art of the bribe. Capone bribed politicians, judges, police officers, prosecutors, congressmen, and newspapermen to help him amass a fortune estimated to be in excess of $20 million. "Big Bill" Thompson, the mayor of Chicago, won election for his third term in 1927 and had received donations of $250,000 from Capone and his associates. In addition to the money he made from alcohol distribution or service through his many speakeasies, Capone operated brothels and gambling houses. Extorting money from businesses also contributed to his fortune.

Capone became the face of Chicago, and he enjoyed celebrity status in a skewed sort of way. To those in his corner, Capone bravely waged a battle against the federal government while providing a business that answered a public need. Capone himself seemed to buy into that perception, downplaying what he did by saying: "All I ever did was to sell beer and whiskey to our best people."

By the late 1920s, Capone basically controlled the illegal revenue-producing businesses on the West and South Sides of Chicago while George "Bugs" Moran had control of the North Side.

The exploits of Capone and the other players in Chicago's gangster arena were covered by eight different Chicago newspapers, with the daily news followed as religiously as the sports pages, except the reports offered details about federal raids and murdered gangsters rather than game stories and how Joe Smith threw a curveball. Part of the allure came in the detachment of Joe Citizen from the violence, which seemed exclusive only to the participants in gang-land warfare.

Violence among the gangsters had come to be an accepted accompaniment to the Prohibition setting, but on February 14, 1929, the mayhem escalated to a new level with what came to be known as the St. Valentine's Day Massacre. Dressed as police officers, a group of Capone's men made their way through the snow-lined streets of Chicago on a chilly 15-degree morning. Their destination: Bugs Moran's liquor depot, located at the S.M.C. Carting Company on 2122 North Clark Street, about 15 blocks from Wrigley Field.

Moran, a known Cubs fan, had been late to show up that morning at his warehouse and actually arrived to see what he believed was a police raid. Hoping to avoid arrest, Moran fled, thereby dodging his execution. Nobody inside the warehouse had resisted, even though they had the weapons to do so, because they too believed they were being raided. They were lined up, then gunned down, execution-style. By the time a neighbor checked on the noise coming from the building, six men were dead against a wall, while another, who would later die, had crawled away. Capone's alibi had been that he was in Florida at the time.

This episode opened a new chapter of gangland violence in Chicago. Despite the dangers associated with procuring a drink and the fact that by consuming illegal alcohol, those partaking were supporting a vicious gangster like Capone, the drinking continued. A mentality prevailed along the lines of, "somebody else is dealing with the violence, all I want is a drink." After all, prosperity brought rewards.

Hack Wilson could be counted among the thirsty masses. Wilson and his running mate, pitcher Pat Malone, spent considerable time at the speakeasies. Among the clubs they frequented was the Green Mill jazz club on the North Side, run by "Machine Gun" Jack McGurn, who was believed to be Capone's henchman for the St. Valentine's Day Massacre; and they often patronized Capone's Cicero speakeasies.

While the Cubs might not have benefited from the climate of crime and vice, they certainly benefited from the prosperous times and the city's large population. Plenty of people coupled with disposable income equaled the perfect scenario for a Major League team. Getting paying customers to attend a ballgame required only a quality product, which the Cubs were more than willing to put on the field. And the rewards were great.

Over a million and a half Cubs fans pushed through Wrigley Field's turnstiles in 1929 to set a new single-season attendance record for the franchise. By winning the National League pennant, the Cubs achieved unprecedented popularity in the city. Their opponent in the World Series would be the American League champion Philadelphia Athletics.

William Wrigley Jr. owned the Cubs and personified the American dream. A door-to-door soap salesman as a youth, he became a business magnate with few peers holding his wealth.

Part of Wrigley's shtick when selling soap had been giving away chewing gum when customers bought his cleaning product. Finally the thought occurred to him that his customers were buying his soap in order to get the free gum. Once that part of the equation hit home, Wrigley had an epiphany and decided to concentrate on the gum. What money he had put away from selling soap, Wrigley invested in his efforts toward building a chewing gum business. America loved Wrigley's gum and while his customers chewed, the profits mounted. Ultimately, the decision to get into the gum business turned a soap salesman into a tycoon, wealthier than most anybody in the country. To Wrigley's credit, his wealth did not cause him to lose his charm. People gravitated to the outgoing Wrigley, who usually could be found in the bleachers during Cubs games. If the Cubs were playing, Wrigley wasn't at work; he was at the ballpark. He had worked since the age of 10, which prevented him from attending games as a kid, something he had always regretted. Once he owned the team, he began making up for lost time.

Wrigley had many attributes that made him a good owner, but the most attractive of those was the fact that he resisted the temptation to meddle. While he loved his team, he knew that he did not have the necessary qualifications to run the ballclub properly. Players often recalled conversations in which the Cubs owner would tell them that it wasn't his way to tell them how to play the game. But he would offer to assist them if they needed a helping hand. Not only did Wrigley develop personal relationships with most of his players, he paid them better than most owners paid their players, and he would regularly invite them to social functions.

Bill Veeck Sr. became Wrigley's general manager shortly after Wrigley bought the team in 1925. Veeck worked as a Chicago sportswriter at the time and according to legend, Wrigley took note of Veeck's constant criticism of the team. He hired Veeck, telling him that if he had all the answers he should give running the club a shot. Veeck's answers worked pretty well, and the Cubs became contenders. Of course, Wrigley's willingness to open his checkbook helped Veeck obtain many of the players on his wish list, turning the Cubs into a popular and successful franchise. The Cubs became the first National League team to draw a million fans in home attendance when they turned the trick in 1927, and they were able to exceed a million fans in 1928 and 1929 as well.

Aside from having put together a quality product on the field, Wrigley took pains to make sure the fan experience would be of equal quality. Upon taking control of the team, Wrigley targeted the mainstream of society rather than the hard-core baseball crowd that could get a little rough. Initially he sought to improve the physical facilities, coughing up approximately $2.3 million to improve cleanliness, convenience, comfort, and aesthetics at Wrigley Field. In short, he converted a decent facility into a baseball showplace. Wrigley also had the foresight to seek female fans. Sound logic told him many men were not allowed to attend games because they would be leaving their wives at home. "Ladies Day" promotions helped fuel the demand, which, in turn, helped grow the attendance by attracting not only husbands and wives, but also entire families.

The 1929 World Series would be the Cubs' first appearance in the Fall Classic since 1918, and World Series tickets were in great demand among the team's loyal legions of fans. Disposable income had never been higher, the speakeasies swelled, and the good times rolled in Chicago, which had a rollicking feeling like Las Vegas would years later. Prior to the start of the World Series, fans swarmed the Cubs' ticket office hoping to purchase seats. If Wrigley Field's capacity had been tripled, they could easily have sold out. Cubs management had to return over half a million dollars to fans sending in money for tickets.

━━━━

Connie Mack arrived late to Wrigley Field prior to the start of Game 1 of the 1929 World Series between his Philadelphia Athletics and the Cubs. While the World Series reigned as sports' marquee event at the time, the media hype that would engulf sports decades later did not exist. Managers were not forced to attend mandatory press conferences where their decisions and insights could be scrutinized thousands of times during the daily news cycle prior to each World Series game. Managers and players alike had to deal with one creature: the print media. And the sportswriters who fed the beast were a primitive form compared to the probing lot that would evolve decades later. Mack's ploy served him well: show up later than usual and avoid the baseball hacks as well as the countless handshakes and conversations.

Fifteen years had passed since the last time one of Mack's teams played in the World Series. Now 66 years old, Mack had witnessed a great deal since first leading the Athletics to a pennant in 1902. Longevity separated him from other managers, as did the fact that he also owned the team, meaning he did not have to worry about getting fired by an owner who questioned his moves. To most, Mack stands out in history because he managed games while wearing a suit and tie with shirts boasting white starched collars. Sitting stoically on the bench, Mack would always hold a scorecard, which he occasionally brandished to position his outfielders. Mack treated players and umpires respectfully, which contributed to his becoming one of the more beloved figures in baseball.

When Cornelius McGillicuddy's full name could not fit into the limited space of a newspaper box score in 1884, "Connie Mack" became his alias. He had been a catcher with the Pittsburgh Pirates and was considered the National League's outstanding catcher in 1893 when he fractured his ankle during a game. The injury ended Mack's playing career and led to his first job as a manager in 1894 with the Pirates. When the team finished sixth in 1896, Mack was fired.

Mack put together the Athletics in the early days of the American League—formerly known as the Western League—when the upstart league wanted a team in Philadelphia to rival the Phillies. By 1901, he had a club in place known as the "White Elephants" in a sarcastic tribute to surly New York Giants manager John McGraw, who made the comment: "Looks like the American League's got a white elephant on its hands in Philadelphia." Those White Elephants became the Athletics.

Mack's early Athletics teams had been the first true dynasty in Major League history with the likes of Eddie Collins, Frank Baker, Chief Bender, and Jack Coombs in uniform. After the heavily favored Athletics lost the 1914 World Series to the Boston Braves, Mack dismantled the team, and by 1916 the Athletics had declined to the point where they had a record of 36-117. Meanwhile, Babe Ruth and the New York Yankees emerged to dominate the American League, making real the possibility that Mack might never return to the Fall Classic. But there in the fall of 1929, baseball's grand statesman stood perched at the doorstep of the World Series with a legitimate chance to once again rise to the top of the baseball world. In the Cubs, the Mackmen had a formidable obstacle to overcome.

A typical Cubs mauling occurred September 2 during a morning-afternoon doubleheader against the St. Louis Cardinals at Wrigley Field. During the morning contest, the Cubs pounded out 11 runs on 16 hits, and in the afternoon 12 runs on 20 hits. Fueling this potent collection of offensive talent were Wilson, Rogers Hornsby, Kiki Cuyler, and Riggs Stephenson, who were known as Murderer's Row. The nickname Murderer's Row, of course, had already been issued to the 1927 Yankees, but that did not keep the Chicago newspapers from adopting the name for the home team's sluggers. Based on this group's potential to score runs, Mack needed to properly calculate his pitching. According to a report in the *New York Times*, indecision haunted Mack about whom to start in the opening game on October 8. Mack had a highly touted staff that included Lefty Grove, George Earnshaw, and Rube Walker, but Mack threw Howard Ehmke into the mix and narrowed down his choices to Ehmke and Earnshaw. John Kieran of the *New York Times* wrote: "A few minutes before game time Connie Mack was in the Philadelphia clubhouse matching straws and tossing coins to see whether he would pitch Howard Ehmke or George Earnshaw."

Imagine the commotion such a play by the manager would cause with today's media. Ehmke ended up being the choice, which caught everyone off guard, including Philadelphia outfielder Al Simmons.

"Is he pitching?" Simmons asked Mack.

"Yes, don't you like him?" Mack said.

Simmons glanced at teammate Jimmy Dykes before looking back at his manager and shrugging his shoulders.

"If it's all right with you, it's all right with me," Simmons said.

Mack gave the impression that the decision had been a spur of the moment, fly by the seat of his pants move, which in fact it was not. In late August, Mack called the 36-year-old Ehmke to his office with the intention of giving him his unconditional release. Ehmke had been a 20-game winner for a last-place Red Sox team and had even thrown a no-hitter. But that had been six years earlier and despite the side-arming right-hander's ability to keep hitters off balance with his soft stuff, the end of his career was near. Once in Mack's office, Ehmke looked at his manager and spoke.

"I have always wanted to pitch in a World Series," said the 14-year veteran. Ehmke then lifted his right arm. "There is one great game left in this old arm." Mack had heard enough. "All right, Howard, when we go west I want you to stay here," Mack said. "When the Cubs come in to play the Phillies, you watch them. Learn all you can about their hitters. Say nothing to anybody. You are my opening pitcher for the World Series."

Ehmke spent most of September scouting the Cubs, scrutinizing their every move and hoping to find a tendency or weakness to exploit for the chance he might get to face them on the grandest of all stages.

Joe McCarthy wasn't caught off guard by Mack's move, though. Prior to the end of the 1929 season, the Cubs manager told famed sportswriter Ring Lardner, who had begun to write fiction and plays by 1929, that he wasn't afraid of the A's using Grove or Earnshaw.

"We can hit speed," McCarthy said. "But they've got one guy over there I'm afraid of."

McCarthy used an expletive in describing the pitcher as a junk ball pitcher.

"His name is Howard Ehmke," McCarthy continued. "And he's the sucker we're going to see in this Series."

Fans swarmed outside Wrigley Field prior to Game 1. Amid the chaos, one of the disturbances saw Chicago police arrest two Cubs employees and two Wrigley Field vendors who had assaulted independent vendors selling hot dogs to the fans waiting to enter the park. Many of those attending the game had left work early, which was reflected at the Chicago Board of Trade, where the normal number of brokers and speculators had been culled to half. Babe Ruth could be counted among those in attendance, looking oddly out of place sitting in the Philadelphia dugout prior to the game.

Wearing a brown suit instead of his customary Yankees pinstripes, the famed slugger would be watching the World Series rather than playing in it after taking part in six of the previous eight. Wilson spoke briefly with Ruth and posed for a photo before working his way back toward the Cubs' dugout, chatting with fans as he walked.

Contrary to the many stories that have been perpetuated over the years, Capone was not in attendance that day. Weeks after the St. Valentine's Day Massacre, Philadelphia police arrested Capone and charged him with carrying a concealed weapon. Based on the ease with which Capone was captured and the relatively petty charge for which he was captured, speculation suggested he wanted to get caught to let the heat die down in Chicago while he served a one-year sentence.

Around 1:00 p.m., the Cubs took fielding practice as photographers flocked to the Athletics' dugout for a photo shoot of the two managers shaking hands. Five radio stations covered the game to help satisfy the Chicago public's insatiable appetite for the Cubs. By the time the game started, Wrigley Field swelled with fans. Arch Ward of the *Chicago Tribune* dismissed the Game 1 attendance figure of 50,740 when he wrote, "The statisticians must have made a mistake. There were that many photographers on the field."

The umpires arrived late, causing a delay to the game that had been scheduled to start at 1:30 p.m. If the start of the game seemed slow in coming, Ehmke's pitches appeared to take days to arrive at home plate. Changing speeds from slow, to slower, to slowest best described the manner in which Ehmke approached the heavily right-handed Cubs lineup. He simply frustrated the powerhouse lineup to no end. In addition to changing speeds, the right-hander alternated arm angles throughout the game, employing a submarine delivery on occasion. Cubs hitters couldn't lay off the slow stuff, nor could they make contact.

Not until the ninth inning did the Cubs mount any sort of formidable threat to Ehmke's masterpiece. By then the hitters had seen Ehmke several times, allowing their timing to adjust to meet his pitches. Wilson alerted the Athletics to this fact when he led off the ninth by lining a shot back up the middle at Ehmke. The line drive struck Ehmke near the groin, but he had the presence of mind to pick up the ball and throw out Wilson at first base. Ehmke appeared dazed as he fell to the ground, but he recovered to squash a Cubs' rally after allowing one run; he struck out Chick Tolson to end the game. Ehmke finished with 13 strikeouts to set a World Series record, and the Athletics had a 3–1 win to go one up in the best-of-seven Series.

"None of us figured on batting against Ehmke, who had a three-quarter side-arm delivery," Rogers Hornsby said. "It made Mr. Mack look like a smart gambler, and he won. But Ehmke got the breaks and I'm not taking anything away from him when I say that. He could have been a bum just as easily. In the first inning we got a man on base when I came up. I hit a fair ball straight for the right field bleachers, which certainly meant Ehmke was finished in this game. But the wind was blowing in off Lake Michigan, and the ball landed foul. Then I struck out and we didn't score."

Any Cubs fans who went to the movie theater following the game were treated to an interview with Wilson that had been conducted by Westbrook Pegler prior to the start of Game 1. Wilson fielded the question of whether he would be doing any slugging during the game and he answered: "Yes, but it will be the ball." There were several highly publicized incidents involving fisticuffs on Wilson's resume.

Chicago turned chilly and gray prior to Game 2 on October 9, prompting fans to huddle under any kind of coat, sweater, or covering they could find. Even Wilson, Cuyler, and Stephenson could be seen huddling together under a blanket.

Malone took the mound for the Cubs. The hulking Irishman ran with Wilson, which translated to his being quick to tip the bottom up at any speakeasy in Chicago and equally as quick at throwing down with his fists. The son of a section foreman for the Pennsylvania Railroad, Malone cut a figure few would dare cross. Described as "colorful" by some and "crazy" by others, he had put together an outstanding season in 1929, posting a 22-10 mark with a 3.57 ERA. Any time he pitched, he brought confidence to the team because in addition to talent, he possessed a certain tenacity on the mound. The Athletics likely would have selected "crazy" based on Malone's behavior prior to the Series, when he made clear that he did not like Al Simmons and had "sinister intentions" toward him. But the Athletics outfielder, who hailed from nearby Milwaukee and had scores of fans there to cheer him on, singled in two runs at a critical period in the fourth and later homered to lead a 9–3 Athletics win, putting the Cubs two games behind with the Series shifting to Philadelphia's Shibe Park.

Simmons stood out among the vocal Athletics smelling a Series sweep. "We will be a rough, tough team to beat from now on," he said.

A cranky McCarthy rationalized to reporters that if the Athletics could win two games, "so can we."

"This thing is not over until the fourth game is won," McCarthy said. "It has been done before, this business of one club coming back after losing two, or even three games."

McCarthy appeared to be feeling the pressure of the situation and took out some of his foul mood on first baseman Charlie Grimm, who played the banjo. The Cubs manager instructed Grimm to leave his instrument at home, making his point that another loss would put the Cubs in a dire situation. Banjos were for fun and horseplay, the kind of stuff reserved for teams on the winning side of the ledger.

After a travel day, Game 3 took place on October 11 with the temperatures dropping on a chilly fall day in Philadelphia. Fans stood or sat in rocking chairs next to fires to stay warm while waiting outside Shibe Park for bleacher seats to a game attended by just 29,921, which paled in comparison to the anticipated crowd of 35,000. A reasonable explanation for some of the dip in attendance had to do with the $1 bleacher seats. Three thousand such tickets were available, but fans had to endure a long wait in line for the ticket office to open. Looking to make a buck, a seedy element arrived way in advance to procure the front spots in the line, hoping to parlay their position into a profit by asking folks for $5 in exchange for their place in line. Evidently the strategy backfired and attendance suffered.

Wilson led a 3–1 Cubs win, going two for three at the plate and robbing Simmons of extra bases by going to the wall in center field to flag down his drive. Guy Bush started for the Cubs despite going winless over the final six weeks of the season, and he proved up to the task by allowing just one run on nine hits. The banjoless Grimm, who entered Game 3 hitting .667 for the Series, went hitless. Later at the Benjamin Franklin Hotel, Grimm's teammates took up a collection to rent him a banjo.

Winning Game 3 gave the Cubs a much-needed lift. They had put themselves back into position to win the Series. They needed just one more win in Philadelphia to force the Series back to Chicago where, despite losing the first two games, they felt confident of their advantage. Fans shared in the Cubs' optimism and were elated with the Game 3 victory, evidenced by more than 500 Western Union messages wired to McCarthy, 75 sent to Wilson, and 50 to Guy Bush. Woody English, the Cubs shortstop, who had made four errors in three World Series games, received 25, most of which were of the encouraging variety, insisting he remained the best shortstop in baseball.

Bench jockeying reached a crescendo in this Series. Bawdy language punctuated barbs that were loud enough to be heard throughout the ballpark. The idea of the practice: to upset players on the opposing team. Master bench jockeys understood that the timing of the cracks was almost as important as the cracks themselves. For example, if the opposing pitcher had just struck out three in a row, that wasn't the time to remind him that his wife had a wide seat. Instead, the seasoned bench jockey chimed in after a call went against that pitcher or he had walked a couple of hitters in succession. The Cubs did not have to worry about having someone who knew how to stir it up. They knew they could count among their numbers one of the best bench jockeys in the game, Hal Carlson.

Prior to the series, Carlson, and those whom he employed to help pepper the Athletics with their morsels of wisdom, figured that Lefty Grove, Al Simmons, and Mickey Cochrane were ripe targets. Each had been known to grow visibly agitated when the bench jockeying reached a crescendo. Living up to expectations, the Cubs' barrage of bench jockeying had been of such quality that Cochrane even offered what amounted to a compliment when he noted of the Cubs: "They should be in the Kentucky Derby instead of a World Series. They're the best bench jockeys I ever heard."

Cochrane said the Cubs were riding him, Haas, and Simmons, which got him stirred up.

"But maybe it's a good thing at that," Cochrane said. "It seems to help my hitting."

Wilson had no sympathy for Cochrane or the Athletics.

"I'm glad they liked it," Wilson said. "They started it in Chicago and we says, 'If you want it, we'll give you plenty,' and that's what we're doing."

Everything went the Cubs' way at the outset of Game 4. Grimm, who obviously depended on his musical hobby, hit a two-run homer in the fourth for a 2–0 lead. In the sixth, the Cubs got successive singles by Hornsby, Wilson, Cuyler, Stephenson, and Grimm, and an error by Athletics pitcher Jack Quinn to go up 6–0 with no outs in the inning. The Cubs had a chance to bury the A's at this point, but Quinn managed to escape the jam by getting Zack Taylor to fly out, which scored Grimm for the Cubs' seventh run, before striking out Charlie Root and Norm McMillan to end the inning. Despite not cashing in for more runs in the sixth, the Cubs looked like they would cruise to their second win after adding another run in the seventh against Eddie Rommel, who surrendered a one-out triple to Hornsby and an RBI single to Cuyler to push the Cubs' lead to 8–0. Mack considered raising the white flag and regrouping for Game 5 by sending in his substitutes at the beginning of the eighth inning, but that line of thinking changed after the developments that took place in the bottom of the seventh.

Root had pitched six scoreless innings when Simmons led off with a home run onto the left field roof, just fair by inches. Jimmie Foxx then singled to bring up Bing Miller.

Back in the fifth inning, Wilson had muffed a fly ball by Dykes, which should have been a wake-up call that his sunglasses were not adequate and prompted him to equip himself with darker shades. But he kept the same lenses, and Miller lofted a fly ball to center that Wilson lost in the sun, turning the first out of the inning into a single. Dykes and Joe Boley followed with run-scoring singles, and one out later Max Bishop's RBI single chased Root in favor of Art Nehf to pitch to Mule Haas.

Nehf entered the game to the public address announcer calling him "Cvengros," mistaking him for another Cubs pitcher. Unfortunately for Nehf and the Cubs, the introduction mistake would rank low on the list of embarrassments before the day was over.

"While Art Nehf was taking his warm-up pitches, one of the returns from catcher Zack Taylor was a trifle high," Chicago newspaperman Warren Brown said. "Art looked up, and as the blazing sun got in his eyes, he ducked hastily and the ball went on past him to be retrieved by one of the infielders. No one paid much attention to that—then. What if the sun is in a direct line from pitcher to catcher?"

Haas hit the ball to center field and Wilson could not find it in the sun, blindly reaching for the ball with his bare hand at the last instant with no luck. The ball rolled to the wall allowing Haas enough time to round the bases. Once he touched home the Athletics still trailed by a run, but the damage had been done. By the time they retired the Athletics in the seventh, the Cubs trailed 10–8. Lacking a score panel with a 10, Shibe Field's scorekeeper hastily found some white paint and scripted a panel reflecting the number of runs scored by the A's in the seventh.

"There was talk that I danced with joy during that big inning," said Mack years later. "It's not true. I just sat there, and when we won the game I walked off with hardly a word to the boys. It doesn't help any to appear to be too pleased before such an important series is won. Such an attitude might lead to overconfidence, and that's fatal."

An emotional Mack did tell his team: "I'd just like to be able to express to you the things I feel, but I can't. I . . . I have to let it go at that."

After leaving his players he told reporters he had never seen anything like the rally his team put together.

"There is nothing in baseball history to compare with it," Mack said. "It was the greatest display of punch and fighting ability I have ever seen on a ball field."

McCarthy tried to sound optimistic after Game 4 when he said: "The breaks of the game beat us today, but we're not whipped in this series yet by any means. It took the worst breaks I've ever seen. The sun had a lot to do with it. In the seventh the sun shone directly out there. It was just going down behind the grandstand. Artie Nehf was almost blinded and poor Hack was in a terrible fix out there in center field."

McCarthy surmised: "You can beat a ball club and even move a ballpark, but you can't do either to the sun."

Dykes, who had three hits in Game 4, had the cockiest remarks following his team's comeback, telling reporters the series was "all over" before adding, "I wish I could bat all the time in the National League. I'd sure lead that circuit. All you have to do against these Cub pitchers is stick your bat out and you get hits."

Cuyler, who penned a column for the North American Newspaper Alliance, wrote the following after Game 4:

There have been some hard luck stories told about losing ball games, but I doubt if any team ever got the tough breaks we did today in losing to the Athletics, 10 to 8, in the fourth game of the World Series.

In a game like that there's always a breaking point—one play that decides the issue. In our case today it wasn't any one particular play in the seventh, when the A's scored all their 10 runs, that caused our defeat. It was the unusual brilliance of the sun, which blinded Charlie Root, Art Nehf, and Hack Wilson.

When Bishop singled to center in the seventh, his hit was a ball which Root would have fielded but for the blinding sun. Root tried to shield his eyes a bit and in doing so just touched the ball and it went to center field. If he had fielded it, there was a chance for a double play.

Then when Nehf came in to pitch to Haas, the sun shone so brightly that Nehf couldn't even see the return throw Zack Taylor was making after every pitch. Then Haas hit an easy fly to center and it looked like a certain out. When Wilson appeared to be under it he staggered and made a blind effort to catch it but the ball went past him for a home run and the A's were within a run of a tie.

Imagine that kind of a situation with a ball club like the Athletics. They couldn't be stopped then. Sheriff Blake tried and so did Pat Malone, but the Athletics were riding high and firm of purpose. The way they lashed out at those balls was a pity.

It was an awfully tough break for Root and all of us, for we thought we had the game in the bag and were on our way to a world's championship.

Despite reports to the contrary, Wilson left Shibe Field without hanging his head or looking the part of a man who felt like he had lost his best friend. But he appeared inconsolable in the clubhouse afterward. He brushed past McCarthy when the manager tried to cushion his failures. According to one reporter's account, "There was fire in his eyes and who knows what was in his heart that minute. . . . He seemed dazed as he stepped outside." And according to Sam Murphy's report in the *New York Sun*, Wilson picked up his four-year-old son, Bobby, once he was outside and hugged him and kissed him and while doing so "his sturdy frame shook with emotion. He wept."

During the taxi ride from Shibe Field to the hotel, Bobby sat up in his father's lap and told his father, "The devil with them, daddy, we'll get them next year."

Other accounts said Wilson returned to the team hotel and spent some time in the lobby talking to friends and others who wanted to make conversation. He didn't start to beat himself up until the following day when he told reporters, "Looks like I'm the big chump of the Series."

"I play good ball all season, and in the most important game I'm ever in I blow up," Wilson said. "The bugs will have all winter in which to think up wisecracks to hand me next season, and I won't be able to do anything except tip my cap to the greetings."

In the brief history of baseball prior to 1929, two noted goats stood out: Fred Merkle and Fred Snodgrass. Merkle is remembered for what happened on September 23, 1908. Merkle had been the runner on first for the New York Giants and returned to the dugout rather than touching second base after what appeared to be a game-winning hit by Al Bridwell at the Polo Grounds. With Giants fans celebrating on the field, alert Cubs second baseman Johnny Evers retrieved the ball and stepped on second base. Umpire Hank O'Day, who had been alerted to a similar play by Evers earlier in the season—and did not rule a force out—did so on this occasion, thereby nullifying the winning run. The game could not be continued because of the boisterous crowd. The following day National League president William Pulliam declared the game a tie. When the Cubs and Giants tied for the National League pennant, a ruling was made to replay the game on October 8. The Cubs won and took the National League pennant.

Snodgrass also played for the New York Giants and was Merkle's teammate. During the deciding game of the 1912 World Series between the Giants and the Red Sox, Snodgrass committed an error on a routine fly ball in the tenth inning. The play came to be known as the "$30,000 muff" (which was the difference between the winning and losing shares from the World Series). Ironically, Merkle also was involved in a critical play in the same game when Tris Speaker popped up into foul territory between home and first. The ball should have been caught, but neither Merkle nor catcher Chief Meyers made the play, and the ball dropped in between them. Speaker followed with an RBI single that tied the game. The Red Sox went on to win the game and the Series.

Merkle and Snodgrass became synonymous with bonehead plays. Wilson knew all about the pair and understood the significance of his failures in Game 4.

"They'll be calling me a long lost brother of Snodgrass and Merkle, and to think that the weather man promised we'd have a cloudy day! If he had only been right," Wilson said.

Rogers Hornsby, who had few unexpressed thoughts, and even fewer that were not of a critical nature, did not fault Wilson for the Cubs' loss in Game 4.

"I've heard many stories about Hack's forgetting his sunglasses and losing the ball in the sun," Hornsby said. "But I don't think that's the truth. Wilson wasn't my favorite player. I didn't approve of the way he drank and broke training, but I can claim that too much blame was placed on him for that incident. People forget, I guess, that he led both teams in hitting in the Series with a .471 average. In my opinion Norm McMillan let two balls that he should have caught get through him for hits at third base. And if he had made those two plays the side would have been retired and there wouldn't have been any ball hit to Wilson."

A year after the incident, Wilson wrote the following in the *Chicago Times*:

When you can't see 'em, you can't catch 'em. That's an old baseball maxim and isn't it the truth? It certainly was that sunny afternoon in October, 1929, when a couple of fly balls and a whole flock of sun rays started arm-in-arming it and left me in the dark.

But it couldn't be helped.

That seventh inning of the fourth World Series game in 1929 was a nightmare in daytime.

My part in the proceedings was to lose two fly balls in the sun. The first was Bing Miller's short fly to center that I couldn't see at all, and which dropped for a single after Foxx had followed up Simmons' opening homer with a single of his own.

The other was a fly by Mule Haas, five batsmen later.

In between them, Dykes and Boley singled. Pinch hitter Burns popped out and Bishop also singled, thus cutting our lead to four runs and leaving two Philadelphians on base.

I saw Haas' fly leave the bat. The next moment I lost complete sight of it.

The sun shining over the roof of the Shibe stands from in back of home plate was blinding. It was so bad that Art Nehf was having a hard time catching Zach Taylor's throws back to the pitcher's box.

Some have asked why those same sun rays didn't cause confusion all during the regular season. I don't really know. Maybe it was me. Maybe it was the fact the World Series games then started at 1:30 p.m., two hours earlier than during the season, and the seventh inning was being played even earlier than regular games start in Philadelphia. The sun can get out of the way a lot in two hours.

I couldn't see the ball at all after it left Haas' bat until it was almost to the ground. I started after it but it was too late. It bounded to the fence in deep center field for a home run, scoring the other two base runners, too, of course.

*Naturally, I felt pretty badly about it. I should have had
that ball, sun or no sun. But the players were kind enough to say
that it didn't lose the game. It helped, but we were still ahead
even after it happened.*

*But although I hit .471 that Series, leading members of
both teams at the plate, and although I handled more flies safely
than any other player in the Series, I guess the baseball world
always will line me, the 1929 World Series, and "Sunny Boy"
in one and the same breath.*

McCarthy received his fair share of the second-guessing. In particular, why had he not foreseen the potential for Wilson to have
problems in the sunny field? Had any such inkling crossed his mind
he could have moved either Cuyler or Stephenson to center as both
had more experience playing in sun fields. Cubs officials also took
shots at McCarthy's choice of scouts compared to Mack's.

Mack, of course, had engineered the brilliant ploy for Game 1
by sending out Ehmke to scout the Cubs during the latter part of
the season. McCarthy had directed former Cub Joe Tinker to scout
the A's. According to the famed member of the "Tinker, to Evers,
to Chance" double-play trio, Simmons and Cochrane needed to
be pitched inside, which they were in Game 2, and the pair went
a collective three for six with four runs scored and four RBIs. In
a moment of foreshadowing of things to come, Hornsby grand-
standed by letting Cubs officials know his opinion that he would
have pitched the pair outside. Did Hornsby want to undermine the
manager? The question of whether his comments were backed by
intent cannot be answered, but Cubs officials were prompted by the
remarks to wonder why McCarthy had not used a current player to
scout the A's as Mack had done with Ehmke.

Wilson might have taken the events from Game 4 the hard-
est, but William Wrigley Jr. wasn't far behind. For six and a half
innings the Cubs principal owner reveled in the belief his team

22

had righted the ship and that his goal of winning the World Series would be realized.

Once the unlikely occurred, Wrigley took the defeat personally and no doubt added this disappointment to an expanding case against McCarthy. Wrigley also lamented the impact losing the World Series would have on the National League, a concern shared by the other National League owners. The American and National Leagues each were part of the Major Leagues, but the competition between the two—the constant question of which league was best—loomed much larger in the 1920s than it would by the end of the 20th century. A perception existed that the league that led this competition led in dollars as well.

"Baseball is a business," Wrigley said. "The National League in 1927 and '28 suffered Series defeats in four straight games of the present series. Then when it appeared as if the Cubs were coming back to regain the parent League's lost prestige the sun blinded Wilson.

"It makes it look as if the American League was a far stronger organization than the National, and that's why the owners in the latter are nettled. As a matter of fact, the Cubs in a full season probably could whip the Macks easily, but a World Series is not a season."

A Navy dirigible, J-4, loomed over Shibe Field prior to Game 5 on October 15 as it had in the previous two games. Prior to Game 5, Judge Kenesaw Mountain Landis got the managers together and the commissioner of baseball told them the bench jockeying had gotten out of hand, and that if the managers could not control their players and keep them from cussing, then the players would be ejected. Both teams seemed to get a kick out of the warning because Athletics catcher Mickey Cochrane looked over at the Cubs' dugout before the game started and yelled: "Come on out, boys. Put on your bib and tucker. We're serving tea and cookies today."

President Herbert Hoover watched Game 5 from the stands in part to show he believed that the country was not on shaky ground

23

and headed for financial ruin. While he put on that outward display, Hoover had grave concerns about the number of stocks that had been bought on margin to the point where he sold his personal stocks and invested the money in high-grade bonds.

Wilson played center field wearing the six-ply shades many felt he should have worn two days earlier, only the point was moot. The Cubs trailed three games to one and the fourth game had ripped out their hearts.

Malone and Ehmke started Game 5, and the game remained scoreless until the fourth inning when the Cubs chased Ehmke with two runs. Wilson's first chance in the field since the Game 4 debacle occurred in the eighth inning and saw him run deep to a spot where he thought the ball would come down and give the impression he had lost another one before recovering to make the catch.

Rube Walberg came in for the Athletics and held the Cubs through the ninth, allowing a chance for the home team to come back. The Cubs were two outs away from forcing the Series back to Wrigley Field when Bishop singled. Haas then stepped to the plate and connected for a blast he sent over the right field wall. Malone recovered to retire Cochrane on a grounder, but he could not retire Simmons, who doubled before Foxx received an intentional walk. Miller then delivered a shot off Shibe Park's scoreboard to give the Athletics a 3–2 win, which clinched the World Series.

———

Landis shook hands with Cochrane following the game and feigned indignation when he said, "And we're not serving tea and cookies today, Mickey."

The light mood did not extend to the other clubhouse. Wilson took the loss particularly hard.

After the game Wilson joked, "I don't suppose the Martinsburg [Wilson's adopted West Virginia hometown] chapter of Elks will meet me in the station, but we'll have a great winter all the same."

During the train ride back to Chicago, Cubs players were awakened by a loud drumming sound, which turned out to be Wilson down on his knees in the aisle, beating on the floor and lamenting how he had let down the team.

More than 500 fans greeted the Cubs when they arrived back at Chicago's Union Station, where Wilson found a sympathetic crowd ready to embrace him.

"They give me hell with their razzing when I'm going good and now when I deserve it, they give me cheers instead," Wilson said. "You can't figure 'em."

Should Wilson have been considered the goat of the 1929 World Series? He hit .471 and made several dazzling plays in the field. There were others on the Cubs who should have shouldered more of the blame, such as Hornsby, who hit a dismal .238, or English with his four errors.

And though never publicly asked, the question had to be in the minds of many: Had Wilson been drinking?

Wilson had incurred headaches during the 1929 World Series. Years after he was out of baseball Wilson learned of Dr. Stuyvesant Butler's articles citing a relationship between migraine headaches and spots before the eyes. When Wilson was in Chicago, Butler tested him and found that Wilson indeed suffered from migraines and prescribed treatment.

Wilson moved into the long winter stamped as "Sunny Boy," and there were concerns about whether he would ever be the same.

Chapter Two

Hack

By the time he was a star baseball player for the Chicago Cubs, Hack Wilson had risen from a dark, sad background. Given his upbringing, he would have had to have been exceptional not to gravitate toward the saloons, a habit and a way of life for those whose lot made them feel damned.

Lewis Robert Wilson came into the world on April 26, 1900, in Ellwood City, Pennsylvania, a city just 10 years old at the time. Charles Richter was born on the same day in Hamilton, Ohio. Wilson would be adored for what he did, while Richter—who developed a scale for measuring the amplitudes of earthquakes—nobly labored in obscurity. Hack's batting accomplishments, meanwhile, could have been measured by a scale similar to Richter's.

Lewis, who would earn the nickname "Hack" later in life, was the son of Robert Wilson, a laborer in his 20s who worked as a "heater" for Steel Car Forge. His principal duties as a heater were to supervise and work alongside a crew that melted iron ore so the mill could produce grab irons for ladders. The work paid well, which is one of the reasons Wilson had moved to the fledgling city from Greenville, Pennsylvania. Nevertheless, working with one's body to earn a living took a physical toll. Wilson worked hard alongside other men in dire conditions of extreme heat or extreme cold and when the whistle blew to end their shift, the next shift convened on any number of barstools in Ellwood City. Primarily he rooted down at Dugan's, which is where he met Jennie Kaughn, a 16-year-old working girl who traveled to Ellwood City from Philadelphia to take a job on the west side, where roughshod was a way of life.

Wilson lived in a boardinghouse owned by a woman named Grandma Wardman. Mostly he just slept at the boardinghouse, since he spent the majority of his time at work or in the bar. But Grandma Wardman knew him well enough to offer advice to the young man after she noticed he had been staying out all night with Kaughn. Wilson would humor Wardman by listening to her rants about the dangers of cavorting with a fast woman like Kaughn, but he did not take them seriously and soon the news came that she was carrying his child.

Kaughn herself had been an illegitimate child. She and Wilson did not marry due in large part to Wilson's feelings of social superiority over Kaughn. Though Wilson did agree to help with the expenses of raising a child, Kaughn still had to work and she did so right up until delivering Lewis; she also returned to work as soon as possible after the birth. She lived in the factory area near her job, which is where Lewis would spend most of his early childhood alone while his mother worked or went out drinking at the saloons after quitting time. Robert continued to live at Grandma Wardman's, but had little to do with his son save for occasional Sunday walks.

Towns like Ellwood City spotted the geographical landscape of the United States, which experienced a turn-of-the-century growth that saw the country's population increase, according to the census of 1900, from 63,039,756 to 76,295,220. But the country still lagged behind in making strides in equality. Only four states allowed women to vote and if a woman dared light a cigarette, shock and indignation followed. In addition, just 700,000 married women were in the workforce, a figure that would swell significantly by the end of the century.

President William McKinley died at the hands of an assassin's bullet in 1901, leading to Theodore Roosevelt becoming the youngest president in history at the age of 42. In May of 1907, Roosevelt passed through Ellwood City on a train, making a stop and cooing over the advancements of the city. Kaughn took her son to see the president make a speech from the rear platform of the train. Three months after that historic event, Kaughn began to feel acute pains in her abdominal area. Given her tough existence and her need to work, she managed to ignore the pains for two days before a friend took hold of the situation and made her call a doctor. Six days after checking into the Ellwood City Hospital, she died at the age of 23 due to complications from a burst appendix.

Seven-year-old Lewis went to live with his father at Grandma Wardman's, where little had changed. Robert continued to leave for work before sunrise and drink at night until the saloons closed, though the Sunday walks came more frequently. Being the son of two alcoholics, Lewis understood just one way of life and that was a drinking life. Whether or not the patterns of one's parents lead a man to drink or whether alcoholism can be hereditary, Lewis was in for a battle with booze.

Fortunately for Lewis, Wardman had remained in his life, and her husband, Connie Wardman, became a kind of surrogate father. The Wardmans are most often credited for getting Lewis interested in the game of baseball. Connie Wardman had actually received the nickname "Connie" because he was a huge fan of Connie Mack. He had played minor league baseball and had the reputation of being a scrappy player who would do anything to get on base. After leaving the game, he settled down in Ellwood City, working at Steel Car Forge while keeping his finger on the pulse of the city's baseball talent by managing and sponsoring different teams. In addition, he offered lessons on how to play the game. Rich families with absentee fathers married to their work were his biggest customers.

In stark contrast to Robert Wilson, Wardman did not drink. So while Robert spent his after-work hours imbibing, Wardman counseled Lewis on the finer points of baseball, often taking him to games where the youngster learned from watching grown men play in the industrial leagues. He recognized talent in Lewis and nurtured it accordingly. Wardman also had a legendary temper that he often directed Lewis's way when he misbehaved, which also manifested itself frequently in fistfights. While Lewis inherited his penchant for alcohol from his parents, his fighting ability could be attributed to Wardman. Lewis's thick neck might as well have been a warning flare. Once it turned red and the veins began to swell with blood, those who knew him understood that he had been provoked to a point where he planned to rumble.

Kids can be cruel, and Lewis's freakish body invited comments from the other kids who would ask him what tree he had fallen from as if he were a wild animal. Most did not escape retribution from Lewis, who ensured that they did not taunt him again.

Lewis would gravitate toward alcohol later in his life, but he shied away from tobacco use thanks to an episode when he tried to smoke Five Brothers pipe tobacco in a crepe paper cigarette at the age of eight.

"Five Brothers was a very potent tobacco, which my old man had been using for years exclusively for pipe smoking," said Lewis years later in an interview with sportswriter Edward Burns. "Child that I was, I never suspected the difference in tobaccos, so, innocently, I stole enough out of the old gentleman's pouch to cover my plans for dissipation, and with three companions of my own age set out for a nook under a railroad trestle. . . . We smoked, briefly, until all collapsed. We were carried home and spanked by the posse that discovered us, and from that day to this I often have publicly condemned smoking among young Americans who seek an athletic career."

By the time Lewis had reached the age of 10, Wardman's instruction had helped him refine his natural talents to the point where a legitimate baseball player had emerged. Incredibly strong for his age, he had the power boys several years older lacked. Receiving

Wardman's coaching at an early age was one of the biggest breaks of Lewis's young life. He had learned to play the game the right way, and those skills were among the only skills he possessed. But having those skills allowed him to use them elsewhere when Robert picked up stakes and decided to move to Chester, an area west of Philadelphia. Contributing to Robert's decision to move were the whispered allegations that he was a deadbeat father who drank too much and didn't take good care of his son, both of which were true. So the move appeared more like an escape for Robert, who figured that a new area meant new people and fewer opinions about his business.

Lewis, who had acquired the nickname "Stouts," cared little about anything else other than baseball. He did not perform in school and often became a distraction to the rest of the class with his antics. Gaining a formal education did not equate to what it would decades later; Lewis simply wanted to make money and be a grown-up. Following his desires, Lewis quit school at the age of 16, and nobody tried to talk him out of his decision. He went to work at a print shop, where he hauled lead back and forth, adding more girth to his already pronounced muscles. All the while he continued to play baseball whenever he had a free moment. By age 17 he lived on his own and had moved on to take a different job for Baldwin Locomotive and later the Sun Ship Building Company. At both stops, Lewis's task was simple: swing a sledgehammer from starting time until quitting time. He relied on his heavily muscled shoulders and arms to get him through each day. Performing duties requiring heavy physical labor gave Lewis some perspective. Though he could handle the work, he knew he did not want to swing a hammer the rest of his life. Hope for a better tomorrow came to him whenever he played baseball.

Lewis played for the Leipersville Field Club and wanted to pitch for the team, but ended up playing catcher, the position he also played for his next team, the Good Will Fire Company. Those watching him play were struck by the immense power he brought to every plate appearance, which led to his being asked to play for the Chester Athletic Club. There he gained the needed recognition to land a job with the Viscose Silk Mill team. He doubled his pay working at the mill during baseball season, and the job allowed him to bid farewell to backbreaking labor. The only work he did now besides baseball was to assemble boxes. With Lewis behind the plate, Viscose Silk Mill won the industrial league in which they competed.

Lewis's play eventually had to attract a baseball scout or two. Scouting during this era relied heavily on word of mouth and beating the bushes to find undiscovered baseball talent. One such scout took notice of Lewis by doing just that. Clayton Johnson liked what he saw of Lewis and relayed those sentiments to Lewis Thompson, the president of the Martinsburg Blue Sox of the Blue Ridge League. That led to Lewis Robert Wilson getting his first shot at professional baseball.

Unlike baseball's minor league systems in the latter part of the 20th century that saw Major League clubs own their affiliates, minor league baseball existed primarily through independent clubs that offered their respective geographical regions a form of entertainment by providing professional baseball. These clubs would try to field the best teams possible without the benefit of an amateur draft. Thus, the best talent available would be procured with the hope that they would play entertaining and winning baseball along with the even bigger hope that one or two of the players would be good enough to sell to a Major League club for a big sum. Such a sale could sustain a minor league club's finances.

Wilson reported to Martinsburg, West Virginia, in the spring of 1921 ready to pursue a ballplaying career. After the team's regular catcher got injured during spring training, Wilson entered the season as the starter. Unfortunately, his professional career almost ended before ever beginning as he got injured in the team's first game, suffering a compound fracture just below the right calf on his tibia. Wilson's future looked grim. Playing baseball again seemed secondary to being able to walk without difficulties. Wilson could have gotten depressed. What if the injury indeed had ended his career? But rather than fall prey to despair, Wilson managed to keep a positive mindset due in part to his room with a view. What he saw while laid up in the hospital encouraged him to do anything but give up the sport. Outside he saw a daily parade of the town's youth pass by with their baseball equipment in tow and smiles on their faces. During his hospital stay, Wilson also met Virginia Riddleburger, a friend of one of his nurses. Even though he was 12 years younger than Virginia, he immediately became smitten. Riddleburger brought him along further than simply looking through the window could do, paying frequent visits to his room, and taking him out on excursions amid the Blue Ridge Mountains. She also helped him pay for some of his hospital bills.

Eight weeks after suffering his injury, Wilson returned to the field in love for the first time and armed with a renewed enthusiasm for baseball. Back in a Blue Sox uniform, he had a new fan in the stands in Virginia, who began to attend his games, offering him the encouragement he had rarely experienced in his life. Due to his injury, Wilson had just 101 at-bats in 1921, but he made the most of his trips to the plate by hitting .356 with five home runs and 17 RBIs. He accomplished those numbers while playing with a pronounced limp, a remnant of his leg injury.

In 1922, Wilson returned to play for Martinsburg, but at a new position. After a scout told Wilson's manager that the Blue Sox's catcher had potential with his bat, but would never make it to the Major Leagues as a catcher, the club moved him to center field. Wilson wasn't crazy about the move, since he fancied himself as becoming a Major League backstop. But foremost in his mind was making it to the Bigs. He continued to hit the powerful drives that brought fans to the ballpark in Martinsburg, where he reigned as a huge local favorite. He broke Walter Kimmick's league home run mark of 20 early in July and the *Martinsburg Journal* wrote about Wilson and how "Stouts ought to make his record look sort of futile before the present season is over."

Wilson finished the 1922 season with 30 home runs while hitting .366. Martinsburg won the league pennant, then won the postseason championship of the Blue Ridge League. Early in the 1923 season, Frank Lawrence, the owner of the Portsmouth Truckers of the Class B Virginia League, received a tip about this hot prospect named Lewis Wilson. Lawrence took the time to attend a Martinsburg game and liked what he saw, offering the Blue Sox $500 to buy their center fielder. Martinsburg accepted the offer, sending Wilson on his way to the higher league. Once again Wilson thrived, becoming a fan favorite for the Truckers while wreaking havoc on the league with his bat. On days off, Wilson would take the train back to Martinsburg to see Virginia, and she traveled to Portsmouth when she could break free from her job as a clerk, leading Wilson to make a proposal of marriage that culminated with the couple exchanging their vows on August 24, 1923, in a small ceremony conducted in Norfolk, Virginia.

Toward the end of the 1923 season, Lawrence began to toy with the idea of parlaying Wilson's success into a big payday. Believing Wilson had the talent to play at the Major League level—despite Wilson's critics, who ignored his lofty numbers to cite his unconventional build as a reason for his not being big league material—Lawrence contacted an old friend, John McGraw, the manager of the New York Giants who reigned supreme as the premier manager in the Major Leagues.

Lawrence somehow convinced McGraw to leave the Giants during the season to pay a visit to Portsmouth to see Wilson play. With the legendary manager in the stands, Wilson put on a show, hitting a home run and collecting three hits and two RBIs. Despite the performance, McGraw didn't fall in love with the freaky-looking slugger, as he noted to the *Virginia Pilot*: "That guy don't look like a ballplayer. He's too short and has no neck."

McGraw didn't want Wilson, but he did want pitcher Kent Greenfield. Still, Lawrence remained persistent, continuing to tout Wilson's merits. Initially he had set a $25,000 purchase price for Wilson, but given McGraw's reluctance to bite on the slugger, Lawrence proposed a deal in which he accepted $5,000 for Wilson with the caveat of an added bonus for every point Wilson hit over .300 the following season. McGraw did like the idea of a bonus for each point, but he did not necessarily agree with Lawrence that Wilson would thrive at the Major League level. In the end, McGraw made a deal, purchasing Wilson and Greenfield for $11,000 and sending Lawrence two Giants players.

Wilson's final numbers for Portsmouth included a .388 batting average, 18 home runs, and 101 RBIs in 115 games. Once the Virginia League season was over, Wilson and Greenfield traveled by train to Chicago, where the Giants were preparing to begin a series with the Cubs. Upon joining the Giants, Wilson was hardly accorded Cadillac treatment, which was the case for all rookies back in that era.

"The Giants bought Ken Greenfield and me from Portsmouth, in the Virginia League, in 1923, and we were ordered to report to the Auditorium hotel in Chicago," Wilson said. "We reported, but McGraw didn't give us a tumble—no instructions or anything. We had come in light and nearly starved for four days, eating sparingly in a one arm joint on Wabash Avenue. Then Jack Scott saw we were a couple of green peas, and on the train leaving Chicago told us we were supposed to eat in the main dining room and sign the tabs. I never have been hungry since that day, and I'll always have a warm spot in my heart for Jack Scott."

On September 27, 1923, Wilson played in his first Major League game, which the *New York Times* noted by calling him "a broad-shouldered, wide beamed outfielder from the Virginia League" saying that he "hit the ball hard, but not safely, and committed an error in the seventh that let in two runs."

Wilson got his first big league hit on September 28. A couple of days later he would count Babe Ruth as a teammate in an exhibition game for the Giants against the Baltimore Orioles. Ruth played for the Giants that day to help raise money for charity. During the exhibition, Ruth hit a ball completely out of the Polo Grounds before leaving the game during the late innings for his replacement, Wilson. A week later, Ruth played for the Yankees, who met the Giants in the World Series. Wilson was not eligible to play due to his late arrival date to the Major Leagues.

Wilson finished the season with the Giants, hitting .200 in 10 at-bats compiled over a three-game period, which the *Sporting News* put into proper perspective in a story that noted: "The kid who doctors said would never walk again is now occupying a space on the Giants bench and drawing his salary from John McGraw, the leading major league manager."

At the start of Hack Wilson's career, John McGraw was already an iconic figure in the Major Leagues. He had played in the majors for 16 seasons and got the most out of his 5'7", 155-pound body, taking whatever steps he deemed necessary to win. He batted left-handed and possessed incredible bat control, which made him a master at the hit-and-run. He drew 836 walks and stole 436 bases during his career. During one nine-year stretch, McGraw hit no lower than .321 in any season. And he wasn't beyond a little gamesmanship, which many would have classified as dirty baseball, primarily involving opposing baserunners. If he noticed the umpires watching where the ball went on a play, McGraw took liberties teeing off on the baserunner by tripping, blocking, or pushing them or just making it difficult for them to pass on a play. Fights would often result from such behavior, and McGraw never backed down.

McGraw became a player/manager for the Orioles in 1899 at the age of 26 and continued to manage the Orioles for three seasons before taking over as the manager of the New York Giants in 1902. Based on his egotistical nature, harsh manner, and aggressiveness, McGraw received the nickname "Little Napoleon." Players did not want to find themselves on the wrong side of their fiery manager, who got results. By the end of the 1923 season, McGraw had managed his teams to nine National League pennants and three World Championships. In hindsight, the marriage between Wilson and McGraw had been destined for a divorce from the beginning. For starters, McGraw had never played the kind of baseball that came into fashion in the 1920s. His team played small ball, which meant hitting behind the runner, bunting, and never taking a button-popping cut at the baseball at any time in the count. While the Giants won National League pennants in 1921, 1922, and 1923, they lost the World Series in 1923. McGraw's preferred style of play was going by the wayside and the future Hall of Fame manager reluctantly clung to the past.

Prior to the 1924 season, the Giants traded Bill Cunningham and Casey Stengel to the Boston Braves for outfielder Billy Southworth, who became Wilson's main competition to win the Giants' center field job. Most believed Wilson a far better player than Southworth—save for McGraw, who seemingly could not see past Wilson's squatty build. On the other hand, the fans loved watching Wilson go through the motions whether in the field or at bat. From the moment he took the field his uniform instantly seemed to be the dirtiest by far of any of the players, and when he hustled he cut an endearing figure, churning stumpy legs and humping it after any ball hit his way. Despite his unorthodox form, he could cover a lot of ground, which was critical to any center fielder playing in the vast spaces of the Polo Grounds.

McGraw seemed to have no logical pattern for how he used Wilson. For example, after entering the game only as a late-inning replacement for the first several weeks of the season, Wilson got a start on May 5, 1924, when Ross Young had to miss the game with a leg injury. Southworth moved to right from center and, according to a story in the *New York Times*, "Lew Wilson, recruit from the Virginia League, filled the gap in center field." Wilson made the most of his start by getting two hits—including a double—in four trips to the plate in an 8–7 Giants loss to the Philadelphia Phillies. But he did not start again until May 30 in the second game of a doubleheader against the Phillies. Once again Wilson stood out, getting two hits in five at-bats, including a game-winning double to right field that scored Southworth.

When Southworth broke his hand, Wilson became a regular in the Giants' lineup. Some time during this period, Lewis Wilson became "Hack" Wilson. The origin of the nickname is not certain, though two solid theories exist. One suggests the name came from his resemblance to George Hackenschmidt, a well-known wrestler and muscle man; the other theory was that Wilson's strength reminded fans of Cubs outfielder Hack Miller, who was believed to be the strongest man in baseball.

Wilson had some initial success once in the lineup, hitting a game-winning triple against the Pirates on June 9, a day in which the *New York Times* referred to him as Hack for the first time and explained the reason why in the following passage, which also exemplifies the prose used to describe the national pastime in the 1920s:

> *The lucky seventh was all of that for the Giants yesterday. Tearing into Wilbur Cooper with an ill-concealed indignation, the champions scored five runs all in a heap, knocked the Pirates for a 6–4 loss at the Polo Grounds and built up their lead to two full games over the Cubs, who lost to the Dodgers.*
>
> *For all of which thank Hack Wilson, whose triple with the bases full was the big noise of the afternoon. From one run behind, the Giants became two ahead when Wilson stepped up and socked one of the justly famous Cooper deliveries to the far corner of the lawn in left centre. Hack, who is labeled because he*

has the same general architectural scheme as Hackenschmidt, was prodigal with his hitting. A single would have done just as well, as the Giants were only one run behind.

But when Mr. Wilson hits one, he has great difficulty in restraining it to an ordinary single. He likes left handers in general and Wilbur Cooper in particular, and for that reason John McGraw keeps him on the Giant bench to turn loose on defenseless southpaws who chance along. A week or so ago Hack knocked Dutch Ruether loose from his bearings with a two-bagger against the fence. This one yesterday was even longer. It wasn't any mere roller between two outfielders. This ball was hit. It was a combination fly and line drive, and although Cuyler and Max Carey turned and chased back at top speed, the pill hit several yards behind them and almost reached the fence on the first bounce. Mr. Wilson aimed for the bullpen and he hit it.

Wilson connected for his first home run on June 25. On July 12, his average stood at .373 and he put together a streak that saw him hit four home runs in five games. Unfortunately for Wilson, he caught his spikes in the turf in a game on July 13 and had to miss several weeks while his ankle mended. Once he returned he continued to play like a man on a mission, which he truly was, and that mission was to win McGraw's favor—a seemingly impossible task.

Aside from the way Wilson looked on the field, McGraw took issue with Wilson's strikeouts. In fairness to McGraw, strikeouts were viewed differently than they would be in the generations that followed. Hall of Famer Bill Terry recalled McGraw in a November 1971 *Baseball Digest* article and spoke about the different mindset in hitting that existed in that era.

"We had a different idea about hitting," Terry said. "We had very few strikeouts. Look at the records and you'll find that in comparison with players of today, we didn't strike out much. I

was taught by John McGraw, and he himself was a fine hitter. I learned from fellows like Hornsby. They impressed on me that with two strikes you get up to the plate and protect it.

"Consequently you got hold of the ball more frequently. These fellows today are back in the same position with two strikes as they are with no strikes. And they're still swinging away. Therefore, they strike out 100 or 110 or 120 times. That naturally hurts a batter's average."

Despite having to fight the odds that seemingly were stacked against him, Wilson continued to play hard. A game at Brooklyn's Ebbets Field on September 7, 1924, demonstrated Wilson's approach to the game.

Brooklyn, known as the Robins in 1924, gave the Giants a run for the pennant, and the excitement of the race spilled over into crowd interest. Attendance drove the fortunes of teams in the 1920s, so the Brooklyn management wanted to accommodate as many paying customers as possible for the game. They did so by allowing fans onto the field, which was not out of the ordinary for the era. By the time the game began at one in the afternoon, fans were lined up in foul territory from the end of the Giants' bench down the third base line all the way around the perimeter of the outfield to the Robins' bench on the other side of the field. Only a rope restrained the field-level crowd from becoming a part of the action.

By the time all the fans were packed inside the cozy ballpark, an estimated crowd of 32,000 watched while a frenzy about half that size tried to storm the locked ballpark gates from the outside. One surge through a gate in left field proved successful, granting several hundred fans entry to the park so they could squeeze in among the masses.

Initially there were few police inside the ballpark, but additional officers were called to help get the crowd off the playing field in the fifth inning. Extra police were brought in to fight back the crowd outside the field too, as the pack of baseball-hungry fans continued to try to find a way inside the gates throughout the game.

Young boys scaled the walls in left and center fields to reach the other side, while others sat atop the walls content to watch the action from the lofty, albeit dangerous, perch. One 13-year-old boy attempted to scale the wall and fell, suffering a concussion from the impact of his fall.

Eventually the Giants took control of the game and carried an 8–4 lead into the bottom of the ninth. However, the Robins did not go gently in the bottom half of the inning. After their first two batters reached, Johnny Mitchell hit a ball to deep center field. Wilson gave chase for the ball and boldly darted into the partisan Brooklyn crowd, which seemed to swallow him whole. Wilson could not be seen for a prolonged period, but his hat flew out from the crowd, as did his glove. Almost a minute passed before Wilson emerged holding the baseball.

Bill Klem could not see what had happened on the play, nor could anybody else inside Ebbets Field, but the veteran umpire ruled the hit a double, which allowed one runner to score while putting runners at second and third and instigating a prolonged argument.

The Giants managed to hold on to win the game 8–7, and they would eventually win the 1924 National League pennant. Wilson always maintained he caught Mitchell's drive, noting that when he went into the crowd he had just twirled in the air to haul in the ball when he noticed a young girl he estimated to be no older than five occupying the space where he was about to land. He quickly adjusted his legs, spreading them out, which allowed him to avoid stabbing the girl with his spikes and seriously injuring her. While down in the crowd, a fan stole his glove and his hat, but he held onto the ball. Wilson came around to understanding Klem's basis for making the call, which centered on the fact that Wilson took so long to reappear from the crowd. Klem felt Wilson had been scrounging around on the ground to find the baseball.

Wilson finished the 1924 season with a .295 batting average, 10 home runs, and 57 RBIs in 107 games. He played in his first World Series when the Giants met the Washington Senators that fall and hit .233 in 32 plate appearances, which included a double and three RBIs. Much to the chagrin of McGraw, Wilson struck out 47 times during the season—a number any manager in future decades would love to see his slugger replicate—and he also struck out nine times in the World Series, which the Giants lost. McGraw never fully embraced Wilson, and surely the strikeouts were a contributing factor to his feelings.

Wilson got off to a torrid start in 1925, but quickly fell into an abysmal slump. Wilson and his wife, Virginia, were expecting their first child. Wilson would later tell friends that the situation brought him a great deal of anxiety and that worrying about her well-being caused him to lose his focus. Others believed his lackluster performance could be attributed to the fact that he had not shown an ability to hit breaking pitches, and National League pitchers had simply begun to exploit that weakness. That, in turn, led Wilson to seeing less playing time. But what playing time he did see often proved memorable, like the doubleheader the Giants played against the Phillies at Philadelphia's Baker Bowl on July 1, 1925.

In the first game of the twin-bill, Wilson was beaned in the ribs by a pitch. Calmly, he took his base, but clearly the ache in his side got his juices flowing. Later in the game, Phillies infielder Lew Fonseca went too far. Wilson had grown conditioned to the relentless name-calling he received over the years, most of which addressed his odd physical stature. But there were limits, and Fonseca escalated whatever anger stirred within Wilson by continuing to taunt him in a manner, and about subjects, the Giants slugger felt were over the line. Finally, Wilson erupted like a volcano. Nothing had changed from his childhood days, and those around him could see the sudden transformation take place. Veins began to show in Wilson's neck, and he turned red before attacking Fonseca. Once Wilson went into attack mode, restraining him became a difficult task. Eventually four players and an umpire managed to harness the powerful slugger.

Wilson was well under control by the start of the second game, and he took out his frustrations on the baseball. He hit two home runs in the third inning, an inning that saw the Giants get eight hits and score nine runs en route to a 16–7 win. Both of Wilson's home runs sailed over the center field fence to the deepest part of the ballpark. After Wilson hit his second home run, a fan was heard to say, "Stop: You are breaking my heart!"

Despite that performance, Wilson found himself on the bench more often than not. On August 6, 1925, the Reds defeated the Giants 9–1 in Cincinnati. McGraw used Wilson as a pinch hitter that day and he struck out. That at-bat turned out to be the last time he would ever step to the plate for the Giants.

The Giants were struggling and McGraw had seen enough, prompting him to make a move. The fiery manager looked at Wilson and staring back at him were his .239 batting average, 30 RBIs, and 33 strikeouts in 62 games. Hoping to find a spark, McGraw optioned Wilson to Toledo of the American Association and got Earl Webb in return.

McGraw told Wilson: "I want you to go to Toledo for the rest of the season and cure yourself of the strikeout habit. I'll bring you back next spring, and you can make a fresh start."

Wilson reported to Toledo and suddenly the weight of the world seemed to be removed from his shoulders. Virginia returned to Martinsburg to prepare for the delivery of their baby, which relieved Wilson to no end. He knew she would be able to receive considerable help in their hometown and wouldn't be at the mercy of a baseball schedule. Toledo's manager also served as a positive influence for Wilson's ailing bat. McGraw micromanaged his hitters and Wilson had never felt totally comfortable being told when he could and could not swing the bat. At Toledo, there were no such instructions and he thrived, hitting .343 with four home runs and driving in 36 runs.

Whether McGraw had completely given up on Wilson remains unknown. What is known is that the Giants lost him through somebody's mistake, and the Cubs were able to grab him.

Somehow the Giants botched the process by failing to renew Wilson's option after the 1925 season, which allowed the slugger to become eligible to be drafted by another club. Most blamed McGraw for the oversight, and given McGraw's controlling nature it's difficult not to do so. There were few, if any, things relating to the New York Giants that McGraw did not have his finger firmly on the pulse of, but McGraw managed to pass the blame off on James Tierney, the team secretary.

Wilson believed the most obvious of explanations, that McGraw had simply given up on him. He would later say: "I was sent to Toledo with the understanding the Giants had strings on me and that I'd be recalled for 1926. But [McGraw] was down on me, and said thumbs down. The Cubs then drafted me."

The Cubs swam at the bottom of the National League in 1925, but it took a botched play by a future Hall of Fame catcher to put into place the events that would bring Wilson to Chicago.

Gabby Hartnett muffed a pop foul on the final day of the 1925 season. The miscue opened the floodgates for a 7–5 Cardinals win, breaking a three-way tie for last place in the National League by leaving the Cubs in the cellar for the first time in team history. Finishing in the basement put the Cubs in position to draft the unprotected Wilson.

The Giants also may have left Wilson unprotected because they expected the Boston Red Sox—who had first pick in the draft—to pick Wilson's teammate, Toledo third baseman Frank McGuire. If that scenario had unfolded as they expected, the Giants would have been safe from having any other players from the Toledo team selected. When the Red Sox selected another player, Wilson was available for the Cubs to take with the second pick, which they did, picking up Wilson for the price of $5,000.

Joe McCarthy later recalled the circumstances that brought Wilson to the Cubs.

"We stole him from the Giants," McCarthy said. "That's right. They had sent him to the minors and then had forgotten to recall him. A clerical mistake. So he was unprotected when the draft came around." After the Cubs took Wilson for $5,000. McCarthy said, "McGraw hit the ceiling when he heard about it. I don't think he ever got over it. Wilson led the league in home runs four out of the next five years."

Despite McCarthy's comments, suggestions that the Giants—and McGraw—had experienced an oversight or a mistake by leaving Wilson are likely false. "Little Napoleon" had controlling, calculating ways. Forgetting to protect a player McGraw wanted would have been reckless behavior from an individual who simply did not make such mistakes. McGraw and the Giants also never offered an excuse for losing Wilson until he began to perform well for the Cubs, suggesting that there had been no mistake.

Free from McGraw's iron hand, Wilson began to hit like he knew he could during his first season with the Cubs. He became an instant fan favorite as much for the way he looked and played as for the exalted numbers he put up. With Wilson in the lineup, the Cubs' fortunes began to improve. Following fourth-place finishes in 1926 and 1927, the Cubs moved to third in 1928 before winning the National League pennant in 1929.

Wilson's numbers jumped immediately once he joined the Cubs. He hit .321 with 21 home runs and 109 RBIs in 1926; he followed with a .318 average, 30 home runs, and 129 RBIs in 1927, and he hit .313 with 31 home runs and 120 RBIs in 1928. Those three seasons established Wilson as one of the premier hitters in the major leagues. After Wilson's 1929 season, when he hit .345

with 39 home runs and 159 RBIs, the inevitable comparisons to Babe Ruth began to grow, though sometimes these comparisons were far from flattering.

Sportswriter Thomas Holmes of the *Brooklyn Eagle* compared Wilson's swing to Ruth's and concluded: "The Babe's sense of timing at the plate is far superior to that of Wilson's."

Holmes also described Wilson as a "chunky young upstart from the coal hills of West Virginia" and as "perhaps the most malicious mauler known to baseball science, the most incorrigible exponent of brute strength versus a pitched ball."

In addition to putting up the numbers for the Cubs, Wilson always seemed to do something special on the field. During one stretch of games in 1926, he hit walk-off home runs on July 1 and July 10, endearing himself to the fans at Cubs Park—which would be renamed Wrigley Field prior to the 1927 season. Wilson walked in the 22nd inning of a May 17, 1927, game against the Boston Braves, moved to second base on a sacrifice by Riggs Stephenson, and scored what turned out to be the winning run on a single by Charlie Grimm. That game remains the longest played in Cubs history. He drove in six runs on April 19, 1928, then opened eyes in Cincinnati on June 30 when he became the first right-handed hitter to homer into the right field stands at Redland Field. Wilson celebrated his feat by repeating it later in the game. While best known for his slugging, Wilson proved to be amazingly consistent, putting together hitting streaks of 27, 25, 22, and 20 consecutive games during the years from 1927 through 1930.

While Wilson's bat grew legendary, it might have been exceeded by his legend off the field. The average Joe in Chicago could relate to Wilson's blue-collar personality—go bash around some baseballs by day and quaff down a few cold ones at night. Stories abounded about Wilson's exploits around the city.

Chicago liked to have a drink, which the large number of drinking establishments during Prohibition validated. Wilson did not have to go far to find a place to wet his whistle after the games since the "Beer Flats" were located around Wrigley Field. These were apartments that had been converted to establishments where patrons could guzzle whiskey and beer. They were illegal, but they enjoyed a vibrant existence.

One story has Wilson drinking in the apartment of Michael and Lottie Frain on May 23, 1926. Earlier in the day, Wilson had homered off the left-center field wall approximately 450 feet from home plate, becoming the first player to do so. Afterward he headed to one of his favorite watering holes, and that's where the trouble began at approximately 11 p.m. Several versions of the story exist, but the gist was that the police raided the premises and found Wilson there. In one version, he was simply arrested. Another had Wilson trying to flee through an open window only to have his stocky body prevent him from slipping through the opening. And yet another said that after the raid the Frains were led out in handcuffs while Wilson walked through the front door with a smile on his face.

The standing joke around Chicago was that Wilson eventually would meet and befriend everybody in the city while sitting on barstools at various drinking establishments. The star outfielder wasn't about to give up the bottle, but he did have his own code of ethics where his drinking was concerned.

"I've never played a game drunk," Wilson said. "Hungover, yes. But drunk, no."

Cubs players parked their cars across Waveland Avenue during games. Afterward, a large group of Wilson's friends would be waiting for him.

"And they'd head off to a road house where they knew Hack would pick up all tabs," Bill Veeck Jr. said.

Though a generous man, Wilson forever remained a man not to be provoked. He looked the part of a brawler, and he acted as such on occasion. Those choosing to poke the bear in the cage quickly discovered another side of Wilson.

In Wilson's first year with the team he went to a speakeasy to sign some autographs. On this occasion, it turned out he was not imbibing, a fact two North Side police officers weren't buying once they entered the premises. They contended that Wilson had gone there for illegal purposes. Before long this led to Wilson getting upset, at which point he suggested they settle things with their fists. Looking at a bulldog that had broken loose from his chain, the officers opted to draw their guns, taking aim at the Cubs star before slapping handcuffs on him and taking him to the police station. After spending a good portion of his day in jail, Wilson somehow managed to convince the police that he indeed was autographing baseballs and not swilling illegal alcohol. He was released. Understanding Wilson's popularity, the two arresting officers were said to avoid future trips to the North Side fearing retribution from Wilson's many admirers.

Wilson had countless nicknames, few of which were flattering, such as Caliban, after Shakespeare's beast man character in *The Tempest*. Thick skin developed to endure the barbs, but Wilson could take only so much. On June 21, 1928, Edward Young, a heckling milk wagon driver, crossed the line.

Young, who admitted to visiting an "oasis" prior to the game for a few beers, maintained that he called Wilson a "big tub" while telling him he should take himself out of the game "for the good of the team." According to Wilson's version, after grounding out for the second out in the ninth inning of a 3–1 loss to the St. Louis Cardinals, Young moved closer to the field and yelled: "Why in the hell don't you bench yourself you fat so and so?" Wilson went into the stands and began to pound Young. Wilson's teammates Gabby Hartnett and Joe Kelly, who entered the box under the guise of breaking up the fight, managed to deliver a few well-placed licks to Young as well. A report in the *Chicago Tribune* estimated that about 5,000 people flooded onto the field, which caused the game to be delayed 12 minutes.

When Young tried to fight back he found Wilson to be "too large a bundle to handle." He left the fracas with a wrenched back and a fat lip that required three stitches.

Wilson broke a National League rule by charging into the stands to fight with fans. Accordingly, National League president John Heydler fined Wilson $100.

Just over a year later the Cubs were playing the Cincinnati Reds in a morning/afternoon doubleheader at Wrigley Field on July 4, 1929. In the fifth inning of the second game, Ray Kolp began to ride Wilson, who had just hit a single. Among other insults, Kolp called Wilson a bastard. Kolp, who pitched for the Reds, was nicknamed "Jockey" for his skills in needling opponents. The episode escalated when Kolp made the mistake of daring Wilson to join him in the Reds' dugout. Wilson didn't bother to call time-out. He took up Kolp on his dare, landing two rights to Kolp's face before Reds players broke up the fracas; a policeman accompanied Wilson back to the home dugout. Once the dust settled, Kolp came away with a black eye. Since Wilson left the base without ever calling time-out, a Cincinnati player tagged him out. Umpires then ejected him from the game.

Later that day at Union Station, the Reds and Cubs were preparing to board the Gotham limited train to New York and had to move through the depot gate at the same time, leading to an exchange between Wilson and several Reds players. Wilson made clear what he had on his mind: Either Kolp would apologize or they would pick up where they had left off that afternoon. Jack May of the Reds attempted to play peacemaker by telling Wilson that Kolp was in the Pullman and to "take it easy." Pete Donohue, also a pitcher for the Reds, who stood 6'2", 185 pounds, wasn't as tactful as May.

"You go in there and you'll never come out," Donohue said.

Enraged, Wilson snapped back: "Well, I may not come out, but I'm going in all the same. No one can call me that word and mean it."

Wilson felt like the matter with Kolp needed to be settled and did not appreciate Donohue's interference. Using his fists to express his displeasure, Wilson's first punch landed square on Donohue's chin, sending him reeling to the concrete floor. Donohue managed to get to his feet and Wilson landed a second punch to his mouth, leaving him bloodied and once again on the floor. "That's the way it was with Hack," Joe McCarthy said. "Good-natured as could be, but things seemed to happen to him. I guess people picked on him because he was small. They never did it twice, I can tell you."

Wrote the *Chicago Tribune* of Hack Wilson's memorable Fourth of July: "Hack Wilson, pudgy outfielding star of the Chicago Cubs, yesterday hit three baseballs for singles and two Cincinnati pitchers on the nose."

Wilson's actions prompted an investigation by Heydler, during which the National League president listened to the testimonials of Wilson and players from each team. He exonerated Wilson of the charges that he had viciously attacked Donohue without a cause. After dismissing the charges, Heydler issued a warning and a reprimand to Wilson.

"In discussing the charge," Heydler said. "I wish to make it plain that I consider Wilson the aggressor, and that he is to be censured for initiating a fight in a public gathering place, and to warn him of the serious consequences which must ensue unless he learns to control himself more properly."

Controlling Wilson's fists was one thing; containing his bat was quite another.

CHAPTER THREE

Marse Joe

JOE MCCARTHY BECAME MANAGER OF THE CUBS PRIOR TO THE
1926 season, a bold move inspired by general manager Bill Veeck, a
former sportswriter for the *Louisville Courier Journal* in Louisville,
Kentucky. Some of Veeck's buddies from his old job spoke highly
about the bang-up job McCarthy had been doing during his seven
seasons as the manager of the Louisville Cardinals, a position that
had been just a part of a lifelong foundation he had been laying
toward reaching his goal of managing in the Major Leagues.

McCarthy grew up in Germantown, Pennsylvania, where his
father, who worked as a carpenter, died when he fell from a scaf-
fold when Joe was three. McCarthy never seemed to carry baggage
from not having a father present for most of his life, though it's
unlikely anybody would have known if he did since most considered
McCarthy a private person. At an early age he appeared content to
head down the path on which he traveled, which would have led
him to become a plumber. The plan called for him to quit school and
become a plumber's apprentice, after which he could earn a living
through the trade for the rest of his life. McCarthy's mother fully
approved of the plan. Only baseball interrupted. Aware of McCarthy's talent for the game, local priests intervened to get him into college at Niagara University where he could play for the baseball team.
Even though he had not finished high school, McCarthy enrolled at

Niagara in 1905. In the spring of 1906, he performed well in a game in which Niagara played the Rochester Hustlers, helping his team defeat the professional Eastern League club 10–5. That game helped convince McCarthy that he could play professional baseball.

In 1907 he left college and signed to play professional baseball with the Wilmington Colts of the Tri-State League. McCarthy figured Delaware would be a quick stop on a trip that would take him to the Major Leagues. Those expectations were tempered when McCarthy found the quality of play to be of a higher caliber than he ever imagined. Breaking pitches brought a particular brand of frustration to McCarthy. He just couldn't hit them. His first taste of managing came during the spring of 1911 with the Toledo Mud Hens. During that spring, the club split into two squads as they traveled by train to different destinations to tour as two teams, competing against one another. The Mud Hens' manager, Harry Hinchman, managed one team and McCarthy the other. Though young at the time, McCarthy showed acumen for running a team, which the Toledo paper noted with the following passage about him:

> *The youth has reached a point where he knows as much baseball as any man on the club outside of probably Manager Hinchman. Joe is a capital inside worker. He is a student of the game, and anytime there is a discussion of plays after or before a contest, "Mac" is always there with his opinion. That's the reason President Armour and Manager Hinchman put him in charge of the second team.*

McCarthy continued to kick around the minor leagues, and by 1913 he found himself playing for Wilkes-Barre. When Billy Clymer quit as the manager of the team, McCarthy succeeded him as a player/manager. He did well on the field, hitting .328 for the season, and he managed his team to a second-place finish in the New

York State League. McCarthy had established himself as a smart player with good judgment on the field, but he was limited in his progress due to his subpar athletic ability. Yet he continued to play. In 1919 he was playing for the Louisville Colonels when manager Patsy Flaherty resigned. McCarthy, who had managed just one season at Wilkes-Barre, was hired again to be a player/manager. By 1921, McCarthy had led the Colonels to the American Association Championship and was being hailed by baseball insiders as one of the finest managers in the game.

McCarthy also quit playing during the 1921 season. He loved playing the game so much that he may have been blind to his own inadequacy. That is, until one of his players opened his eyes.

McCarthy had criticized infielder Jay Kirke after he had made a wild throw, to which Kirke offered a rebuttal.

"Who are you to be telling a .380 hitter how to play ball?" Kirke said. "Why don't you go home and take a look at yourself."

McCarthy did just that. He went home that night and evaluated himself as a player. That reflection resulted in his returning to work the following day and announcing that he would only be the team's manager and that his playing days were complete.

In addition to his acumen managing game situations, McCarthy could spot talent, which became evident from the manner in which he developed outfielder Earle Combs, who would go on to thrive with a Hall of Fame career in the Major Leagues. McCarthy understood the personalities of the players, knowing what buttons needed to be pushed in order to get top performance, and he had a feel for the game. With that feel for the game came a healthy respect for the game, which led him never to underestimate an opponent. Even when his team led in the standings, often by large margins, he never deemed a lead safe. Keeping the pedal to the metal throughout the season was the only line of attack in McCarthy's mind. The players and the manager had plenty of time to relax once the season was over. McCarthy's attitude rubbed off on his players, who played hard every day. Opponents couldn't help but take notice of his approach either.

When asked about McCarthy, rival manager Jimmy Burke of Toledo answered: "What do I think of Joe McCarthy? Why I think he would take a dead fly from a blind spider."

By the end of the 1925 season, McCarthy had won two pennants and finished out of the first division just once. In essence, the perfect manager had been developed. He had experience as a player and a manager, and he had shown a propensity for winning. All he needed to thrive at the Major League level was a chance.

While McCarthy continued to flourish, the Cubs floundered. After a 33-42 start, Bill Killefer, who took over as the team's manager in 1921, opted to resign his post in early July. The Cubs compounded their problems on the field by making Walter "Rabbit" Maranville the manager. Only 33, the veteran infielder had been in the Major Leagues since 1912 by the time he took over the reins as the Cubs player/manager. None of his employers ever questioned how he played on the field—he brought intensity to the game every day. But the nights that followed the games were bothersome. He made a habit of finding the speakeasies and carried with him a well-established penchant for going over the line after drinking too much. The Cubs' management figured that putting him in charge of the team might have a sobering effect on the future Hall of Famer. That didn't happen. If anything, Maranville seemed to turn it up a notch once he had control of the team. One incident saw him get arrested by New York City police after he went berserk on a cab driver he felt had charged him too much. That incident came on the second day after being named manager. Another episode saw him pass from one end of the train to the other spraying tobacco juice on any passenger who happened to be in his line of fire. The Cubs were a bad team with an even worse manager, which could be seen in the team's 23-30 mark after Maranville took over. Even Maranville recognized that the experiment was failing miserably, and he resigned in September, leaving George "Moon" Gibson to finish out the season as the team's skipper.

Baseball had become a huge part of the fabric of Chicago and owner William Wrigley Jr. understood that fact. The 1925 season had been a major embarrassment, so Wrigley was looking to resurrect the team's fortunes, as he told the *Chicago Herald Examiner*:

> *In 1896 I was traveling. I was bragging about Chicago being "the greatest town on earth." A fellow in Cincinnati stopped me cold one day. "Why that town of yours doesn't even own its own ball club." That was right, and to rub it in I learned that the team [then called the White Stockings] was owned by Cincinnatians . . . I resolved that some day I would give Chicago a ball team of its own . . . Yes, they're in the cellar, those boys of mine, [but next year] we'll have the ability. I'll shoot another quarter million dollars.*

In the backdrop of their worst season in franchise history, the Cubs formulated a plan. The solution to their problems would be to find a manager of high quality, one who understood the game and always remained a step ahead of the manager in the other dugout. They also needed a strong manager, a man who understood discipline and how to dole out punishment to those deserving of it. Patsy Flaherty, the former Louisville manager, had become a field scout for Cubs president William Veeck, and upon his recommendation they began to court McCarthy to become the team's manager in 1926. Rumors that McCarthy had signed to manage the Cubs began circulating when Maranville took over the club. He denied the rumors time and again. And in truth, he had not yet signed on to manage the Cubs. As late as October 9, 1925, Cubs president Bill Veeck would not confirm or deny that the Cubs had signed McCarthy. Two days later McCarthy signed a deal to manage the Cubs for $7,500 per season.

McCarthy received a favorable reception from the Chicago press. The track record he had established at Louisville along with Wrigley's enthusiasm about his new manager went a long way toward the initial perception. Wrigley told the press: "We have a man who knows baseball with us and don't forget that."

But there were several hurdles that McCarthy had to clear to gain complete confidence from Chicago. He had never played in the Major Leagues. Many felt that you could not successfully manage in the Major Leagues if you had not been a player in the Major Leagues. In addition, hiring a manager from outside an organization was an unusual practice for the era. Most organizations had a successor in line on the roster, or knew the guy the players respected and looked up to the most. The final hurdle in front of McCarthy: assembling a team for the 1926 season. Not only did the Cubs need to build a team that could win to gain the public's confidence, they needed to show that they had a team that could eventually *win it all.*

At age 35, McCarthy began the building process that would take the Cubs to the World Series. The acquisition of Wilson highlighted the moves. Harry Neely, who wrote for the the *Chicago American*, tabbed him as "Marse Joe," Marse being a Southern term for "master."

In McCarthy the Cubs got a disciplinarian who believed in endless drills stressing the fundamentals of the game. He carried preconceived notions about Southern and Polish players—whom he believed were hotheads, drunks, or both. If a player smoked a pipe, he was better served by not letting McCarthy know since McCarthy deemed pipe smokers as too easygoing. He liked position players better than pitchers, and he preferred not to have a set rotation.

While Wrigley had said he would kick in $250,000 for the new manager to spend on players for the 1926 season, McCarthy used prudence. In the end he spent approximately $50,000, coming up well short of his limit of which he said: "I can't use this. The only players I want to buy can't be bought, and there isn't any sense in spending your money on players that won't do the club any good."

McCarthy earned respect from the players from the beginning, even though he had not played in the Bigs. In part, he earned respect from his obvious brilliance in managing the game. He seemed to grasp things others did not.

McCarthy kept a low profile during the games, which extended to his treatment of the umpires. He figured out that arguing with the umpires never paid off, and he did not want to get ejected because he wanted to manage the games, so he remained seated in the middle of the bench without ranting and raving. Perhaps by avoiding the negative qualities of other managers he enabled himself to push more of the right buttons than the others, but chances were he just simply possessed a keener baseball intellect. McCarthy always seemed to be in thought, as if he were calculating moves for a chess match. And without fail, he always appeared to trump the moves of the other managers. In fairness to the managers McCarthy trumped, more managerial moves work out when you have better players, which McCarthy eventually had with the Cubs.

McCarthy thought outside the box, employing strategies that we now consider de rigueur in baseball. For example, he would become the first manager to divide his pitching staff into starters and relievers.

In the public eye, McCarthy was seen as a wise choice for the job, but he came off as dull, a square-jawed man with a squatty body who smoked big, black cigars. The only offseason hobbies he had were hunting and fishing and he didn't like to read, nor did he associate with his players. Baseball served as his one true passion.

After breaking camp, McCarthy felt good enough about his first Cubs team to write a short article in the *Chicago Herald and Examiner*. Here's a passage from the article that appeared on the morning of opening day:

We do not start tomorrow in a dash after the pennant. We are going out to prove we are a ball club that is capable of playing intelligent baseball and of taking advantage of every opportunity that comes our way. We may not be the best ball club in the National League, but we are a long way from the worst. This we will prove, perhaps before the week is out.

McCarthy exuded confidence to the public and to his players. But not everybody bought in.

In McCarthy's first season managing the Cubs, he found a major obstacle in the road in Grover Cleveland Alexander. McCarthy and Alexander were water and oil from the beginning, which could have gone badly for McCarthy since Cubs fans revered Alexander. The pitcher had been with the team since 1918 and had twice been a 20-game winner. That status coupled with the relationship he had with Bill Killefer made Alexander feel as if he had no rules. Killefer had been a catcher and he had caught Alexander, which meant that their friendship dated a long way back. That friendship included a lot of nights out knocking back the spirits. Alexander suffered from epilepsy, which would be widely known years later, but he also had an alcohol problem. Alexander crossed McCarthy countless times when alcohol was involved and Alexander's act quickly grew old.

When the veteran hurler sprained his ankle in spring training, the Cubs manager showed little sympathy, noting that his team was in good shape except for Alexander. Alexander would not hesitate to call McCarthy "bush league" behind his back, and he constantly pressed McCarthy's limits. After all, he was "Alexander the Great" and McCarthy was simply a minor league manager destined to fail in the Major Leagues. In one instance, Alexander arrived late to a team meeting that spring, and he had obviously been drinking. McCarthy had been discussing some new signals regarding situations with a runner at second base when Alexander, who had just lit a cigarette, chimed in with: "You don't have to worry about that Mr. McCarthy. This club will never get a man that far."

Alexander carried a rogue image, which caught on with Chicagoans during Prohibition. Early in the season the Cubs even staged an "Alexander Day," during which Cubs boosters rained gifts upon the beloved right-hander, including a new Lincoln. McCarthy knew he might lose the popularity contest if matters with Alexander came to a head—and they did. Alexander showed up deep in his cups at a June 15 game in Philadelphia. McCarthy euphemistically claimed Alexander had showed up "out of condition," prompting the Cubs manager to suspend the pitching icon. Wrigley backed McCarthy on the move. A week later the Cubs put Alexander on waivers and the Cardinals claimed him. A month after the transaction, Alexander sent a telegram to Wrigley, which, in essence, paid tribute to McCarthy as it read: "Congratulations. For years I've been looking for a manager who had the nerve to do that."

McCarthy would handle Hack Wilson much differently than he did Alexander. McCarthy understood Wilson like no one else. On the field, Wilson needed to be allowed to swing whenever he felt like swinging. And foremost, Wilson needed approval. McCarthy employed a radical method for the era in handling Wilson. Discipline defined the period: Either a player followed the manager's way or he took the highway, as the saying goes. McCarthy the disciplinarian actually spared the whip with Wilson, employing kindness instead. When Wilson did not receive his much-needed approval from the crowd, McCarthy could be counted upon to do so. And while McCarthy took a hard line with Alexander's drinking, the manager took a boys-will-be-boys attitude with the slugger. The reward came in performance. McCarthy got everything he could get from Wilson.

McCarthy once tried to impress upon Wilson the dangers of drinking. In the well-chronicled story, the Cubs manager put on a demonstration for Wilson. He dropped a worm into a glass of water and they observed the worm happily wiggling around. He then dropped the worm into a glass of whiskey and the worm died.

"What did you learn from that?" McCarthy said.

"I guess it means that if I keep on drinking liquor, I ain't gonna have no worms," Wilson replied.

Warren Brown covered the Cubs for the *Chicago Herald-Examiner* and remembered a story about Wilson during spring training. Brown was preparing to leave the team hotel and head to church on a Sunday morning when he saw Wilson storming in through the hotel lobby from his night out. A few minutes passed before he saw Wilson go back through the lobby to return to the car and drive off.

Brown hurried to the ballpark after church, wondering all the way in what condition he would find Wilson for that afternoon's exhibition game, if indeed he made it to the game at all. He did.

The Cubs accorded Brown the privilege of watching the games from the team's bench. He saw Wilson up close. Expecting to see a sorry performance from the slugger, Brown instead saw Wilson hit a home run in his first at-bat. He then repeated the act in his next at-bat. Brown noticed dirt caked to Wilson's uniform, clinging to the fabric drenched with sweat from the alcohol running through his pores. During spring training games, the custom is for most of the regular players to get one or two at-bats and take the remainder of the afternoon off. McCarthy allowed all of the regulars to do so that afternoon, with the exception of Wilson, who connected for his third home run of the contest in his third at-bat. Wilson never complained, though the toll from the night before could be seen in the manner in which he barely made his way around the bases. Once Wilson reached the bench, Brown observed McCarthy congratulating Wilson and telling him to hit the showers.

"You better go in now," McCarthy said. "You look awfully tired to me."

"Thanks," Wilson said. "It was so damned hot and sticky I couldn't get my regular sleep last night."

Once Wilson had left the dugout, McCarthy turned to Brown. "It's a good story, don't you think?"

Another variation of the same story had McCarthy driving to mass on Sunday morning when he had to swerve to miss a car speeding at him. Several men were hanging out of the car with whiskey bottles evident everywhere, and who should be behind the wheel but Wilson. According to that one, McCarthy made Wilson play that day, and he hit three home runs. When McCarthy took Wilson out of the game he explained why: "Otherwise you won't have the strength left to go out riding tonight."

Ralph "Buzz" Boyle, a teammate of Wilson, called him "the best night clubber that ever came along."

"People knew him everywhere he went," Boyle said. "He'd go from bar to bar, buying drinks. Joe McCarthy, who managed him on the Cubs, never tried to stop him from drinking. He knew it was impossible. But when they had a tough series coming up, he would ask him to cut down a little."

Pat Malone joined the Cubs in 1928 and became Wilson's best friend and drinking buddy. Around the clubhouse the pair could always be seen roughhousing and comparing muscles like teenaged boys. After hours they could often be found sitting next to one another at one of the many speakeasies they frequented. Not only did Wilson and Malone drink a lot, they enjoyed getting things stirred up after they had downed a few, whether this meant fighting or provoking others to fight. One of the pair's favorite rituals to get a few smiles—or prompt someone to fight—was to pass through a hotel lobby and set fire to newspapers while hotel guests were reading them. Malone even antagonized his roommate, Percy Lee Jones. After Malone trapped pigeons on the ledge outside their hotel room, he then placed them in Jones's bed—while he slept. They ceased to be roommates.

Eventually, Wilson and Malone would become roommates, leading to more advanced pranks fueled by alcohol. In a Philadelphia hotel after midnight, Malone made his way back to the room he shared with Wilson. He went slowly since he literally crawled all the way, first up the stairs and then down the hallway until he reached the room and began banging on the door, yelling for Wilson to let him in. Wilson never came to the door, which only served to make Malone bang on the door even harder. By the time Malone had quit banging, most every hotel guest on the floor had poked his or her head out of their room to see for themselves who was making all the noise. Malone headed back down the stairs.

Malone had been gone from the scene for only a few minutes when Wilson staggered to the room and—to the amazement and ire of the hotel guests staying on the same floor—began banging on the door for Malone to let him in. Nobody knows where the pair eventually slept that night, but the next day at breakfast they fought like a married couple, each accusing the other of not opening the door.

Another night in a Boston hotel during the 1927 season, the pair's behavior grew destructive. Wilson and Malone went on a bender and finished the night, or early morning, with a rampage in their hotel room. By the time they had finished ransacking the room, literally breaking most everything into little pieces, including the toilet seat, they were paid a visit by the hotel manager. After surveying the damage, the astonished manager told the Cubs' traveling secretary that the team had to leave. The Cubs did not end up having to leave, thanks in large part to some shrewd bargaining by their traveling secretary. By the time the traveling secretary had won back the right for the Cubs to remain in the hotel, he had promised the manager that Wilson would apologize and even shake his hand. A meeting between Wilson and the hotel manager was arranged to take place in Wilson's room. And a cordial meeting in fact transpired between the two, but did not take place without interruption as Malone burst into the room when they were wrapping things up. Drunk and disheveled, Malone insulted the manager, no doubt making him immediately regret his decision to let the Cubs remain in his hotel.

Hijinks aside, Wilson finished the '28 season with 31 home runs. Malone picked up 18 wins.

Judging from McCarthy's record of decisions, the difference between his dealings with Wilson and those with Alexander came down to the fact that Alexander openly challenged McCarthy's authority. A manager can choose to ignore errant behavior from great players as long as they don't move into confrontation. Wilson was compliant in the clubhouse and on the field, religiously following his manager's wishes.

Charlie Grimm spoke about McCarthy's handling of Wilson during a 1977 interview with Bob Broeg: "Mac was quite a psychologist. He could get Hack crying like a baby. Wilson would go through a wall for him. He kept him straight."

McCarthy, though perceived as a taskmaster and a disciplinarian, seemed to carry a soft spot for Wilson. Later in his life, McCarthy would speak about Wilson with sadness: "Hack was a much misunderstood man. He needed someone to hold him by the hand. His background was meager. I'm afraid the public jumps at conclusions and decisions too fast and pays too little attention to the handicaps which some of our players have to overcome as youngsters. If you come out of a coal mine into the sunlight, your psychology is not likely to match, at once that of the youngster who went from a good home to college and then into the Major Leagues."

McCarthy brought more to the table than just understanding Wilson. He continued to show a shrewd eye for talent. Take the example of pitcher Hal Carlson. McCarthy wanted the right-hander, and the Cubs acquired him from the Philadelphia Phillies in June of 1927 for Tony Kaufmann, Jimmy Cooney, and $20,000.

Carlson had begun his Major League career with the Pittsburgh Pirates as a spitball pitcher in 1917 before shipping off to France in World War I, where he served as a machine gunner with the 76th infantry. When Major League Baseball outlawed the spitball prior to the 1920 season, those pitchers who relied on it were grandfathered in to continue using it after their respective clubs registered them as such. Pittsburgh failed to do so with Carlson, and he lost the right to use his best pitch. Thus, he had to reinvent himself on the mound and he did so with success. But after Carlson went 12-8 while finishing the 1927 season with the Cubs, he fell to 3-2 the next year after being ill for much of the campaign. Still, McCarthy did not give up on Carlson, and he rewarded the faith of his manager by reeling off an eight-game winning streak in July of 1929. Carlson's performance validated McCarthy's innate ability to see beyond the obvious.

Among the measures of discipline McCarthy insisted upon were that players shave before they arrived to the ballpark. The logic for that rule came from his belief that playing baseball was a man's job, and he should treat the workplace, aka the ballpark, as such. But while he disciplined players, he wasn't one to show them up by doing so in front of the others. McCarthy would simply call the player back to his office and discuss the matter behind closed doors. However, everyone knew making the same mistake twice would not be tolerated. Repeated mistakes usually meant getting traded elsewhere.

McCarthy came up with his Ten Commandments for Success in the Major Leagues, which were as follows:

Nobody can become a ballplayer by walking after a ball.

You will never become a .300 hitter unless you take the bat off your shoulder.

An outfielder who throws after a runner is locking the barn door after the horse is stolen.

Keep your head up, and you may not have to keep it down.

When you start to slide, slide. He who changes his mind may have to change a good leg for a bad one.

Do not alibi on bad hops. Anybody can field the good ones.

Always run them out. You can never tell.

Do not quit.

Do not fight too much with the umpires. You cannot expect them to be as perfect as you.

A pitcher who hasn't control, hasn't anything.

McCarthy continued to hold his belief that at no time should his team pull off the dogs. No lead was safe in a baseball game.

During the 1929 season, well after his team had clinched the National League pennant, the Cubs were throttling the Boston Braves. Judge Fuchs managed the Braves and pleaded with McCarthy to let up on his team, telling him that he was "killing baseball in Boston" and asking him why he always kept trying to score more runs. McCarthy told Fuchs that he would answer his question at some point in the future.

Following Game 4 of the 1929 World Series when the Cubs blew their lead, Fuchs went to the Cubs' clubhouse to console McCarthy.

"Well, you got it today, Judge," McCarthy told Fuchs. "The answer to that riddle you were asking me in Boston."

Chapter Four

The Rajah

ROGERS HORNSBY ARRIVED IN THE MAJOR LEAGUES AT THE AGE of 19 after the St. Louis Cardinals purchased him from a Class D club in 1915. A shortstop, he weighed all of 140 pounds when he made his Cardinals debut on September 10, 1915; he hit just .246 in 18 games that season. Miller Huggins saw potential in Hornsby, but the Cardinals manager also saw a scrawny young man whose 5'11" frame needed beefing up if he was going to handle the rigors of big league baseball. Could Hornsby's body withstand a 154-game season? Did he possess the physical attributes necessary to battle bigger men arriving at second base with red asses trying to break up double plays?

Eaten up with a desire to be the best, Hornsby spent the winter laboring on his uncle's farm and eating everything in sight. By the time he reported to spring training in 1916, he had added 20 pounds of muscle and appeared ready to stand his own on the diamond with men older than him. In addition to having a sturdier body, Hornsby also put into play a new approach at the plate. The great Honus Wagner, who would become a member of the Hall of Fame's original class in 1936, pointed out to Hornsby the virtues of standing in the far reaches of the batter's box to hit. Doing so gave pitchers the impression that he would not be able to reach the outside pitch. But to Wagner's way of thinking, a hitter could drive the outside stuff to right-center field and easily open up to pull the inside pitches. Wagner's advice worked, and Hornsby's career kicked into high gear.

From 1916 through 1920, Hornsby hit .325, reaching .370 in 1920. In 1921, he stepped up his game even further, hitting .397. Averages of .401, .384, .424, and .403 followed. Incredibly, Hornsby walked 89 times when he hit .424 in 1924, a season that also saw him hit 25 home runs and drive in 95. He garnished his .401 season of 1922 with 42 home runs and 152 RBIs. He wasn't a "hit-them-where-they-aren't" kind of hitter—he had power to spare and he could hit the ball to all fields. Hornsby won the National League Triple Crown in 1922 and 1925.

In addition to having gained a reputation as a top batsman, Hornsby was known foremost as a baseball man, who didn't win many friends with his personality, the nature of which could be partially attributed to his singlemindedness. Later in his career a teammate anonymously spoke of Hornsby to *Chicago Tribune* reporter Arch Ward and described him as such:

"Rogers only has one fault, if you can call it that. He lacks tact. He speaks his mind at all times. If you asked him how he liked your new necktie, he would take you at your word and tell you how he liked your new necktie. Sometimes that isn't diplomacy.

"Hornsby has no other interest than baseball. He will talk any angle of the game you want him to discuss from early morning until retiring at 11:30 p.m."

Ever protective of his eyes, Hornsby stayed away from reading books or going to the movies as he felt both practices could be detrimental to his hitting. In addition, he shied away from most all of the vices known to man such as drinking, smoking, and playing cards. He didn't even care for music because it might block out a conversation about baseball he was having in some hotel lobby.

He once noted: "If you live like I do, you can be a great player, too."

Hornsby's only true vice was going to the horse track, where he felt he had the necessary acumen to successfully handicap the ponies.

In truth, as a railbird, Hornsby lost a small fortune and did not endear himself to baseball's commissioner, Judge Kenesaw Mountain Landis, whose stance on gambling became clear when he dealt out lifetime bans from Major League Baseball in the aftermath of the Black Sox Scandal that saw the Chicago White Sox throw the 1919 World Series.

Branch Rickey served as the Cardinals manager from 1919 through 1925 until Cardinals owner Sam Breadon decided he had seen enough of Rickey's outside-the-box antics. He wanted change so he called upon Hornsby to manage the team. Hornsby reluctantly agreed on Memorial Day in 1925.

A frustrated Rickey decided to rid himself of his Cardinals stock. Breadon offered it up to Hornsby, and Hornsby bought more than a thousand shares at $45 per share, which would turn out to be a good move.

Breadon liked Hornsby's confidence. He knew Hornsby would do things the way Hornsby wanted to do things no matter what anybody else thought. He proved as much his first day on the job when he had Rickey's blackboard removed from the clubhouse. Rickey had used the blackboard to teach players about different aspects of the game.

"You don't win ballgames in here," said Hornsby while addressing the team during his first clubhouse meeting. "And if you don't know how to make the plays by now, you're not going to stay."

In Hornsby's second year on the job, the Cardinals advanced to the World Series, an event that coincided with the death of Hornsby's mother. Her maiden name had been Mary Dallas Rogers, which is where Hornsby got his first name. She had forecast that the Cardinals would win the pennant in 1926, and she died the day they clinched. In her last words she expressed her wishes that her son stay with the team until after they had played in the World Series. Accordingly, her funeral was delayed.

Prior to the start of the World Series, Hornsby had a rift with Landis, who declared that the New York Central Railroad would be the line used for both teams and Major League officials during the World Series. Hornsby stood up to Landis by telling him that the Cardinals had traveled on the Pennsylvania Railroad for trips to New York the entire season and that the Pennsylvania Railroad would remain their carrier during the postseason.

Hornsby could be credited for giving Grover Cleveland Alexander another chance after Joe McCarthy placed the 39-year-old on waivers in June of 1926. Alexander rewarded Hornsby by winning two games in the World Series when the Cardinals met the New York Yankees, and he came through in Game 7 by striking out Tony Lazzeri with the bases loaded in the seventh inning to help the Cardinals win the final game 3–2.

Many stories exist chronicling what actually happened when Alexander came into that game. The tales are tinged with accusations that the right-hander entered the game with a hangover from the previous night. Some even suggested he was drunk. But Les Bell, who was a 24-year-old third baseman for the Cardinals at the time, maintained that any reports of Alexander being drunk or under the weather from the previous night were myths.

"Everybody knows that he was a drinker and that he had a problem with it, but he was not drunk when he walked into the ballgame that day," Bell said. "No way."

Bell, Hornsby, Tommy Thevenow, Jim Bottomley, and Bob O'Farrell waited on the mound while Alexander made his way in from the bullpen. Once Alexander reached the meeting the following exchange took place.

Hornsby: There's two out and they're drunk [the bases were loaded] and Lazzeri's the hitter.

Alexander: O.K. I'll tell you what I'm going to do. I'm going to throw the first one to him fast.

Hornsby: No, no. You can't throw him a fastball.

Alexander: Yes I can. If he swings at it he'll most likely hit it on the handle, or if he hits it good it'll go foul. Then I'm going to come outside with my breaking pitch.

Hornsby smiled. "Who am I to tell you how to pitch?"

Hornsby's final self-assessment, while possibly sarcastic, proved correct. Not only did Alexander finish out the seventh, he recorded the final six outs of the game.

Hornsby already owned St. Louis from his playing career. That popularity escalated after the World Series win. Given his popularity and the fact he liked playing in St. Louis, it would have been feasible to picture Hornsby spending the rest of his career in a Cardinals uniform. Had he not embarrassed the team's owner in front of the team that might have been the case. However, in addition to Hornsby doing things his own way, he did not fear his boss and treated him like he would treat anybody else, which meant gruffly for the most part. Breadon found this out during the 1926 season when Hornsby kicked him out of the clubhouse. In the aftermath of the incident, which Breadon did not forget despite the Cardinals winning the World Series, Breadon offered Hornsby a one-year contract worth $50,000 for 1927. Breadon knew the offer would not sit well with Hornsby, who expected a three-year deal. Hornsby balked at the offer, thereby prompting the trade that sent him to the New York Giants for second baseman Frankie Frisch and pitcher Jimmy Ring.

Hornsby liked playing in St. Louis and had not wanted to be the team's manager in the first place, so he did not take the news of his trade well. Seeking his own measure of revenge against Breadon, Hornsby aimed for his wallet by deciding to cash in his stock.

After being advised by a broker friend in St. Louis about the team's stock having increased in value to $125 per share, Hornsby stood to make a nice profit of $80,000 by selling his stock. Breadon stubbornly refused to buy back the stock at its appraised value, which eventually resulted in Landis calling a meeting of the other National League owners. They ended up making up the difference between what Hornsby wanted to be paid and what Breadon offered to pay him.

Hornsby could be stubborn and blunt to a fault, and he always made up his own mind about how to manage the club. For example, he did not believe in unleashing his nastiness toward the umpires, of whom he said: "Hell, they're human beings with a job to do and they don't beat you. The only thing I hated to see 'em ever do was miss the third strike on me so I didn't get a chance to swing."

Al Lopez elaborated on why he figured Hornsby always got along with the umpires. The Hall of Fame catcher spent all of his 19 Major League seasons in the National League, which put him behind the plate on many occasions when Hornsby was up to bat. Lopez started by noting that Hornsby was the best judge of a ball and a strike he had ever seen.

"Everybody knew it, too," Lopez said. "Including the umpires. On any given pitch, he probably did know whether the pitch was a ball or a strike, but having that reputation really helped him with the umpires. They would figure if Hornsby doesn't swing at the pitch, it's probably a ball. He was smart, too. If they did call him out or if they called a strike he thought was a ball, he wasn't about to give them a hard time. They were on his side. No reason to upset the apple cart."

Legendary umpire Bill Klem once called a ball on a pitch that the pitcher thought was strike three. According to the story, Hornsby then hit the next pitch out of the park. The umpire told the pitcher afterward: "You see, Mr. Hornsby will tell you when it's close enough to be called a strike."

After going to the Giants, Hornsby's play on the field remained true to form as he hit .361 with 27 homers while driving in 125 runs in 1927. John McGraw continued to manage the Giants, as he had since 1902, and Hornsby held the Hall of Fame manager in high regard, respectfully calling him "Mr. McGraw." But when Hornsby wasn't swinging the bat, he remained the same unpleasant force he had been in St. Louis. Though Hornsby never presented an affront to McGraw, he managed to reaffirm his reputation as blunt and prickly. Opinions, whether solicited or not, spewed from the Texan's mouth even if they might be hurtful. On one occasion, Hornsby had accompanied teammate Eddie "Doc" Farrell out to dinner when a New York writer dropped by their table and asked an innocuous question about whether he felt the Giants could win the pennant.

"Not with Farrell playing shortstop," Hornsby said.

No doubt that remark led to an interesting dinner.

Hornsby's remarkable achievements on the field and the fact he had managed earned him the job of team captain for the Giants in his first and only season with the team. That designation made him the team's manager when McGraw had to take a leave of absence to take care of some real estate issues in Florida. McGraw stood as the definitive autocrat and ran things the way he saw fit. So in his absence, most assumed Hornsby would simply put the team on automatic and run the team as if McGraw were standing in the dugout. But that wasn't the case. Though Hornsby respected McGraw to no end, he still ran the team the way he saw fit. The difference became evident after Giants third baseman Fred Lindstrom began a double play, using a cautious approach that made certain they would get at least one out. Afterward Hornsby let Lindstrom know that he did not like the way Lindstrom had executed the play.

Lindstrom defended the play by telling Hornsby, "But that's the way the Old Man wants it made."

To which Hornsby replied gruffly: "When he's here, make it the way he wants, but I'm in charge now and I want it done my way."

Hornsby could dish out the criticism, but he bristled at criticism directed his way, which came into play more when he managed. He did not care for Giants owner Charles Stoneham, a dislike that grew in the lobby of a Pittsburgh hotel when Stoneham asked Hornsby about a move he had made during a game. The owner's tone indicated that he was simply interested in finding out about the move for his own knowledge. Hornsby took the question as Stoneham second-guessing him, so he dismissed the Giants owner without answering his question.

Paranoia and insecurity ran through Hornsby, which was surprising given all the success he had enjoyed. He forever remained on the lookout for others trying to undermine him. While with the Giants he believed that the team's traveling secretary, Jim Tierney, worked against him by making adverse comments to the team's management about the way Hornsby did things. Once when Tierney complained to Hornsby about one of the Giants players who had played poorly, Hornsby told Tierney in no uncertain terms that he needed to "take care of the railroad tickets and hotel rooms" while leaving the managing to him. No doubt Hornsby's paranoia about others talking to team management about him stemmed from the fact that he didn't think twice about filling management's ears about a player or a manager in order to better his situation.

Besides being a bad influence in the clubhouse, Hornsby's gambling remained a problem. In 1927, different bookies approached the commissioner's office to report that Hornsby owed them several thousand dollars from bets he placed on losing horses. Hornsby's act quickly got old to the Giants, who traded him to the Boston Braves on January 10, 1928, for Shanty Hogan and Jimmy Welsh.

Emil Fuchs owned the Braves and had long admired Hornsby, which gave Hornsby the influence to have just the sorts of conversations that allowed him to undermine the manager. Hornsby's unbecoming pattern of behavior became apparent to all when he parlayed his friendship with Fuchs into a situation that cost Jack Slattery his job. Slattery had been a popular coach at Boston College before becoming manager of the Braves. Hornsby convinced Fuchs that Slattery was in over his head, which led to Slattery's dismissal 31 games into the 1928 season. Hornsby then became the team's player-manager. Despite the dismal team the Braves fielded, Hornsby managed to hit .387 with 21 home runs and 91 RBIs.

Boston finished in seventh place in the eight-team National League with a 50-103 record. In addition to their problems on the field, the team's finances were in terrible shape. Ultimately, the financial disarray of the Braves spelled Hornsby's end with the team.

Finishing in third place in 1928 were the Chicago Cubs, a team that William Veeck Sr., and Joe McCarthy believed could reach the World Series if they could add one more component to an already potent lineup. Knowing of the Braves' financial difficulties, they made an offer for Hornsby that Fuchs accepted. Hornsby went to the Cubs for Socks Seibold, Percy Jones, Lou Legett, Freddie Maguire, Bruce Cunningham, and $200,000.

When the apologetic Fuchs informed Hornsby of the deal, Hornsby told his friend: "Come on now Judge, you can't afford not to take that kind of offer."

McCarthy should have been apprehensive about bringing on board such a divisive figure. Given Hornsby's background, there were legitimate questions about whether he would try and backstab McCarthy or Charlie Grimm, the team's captain. Then again, how many .400 hitters could be acquired in a trade?

Upon bringing Hornsby aboard, Veeck told him that the Cubs had the "finest manager in baseball" and that he had quality assistants. Veeck went on to tell Hornsby that Grimm gave the team everything it needed in the way of a team captain and concluded with the following statement: "We are not hiring you for any of those jobs. We want you to play second base."

Despite such proclamations, Hornsby quickly ingratiated himself to Wrigley, spending almost an entire practice during spring training talking to the Cubs owner. The visit did not go unnoticed by the other players, who viewed the move as calculating. Nobody wearing a Cubs uniform had ever seen a player act so boldly, and the act bred suspicion among Hornsby's new teammates. Stories got passed around baseball about the character of a player, and seeing Hornsby with Wrigley confirmed much of what Cubs players had heard through the gossip wire. Meanwhile, Wrigley grew smitten with his new acquisition, noting after their session: "I heard more baseball today than I have heard in my whole life."

Hornsby then went out and hit .380 in 1929 with 40 home runs and 149 RBIs. While his personality and actions might have been difficult to gauge, his performance on the field remained incredibly consistent. Players on other teams would try anything to distract Hornsby from doing what he did best, which was hit a baseball.

Al Spohrer, a catcher for the Braves, figured he would prey on Hornsby's love of steak to get his mind to wander. So when Hornsby stepped to the plate, Spohrer told Hornsby that his wife had just discovered a butcher who sold top-of-the-line steaks. The remark piqued Hornsby's curiosity.

"That so," Hornsby replied shortly before strike one passed by.

"Not only that, Rog, but my wife can cook steaks better than anyone I know," Spohrer said. "Grace really can broil 'em."

Strike two successfully blew past Hornsby.

"What Grace and I thought, was that the next time you're in Boston, you might come out to the house and have a steak with us," Spohrer continued.

Hornsby swung and connected for a home run. Upon rounding the bases and touching down on home, Hornsby remarked: "What night shall we make it, Al?"

Following the 1929 season, the Baseball Writers Association voted Hornsby the National League's Most Valuable Player. But that would be the extent of the good news for Hornsby, who had to have bone particles shaved off of one of his heels. Hornsby gathered from his doctors that he would be able to play by the time the Cubs reported to spring training at Catalina Island.

During Hornsby's first season with the Cubs, he had played nice, save for one episode in which he leaked information to a reporter about botched scouting reports for the World Series. Initially he did not seem to want to upset the apple cart in regard to team harmony. When Grimm was injured during Hornsby's first year with the team, McCarthy asked Hornsby to assume his captain's duties and Hornsby happily did. Later when Hornsby received his paycheck he noticed he had been paid extra for assuming the captain's duties, which prompted Hornsby to call Veeck to tell him he didn't want that money—it belonged to Grimm. Veeck assured Hornsby that Grimm had not been docked and went on to tell him that as long as he executed the captain's duties, he would be paid accordingly.

Such selfless acts by Hornsby were few and far between. The poison he brought to the Cubs did not start to kill the team during the first season, but those who would be affected should have known their days were numbered. Someone as smart as McCarthy had to have known that from the day Hornsby was acquired he would have to watch his back. Others, like Hack Wilson, weren't so savvy. In Hornsby's eyes, Wilson's hard-drinking lifestyle made him a low-life. Yet Hornsby could find no fault in his own life, which featured infidelity, gambling problems, and horrible racism. With Hornsby in the Cubs' clubhouse, the future did not bode well for McCarthy or Wilson.

Hornsby's infidelity cost him his first marriage, which ended due to an affair he was having with a married woman. Making him even more of a miserable human being than his adultery and compulsive gambling was the fact he was a racist. He often criticized players in the Negro Leagues, and former sportswriter Fred Lieb maintained that Hornsby told him he joined the Ku Klux Klan.

Les Tietje, who pitched for the St. Louis Browns when Hornsby managed the club from 1933 to 1937 would say of Hornsby: ". . . one guy nobody liked and that was our manager Rogers Hornsby. Now there was a real p-r-i-c-k. With Hornsby, except for his Racing Forms, there was no newspapers, no movies, no beer, nothing. Women and horses, that was his downfall."

CHAPTER FIVE

The Depression, Martinsburg, and the Great Shires

TEN DAYS AFTER THE CUBS LOST THE 1929 WORLD SERIES, "BLACK Thursday" took place. October 24, 1929, saw the beginning of the Wall Street crash.

Black Thursday brought the first large fall in share prices, a loss compounded by incredible falls on October 28 and October 29. Among the causes were the vastly overvalued share prices, a growing lack of confidence in the market, and the falling profitability of blue chip firms, which offered a clear sign the boom years were over.

The market would continue to decline in the coming months until share prices had lost 89 percent of their value by July of 1930, and the market fell to its lowest level since the 19th century. In the aftermath of the crash, jobs became scarce and the nation moved into the Great Depression.

Ballplayers were not immune from the crash.

Rogers Hornsby had been on easy street just two months earlier. Following the advice of a broker friend in St. Louis, the Cubs second baseman had purchased mostly on margin a thousand shares of RCA that he had bought at 52, which meant his shares had been worth $505,000 on September 3 when RCA's price stood at 505. Obviously Hornsby's friend did not foresee the crash, nor did

Hornsby, who held onto the stock until after Black Thursday, taking a major hit.

Despite the disappointment of being labeled the goat of the World Series, Hack Wilson settled back into life at his home in Martinsburg, West Virginia, where he spent his days playing on a basketball team with the locals, deer hunting, and downing drinks with his cronies at the Moose Lodge. Some of the townspeople looked down on Wilson because they believed the only reason he remained in Martinsburg was because his wife hailed from there and would not go elsewhere. Others looked down on Wilson, or any member of Martinsburg Lodge 778, because they believed the lodge brothers gambled and made a practice of gawking at the women who passed by the lodge on their way home from the stocking factory. But Wilson had many friends, including the local police department, who often looked the other way to accommodate the legend living within their midst.

During Wilson's respite from the big city and any lingering memories of having become "Sunny Boy" after the World Series, Art Shires managed to catch his attention.

Shires was a pioneer in the art of self-promotion in the sports world. Outgoing and boisterous, the native of Italy, Texas, gave himself a nickname, "Art the Great."

Long before Reggie Jackson would call himself the straw that stirred the drink for the New York Yankees, Shires went about making a name for himself with the sporting public. Shires thought nothing of stopping somebody on the street to tout the merits of the White Sox first baseman—who happened to be Shires. Like Wilson, Shires had a reputation as a man who knew how to use his fists. The difference between the two was that Wilson had to be provoked for his temper to flare up. Shires possessed a switch that easily flipped on and off. He could be all smiles one moment and throwing fists at an innocent bystander the next.

Shires kicked around several different places trying to find an entry into professional baseball during his late teen years. He knew he had the ability to make a living in the sport. He made a name for himself playing for Waco of the Texas League, which attracted the Chicago White Sox. They bought his contract on July 31, 1928.

Shires was just 21, but he already was outspoken and let everyone know that Waco had not pursued the best deal, which would have been to sell him to the Cleveland Indians. Shires's displeasure was motivated by the fact that he would have made a nice cut of the sale price on the deal. So rather than report to the White Sox, Shires opted to join a semi-pro team. The White Sox were not about to let a player they had interest in—and a player they had purchased—play semi-pro ball, and they managed to bring him into the fold approximately three months after they had initially purchased him.

Cocksure about his abilities and importance, Shires made his Major League debut against the Boston Red Sox on August 20, 1928, at Fenway Park. He had already gained a name for himself through the publicity surrounding his initial balking at playing for the White Sox. Many fans wanted to see him fail. Instead he enjoyed a glorious debut.

In his first Major League at-bat, Shires faced Red Ruffing, who had not yet developed into the Hall of Fame pitcher he would become with the Yankees later in his career. In Shires's first at-bat he tripled to deep center field. By the end of the day, he had four hits. Afterward, instead of employing the "aw shucks," humble approach, Shires told reporters that he figured he would hit .400 based on what he had seen of the American League.

Shires did not hit .400 in his rookie season, but he did hit .341, endearing himself to White Sox fans and the team while earning major points with the media as an up-and-coming superstar. The White Sox were still reeling from the "Black Sox" scandal, so suddenly having a drawing card like Shires felt like manna from heaven for the Pale Hose. In their minds, Shires might just attract the fans back to the South Side. So confident were the White Sox in Shires's ability that they made him a team captain after his rookie season.

Off the field, Shires flaunted his flamboyance with an attention-grabbing wardrobe. Within his closet were the clothes to make him fit in at any sort of social function, from golfing or yachting to the finest black-tie affair. Not only did he like wearing the fancy clothes, which fit him well due to his athletic build, he went a step further by having a collection of canes to complement his wardrobe. What he wore might have been over the top, but nobody would dispute that he had good taste.

Shires had just finished his second year in the majors as a first baseman for the White Sox, and his reputation for being a brawler had grown. He had punched out his manager, Lena Blackburn, on two occasions. After the second incident, a friend of Blackburn, "Mysterious Dan Daly," accosted Shires, clearly hoping to teach him a lesson. Shires hastily arranged for a boxing match to be staged with an accommodating gate. After taking care of Daly in 21 seconds, a bright light went off in Shires's head, and he saw dollar signs on the horizon. He orchestrated a match in which he would fight against George "The Brute" Trafton of the NFL's Chicago Bears. Rather than concentrate on the fight with Trafton, he looked ahead to putting more fights on his calendar. The more fights he booked during his offseason, the more he could augment his baseball salary. He believed the biggest payday to be had would involve a rivalry from Chicago. There were Cubs fans and White Sox fans, and neither side shared any love for the other. What if he could get someone from the Cubs to fight him? Pat Malone loved to mix it up, but Shires wanted big dollars and to get big dollars he needed to be able to promote such a fight. That's when Hack Wilson flashed across his radar. Wilson reigned as Chicago's baseball hero, and he had a well-chronicled history of using his fists. Shires didn't procrastinate after identifying Wilson as the guy he wanted to fight. The publicity would be great. He had no thoughts of losing such a fight, and—given the right promotion—it had the potential to earn him more than he made in a single baseball season. Shires bounced the idea off his manager,

James C. Mullen, who the *Chicago Tribune* referred to as "the same Jim Mullen, folks, who time and again lost his shirt trying to sell skilled boxing to the fans, but who has now struck the public fancy with a gladiatorial vein which has apparently thrown boresome artistry out of the ring."

Mullen and Shires agreed that Wilson would be the best draw he could possibly have for a Windy City bout. Both envisioned a packed house watching while Shires pummeled the Cubs' bulldog of a slugger.

Shortly after Shires and Mullen reached their conclusion, Shires went to the telegraph office and fired off a challenge to Wilson. The message arrived in Martinsburg while Wilson sat at a Blue Ridge League meeting with a large crowd of townspeople in attendance. Rather than hand the telegraph to Wilson, the delivery man handed the telegraph to the man at the podium running the meeting, and he chose to read Shires's message to the crowd.

Wilson's chest seemed to swell when he stood and declared, "I accept. Wire him right away and tell him to name a place."

Cheers erupted, giving Wilson a dose of the much-needed acceptance that he had craved throughout his life. If fighting Shires brought so much satisfaction to those around him, and he made some extra money in the process, it had to be the right move. Wilson did not give any thought to what the Cubs might think or that his wife might not approve. Later in the meeting, Shires's response to "name a place" arrived in another telegraph that read: "Have decided I will fight any place but in the sun."

Shires left little doubt; he knew how to promote. His messages kicked off a winter of verbal sparring between the two. Readers of sports pages around the country knew Wilson had been doing some hunting in the offseason. A wire photo ran in early December underneath the title: "Hack and His Big Game." In the photograph, he was shown holding a shotgun while standing behind a 200-pound buck he had killed in the woods near Huntsdale, Pennsylvania. Wilson credited his hunting exploits with keeping him in excellent shape, but he planned to take his conditioning a step further by going to the gym and training like a boxer. Wilson further planned to bring in quality sparring partners to help him prepare for however many rounds he needed to defeat Shires in the ring. In short, Wilson made his intentions clear: If Shires had ideas of beating him in the ring, he had better be ready for a brawler possessing great toughness, who also knew how to box. Wilson did not engage in the manner of ridicule that Shires employed.

"I haven't thought up any mean things to say about Shires yet but I guess, with the Cubs-Sox angle, we won't have to smoke up any grudge stuff," Wilson said.

Surprisingly, the Cubs seemed indifferent to Wilson's fight plans. Bill Veeck initially said he could see no reason why Wilson should not fight Shires, while Joe McCarthy teased that he would handle Wilson's water bucket during the fight.

Shires continued to publicly humiliate Wilson. Here's just a sample of what Shires dished out on a daily basis:

"Hack will lose sight of my gloves just like he lost sight of the ball in the World Series. But instead of looking at the sun he'll be seeing more stars than there are in the heavens.

"The fact that Hack belongs to the National League, which really is a minor league, doesn't prod my Major League pride. The worst thing I have against Sunny Boy is that he's an outfielder and outfielders for the most part are a worthless lot."

If Wilson had a dog, no doubt Shires would have insulted the canine. Such a tactic served Shires's purposes two-fold by promoting the fight while also trying to goad Wilson into following through on taking part in the exhibition.

If Wilson took part in the fight tentatively scheduled for January 1930, he would be paid $10,000; Shires had an arrangement with Mullen that paid him a percentage of the gate. Both players would be well compensated for the fight, and they would earn every penny of it since Chicago Stadium, the proposed venue for the match, would be packed.

Ever the promoter, Mullen had established that the combatants would sign autographs and pose for pictures prior to the fight. He hoped to enlist Babe Ruth's services as a guest referee for the bout, a move that would first require the Illinois boxing commission's blessing—but Mullen specified he did not want Ruth if Ruth did not feel he was capable of being a competent referee. That thought seemed comical considering the boxing pedigrees of the combatants.

Eventually Veeck reversed his position and tried to put a halt to the fight. He got in touch with Wilson and let him know that he would not be pleased if such a fight took place and that the Cubs were not behind him at all. Contracts at that time did not specify what a player could or could not do during the offseason. Decades later, player contracts would contain clauses preventing players from participating in any number of activities, such as basketball, karate, skydiving, or anything that might damage a team's prized asset. Warnings aside, Wilson could pretty much do what he wanted and have the public on his side given his standing in Chicago. Cleverly, Wilson put the ball back into Veeck's court by suggesting the Cubs could stop the fight by simply adding another $10,000 to his salary. Veeck didn't bite.

Wilson presented one front to Veeck and another when talking to the newspapers later that day, telling them the fight was off even though the money had greatly tempted him.

"Mr. Veeck called me twice on the phone today to ask and warn me not to go into the fight," Wilson said. "This afternoon while I was duck hunting, Mr. Veeck called Mrs. Wilson and asked her to join with him and urge me to abandon the fight."

Wilson added that despite his statement, the reporters should not assume it was his final decision. He might just make a trip to Chicago to straighten out the matter.

Shires and Mullen sensed they might be losing their main attraction and opted to raise Wilson's take from the fight to $15,000. "Don't do that," Wilson told Mullen. "I didn't sleep a wink last night because I was too busy counting $10,000. Now I won't be able to sleep again tonight, for there's $15,000 to count this time."

If Wilson had any second thoughts about taking part, the expanded purse seemed to reel him back in as he told the *Chicago Tribune*, "$15,000 is a lot of bucks. I've been undergoing the most terrific struggle trying to be good and say no, but I just can't turn down that kind of dough."

It looked like the fight would happen, although no date had been set. Wilson would enter the ring using the name "Battling Stouts," and a betting line had been established that had Wilson as a 7–5 favorite over "The Great Shires."

While Wilson continued to train for the fight, he began to receive more opposition to taking part from his wife, Virginia, who issued the following statement to the newspapers: "If president Veeck of the Cubs wishes to disapprove of Lewis's plans to fight Art Shires or anyone else, I wish to voice my opposition too."

And, thus, a daily ritual began to take place in Wilson's little corner of the world. In the mornings while around Virginia, Wilson lacked resolve that he would actually take part in the fight with Shires. As the day progressed, Wilson grew more adamant about taking part in the fight. By the time the day had turned into night, Wilson could be found with his brothers at the Martinsburg Elks Lodge No. 778 demonstrating how he planned to handle Shires, talking loudly while punching the air as if the Great Shires stood before him.

In the public eye, Wilson began to come off as a hen-pecked husband who wanted the money but had to go up against more than Shires to get it: the Cubs' ownership and Virginia. Wilson made attempts to change the perception after Virginia made comments to the press. On one such occasion, he sheepishly explained his wife's comments by attributing them to her being upset because she could not decide what to buy him for Christmas. He then rattled off all the possessions he already had—a list that included "all kinds of haberdashery" and "three pairs of carpet slippers with 'Papa' embroidered on them"—to illustrate Virginia's frustrations, which Wilson somehow believed exonerated him from being considered a member of the hen-pecked husbands club.

Wilson continued to let the prospect of lining his pockets with the $15,000 invade his consciousness. One day he even set up a visit to the local bank where they allowed him to hold $15,000 in bills, then in gold. Wilson explained his infatuation with the sum by noting that he made several thousand dollars more per year than the $15,000, but he never had it all at once. He must have gathered some of what people thought about his being lured by the money, because he went on the defensive. He said he was not being "one of those greedy ball players you read about," though he called himself a spender and as such he needed to keep chasing the dollar. But he also was quick to point out that he had the virtue of generosity, citing the time he tipped a waiter a dollar during spring training. Tipping someone a dollar in the 1920s was a grand gesture, particularly during spring training when the players were paid only for their room and board. Wilson would go further by saying that he had heard Babe Ruth had tipped someone a dollar, but that he really didn't believe that.

The climate for the proposed "Battling Stouts" vs. "Great Shires" changed dramatically on December 16. That night a crowd of 5,000 crammed into the White City roller skating rink to watch from wooden bleachers as Shires squared off against Trafton. Most believed Shires's boasts, and his rants had made fighting Trafton sound routine. No doubt he would take his same tough guy act up against Trafton and quickly send him to the canvas as he had Mysterious Dan Daly. However, Trafton turned out to be a different kind of opponent. At 6'2", 230 pounds, he enjoyed an advantage of one inch in height and 35 pounds over Shires. Trafton, who played center for the Chicago Bears after being a standout at Notre Dame, understood physical contact. He would be elected to the NFL Hall of Fame in Canton in 1964, a place where sissies need not apply.

When the fight began, Shires quickly found himself in over his head. Employing the same hard-charging tactic he had used against Mysterious Dan Daly, Shires threw everything he had at Trafton, who responded as if he had been bitten by mosquitoes rather than floored by a bulldozer. After taking everything Shires had, Trafton landed a thundering left hook to the right side of Shires's head, sending him to the canvas with two seconds remaining in the round. Shires was saved by the bell, which was the only reason the fight continued.

In the second round, Trafton again landed a telling blow. He sent Shires reeling into the ropes where he seemed to hang like a helpless fly in a spider's web. To Shires's credit, he somehow managed to stay on his feet to survive the second round. The final three rounds of the scheduled five-rounder saw both fighters dancing around the ring, huffing and puffing in a fashion that further convinced the booing audience that neither was a trained fighter.

Afterward Shires bled from his lips, but his pocketbook appeared to take a bigger beating. While Shires's share of the gate from the fight paid him $1,800, he understood that by losing to Trafton he had put his big payday with Wilson in jeopardy.

Contacted after Trafton's victory, Wilson told reporters that the result of the fight should end any talk of him going to Chicago to fight Shires.

"I've been undecided all along, what with wanting to grab that $15,000 and yet not wanting to offend Mr. Veeck or cross my wife," Wilson said. "Now I know what I'm going to do. I'm going to stay right here in Martinsburg and get ready to play some great baseball next summer.

"If Shires had licked Trafton I guess I might have had to go to Chicago to talk Mr. Veeck into seeing my point. But there's no use in me bucking the Cubs, and making my wife mad, just to floor a guy who has already been licked."

In Wilson's mind, Trafton had taken $15,000 out of his pocket. Still, he felt thankful that the decision had been taken out of his hands. He could relax rather than leave the Blue Ridge country to head to Chicago for a fight. Wilson had also viewed the fight against Shires as being about more than money. The pursuit would have been almost noble: Shutting up Shires would serve as a proud moment to all the baseball players in the Major Leagues who went about their business with dignity and did not run their mouths. Once Trafton had taken care of business against Shires, Wilson felt as though Shires had been sufficiently humbled.

On December 22, Wilson received a Christmas card from Shires. The card was signed, "The Great, Great Shires."

Upon receiving the card, Wilson replied: "From now on I'm going to follow no sport professionally but baseball. Right now, however, I'm greatly interested in the basketball team that I'm coaching. It won the City League pennant for me last year and I believe the boys will come through again."

Days later, Shires fought again in front of a crowd of approximately 4,500 in Buffalo. This time the results were more in line with the image Shires tried to project, as he knocked out "Bad Bill" Bailey, a former Army amateur, in the first round.

Back in Martinsburg, Wilson was initiated into the local lodge of the Loyal Order of Moose, making him a member of three lodges; he already belonged to the Elks and Eagles lodges.

Wilson received a late Christmas present in the form of work compiled by National League statisticians. They came out with a report on December 30, 1929, that concluded Wilson was the best run producer in the National League based on his 39 home runs and 159 RBIs—despite striking out 83 times. The report emphasized that the unheard of amount of strikeouts was counterbalanced by the fact that his swinging for the fences yielded home runs. In later years the statisticians' concern about Wilson's strikeouts would seem ridiculous, given the high strikeout totals compiled by more modern sluggers.

Meanwhile, Shires and the prospect of a big payday continued to linger in Wilson's mind. After Shires's victory over Bailey, Wilson allowed that Shires had restored his reputation, which gave him license to once again consider fighting him. In early January, Wilson's Martinsburg friend, King Larkin, put out what amounted to a press release on behalf of Wilson. In essence, the release let it be known that Wilson considered Shires to again be legitimate, which again made fighting Shires a desirable pursuit. Edward Burns of the *Chicago Tribune* wrote the following about the realistic chances of that fight taking place: "We now have reasons to believe that Uncle Bill Wrigley and Bill Veeck wouldn't let Sunny Boy go through with it, even if they were forced to have some of Al Capone's or Bugs Moran's efficient sides kidnap their center fielder for a specified period."

Wilson had two reasons for expressing interest in going through with a fight against Shires. For starters, the banter could have been a ploy to get the Cubs to up his salary by $8,000 for the 1930 season, —a prospect some joked might come to fruition if Wilson caught the Cubs on a cloudy day when the sun would not be out, preventing them from being reminded about his fielding performance in the World Series.

Another possibility could have been Wilson's concern about the pending civil suit against him by Edward Young, the milkman Wilson went after in the stands the previous summer. Young originally sued the Cubs and Wilson for $50,000, but he amended his suit to exclude the Cubs and sought to collect damages of $20,000 from Wilson only. On February 11, 1930, the suit was heard in Superior Court by Circuit Judge William J. Fulton. Unsurprisingly the proceedings took just 20 minutes, and Wilson was exonerated. After all, judges had to get re-elected, and few people in Chicago were as popular as Wilson. Any talk about fighting Shires disappeared once

Wilson prevailed in court, adding weight to the idea that Wilson's anxiety about the lawsuit had fueled his interest in fighting.

The more the public found out about Shires, the more it seemed the White Sox first baseman had a past that he would have preferred to have remained private.

Back when Shires had played for Waco, they were facing a team from Shreveport, Louisiana, when Shires had lost his temper and fired a baseball into a group of fans not on his side. The ball he threw struck Walter Lawson at the base of his head. Seven months later Lawson died. The only thing that acquitted Shires from facing serious charges from the matter was the fact that Lawson was black in an era of institutional racism. Lawson's wife sued Shires for a large sum, but Shires managed to get the suit dropped on January 11, 1930, and he paid only $500.

Kenesaw Mountain Landis eventually took a stance regarding any proposed fights between Wilson and Shires when he stated on January 18, 1930: "Professional boxing will be regarded by this office as having permanently retired from baseball." No doubt Wrigley and Veeck had fanned the flames in the background prior to Landis's declaration.

The Shires versus Wilson fight never happened. The Cubs ended up signing Wilson to a contract that would pay him $22,300 for the 1930 season, leaving the slugger to concentrate on one thing: hitting the baseball.

CHAPTER SIX

Home Runs, Babe Ruth, and the Rabbit Ball

FEW THINGS PUT A HITTER IN MORE DANGER THAN A PITCHER WITH a spitball.

A pitcher could ignite a spitball by any number of means: adding lubricants, rubbing the ball in the mud, or simply spitting on the baseball. By employing the spitball, pitchers were, in essence, loading up a live gun and firing it in the direction of the strike zone. Unlike other pitches in which the ball moves in different directions as dictated by the spin put on the baseball, a properly thrown spitball has no spin. A knuckleball also has no spin, but knuckleballs are released at passive speeds that allow the fate of the pitch to be guided by whatever direction the air allows it to float through the strike zone. A spitball is thrown at regular speed, thereby creating a pitch with no spin that arrives at the speed of a fastball. A spitball squirts from a pitcher's fingertips like a bar of soap from one's hands, making the pitch impossible to completely control.

In Lawrence S. Ritter's *The Glory of Their Times*, the author interviewed Lefty O'Doul, who spoke about the difficulty of hitting a baseball when pitchers doctored the ball.

"I marvel at how some of those guys used to hit the ball back when I first started. The pitchers would use dirt and tobacco juice and licorice and make the ball as black as your hat. Why, just imagine Ty Cobb, hitting the emery ball, the shine ball, the spitball, the coffee ball—they used to chew coffee beans and spit it in the seams—just imagine him hitting .367 lifetime for more than 20 years."

In the same interview, O'Doul went on to speak about a banquet he attended at which Leo Durocher declared Willie Mays the greatest baseball player who ever lived. After hearing Durocher, O'Doul stood up and spoke, taking exception with Durocher and pointing out that Mays was a great fielder and he could run, but he wasn't in the same league as Cobb, Babe Ruth, and Joe Jackson as a hitter. After O'Doul finished his rant, a kid in the audience asked O'Doul what he thought Cobb would hit in modern times with a white ball. To which O'Doul replied: "Oh, about the same as Mays, maybe .340, something like that."

The kid followed by asking O'Doul why he thought Cobb was so great if he could only hit .340 or so with the lively ball. To which O'Doul replied: "Well, you have to take into consideration the man is now 73 years old!"

Understanding the dangers of the spitball and all the various doctored pitches—along with the difficulty batters had hitting the pitch—Major League Baseball instituted a rule change prior to the 1920 season. Up until that change, a pitcher could doctor the baseball with any kind of lubricant without any recourse. With the exception of a maximum of two pitchers per club who had been grandfathered in to use the pitch for the remainder of their careers, pitchers using the spitball were subject to disciplinary action, including getting ejected from the game for said offense.

By outlawing the spitball, Major League Baseball might as well have taken out an ad on the front page of the *New York Times* declaring they had decided to open the floodgates for a new era of offense. Ridding the game of the pitch helped trigger an offensive surge never before seen in the national pastime.

Complementing the demise of the spitter was the alleged arrival of a "rabbit ball." Whether the "rabbit ball era" is cooked up baseball history or not, it can't be denied that offense began to pick up after the 1920 season, which some historians have routinely attributed to clandestine meetings between Major League executives and baseball manufacturers, the result of which birthed a livelier ball.

Those who endorse the "rabbit ball era" theory believe that baseball executives wanted to boost attendance in the aftermath of the 1919 World Series, which proved to be fixed by the White Sox and New York City crime boss Arnold Rothstein. Worried about the effects of that scandal, the owners thought about what could be done to make fans forget and feel compelled to want to push through the turnstiles to watch their team. Fans seemed to enjoy the new game of baseball that saw hitters swing for the fences rather than place hits with precision. Home runs were quickly becoming the new be-all, end-all for the game. Thus, the conspiracy theorists had fodder for allegations that a lively ball existed. For a decade, stories went back and forth backing the theory while offense continued to rise.

National League president John Heydler offered this denial: "At no time have the club owners ordered the manufacturer to make the ball livelier. The only stipulation the club owners have made about the ball is that it be the very best that could be made."

Julian Curtiss, president of A. G. Spalding & Company, which supplied baseballs for the National League, made the comment: "There has been absolutely no change in the manufacture of the ball in recent years; that the ball is exactly the same in weight, in size, and in resiliency."

Even after the spitball was outlawed, dangers were still prevalent for the hitters, which became all too clear after the death of Ray Chapman.

On August 16, 1920, the Yankees played the Indians at the Polo Grounds in New York. Chapman stepped to the plate to lead off the fifth inning to face Carl Mays, a right-hander who employed an odd, submarine-type delivery that made the flight of the ball particularly hard to pick up for right-handed hitters.

Mays had struggled in the early going, surrendering a home run to Steve O'Neill in the second inning followed by two more Cleveland runs in the fourth, giving the Indians a 4–0 lead. Hoping to again get his team's offense going, Chapman assumed his normal crouched batting stance that saw him leaning forward to where he hugged the plate. Nobody could account for what happened next. Perhaps Mays's delivery disguised the ball too much. Maybe Miller Huggins had the right explanation. The Yankees manager thought he saw Chapman catch his left foot in the ground, which restricted his movement. Or the discoloration of the baseball could have made the ball undetectable for just a split second, a split second that would have allowed Chapman to get out of the way. Instead Chapman froze and the ball crashed into the left side of his head. Hitters did not wear batting helmets in 1920, and the resulting impact of the baseball boring into an exposed skull made such a profound thud that a palpable gasp by the crowd of 22,000 could be heard throughout the ballpark.

Mays actually thought the ball had hit Chapman's bat, prompting him to field the ball and throw to first base. He quickly learned otherwise.

The unconscious Indians shortstop collapsed in the batter's box. A doctor hustled from the stands to Chapman's side. After a brief delay, Chapman got to his feet with the aid of two teammates and tried to make his way to the clubhouse. He managed to negotiate only a few feet toward his destination before his legs again went out from under him. Chapman's prized possession was a diamond ring given to him by his wife of a year. Prior to the game, he had given the ring to Cleveland trainer Percy Smallwood to hold for him. In the clubhouse, Chapman struggled to speak, trying valiantly to say "ring" before he finally pointed to his finger. Smallwood understood and gave Chapman his ring shortly before they rushed him to St. Lawrence Hospital.

The game continued. Mays asked for a new baseball before facing the next hitter, Indians player/manager Tris Speaker, and the ball that had hit Chapman was thrown out of the game. The Indians held on to take a 4–3 win.

An x-ray of Chapman's injury revealed a depressed fracture on the left side of the skull. When his condition continued to deteriorate, a decision was made to operate. The one-hour operation took place at approximately 12:20 a.m., or roughly ten hours after the injury took place. Surgeons removed a portion of Chapman's skull approximately an inch and a half square and discovered that several blood clots had formed. Not only did the ball cause lacerations on the left side of the brain, but it also had caused trauma to the right side of the brain, which had been whipped against his skull.

Several of Chapman's teammates huddled together at the hospital while the surgery took place. Chapman had spent his entire Major League career with the Indians, having joined the team in 1912. Cleveland fans adored him and he enjoyed great popularity among his teammates, whom he had told that 1920 would be his final season if the Indians reached the World Series. After the surgery, Chapman seemed to be improving based on his breathing and the status of his pulse. Relieved and feeling that Chapman would pull through, his teammates left the hospital and returned to the team hotel only to be told around sunrise that he had died at 4:40 a.m. on August 17.

A firestorm about how to deal with the incident followed.

Initially, Mays took the blame. He had long pitched batters closely and had been known to throw "purpose pitches" to get hitters to quit crowding the plate. So thought was given to banning Mays from baseball. Players from the Boston Red Sox and Detroit Tigers embraced that thought by threatening to boycott games if he pitched. The Yankees hurler could not find a friend among the umpires either.

He had attributed the sailing action of his pitch to a rough spot on the baseball, which he noted had prompted him to ask for a new baseball after the incident. The umpires felt Mays was implying home plate umpire Thomas Connolly had been at fault for allowing the roughed up ball to remain in the game. Addressing that allegation, American League umpires William Evans and William Dinneen issued a statement that read:

> No pitcher in the American League resorted to trickery more than Carl Mays in attempting to rough a ball in order to get a break on it which would make it more difficult to hit. Until the new pitching rules came into force which put a severe penalty on a pitcher roughening the ball, Mays constantly used to drag the ball across the pitching rubber in order to roughen the surface. Hundreds of balls were thrown out every year because of this act.

Cooler heads prevailed and cries to have Mays banned eventually subsided. But the problem still remained about what to do to prevent future accidents from occurring.

One suggestion coming in the days following Chapman's death was to have players begin wearing helmets like those worn by football players at the time. That suggestion gained little steam, leaving baseball owners to consider other factors such as whether the accident could have been averted had Chapman been able to see the ball better. Nobody will ever know if the baseball's discoloration had indeed been a factor in why Chapman did not move, but the owners made a decision to remove that question from the equation. Before Chapman got hit, changing balls had not been a common practice. In fact it wasn't unusual for only one or two balls to be used the entire game, leading to discoloration. Chapman's death prompted the owners to instruct umpires to keep white balls in the game that could easily be seen.

While the existence of a whiter baseball—which could be confirmed, and perhaps a livelier baseball—greatly affected the offense, Babe Ruth's arrival likely had the biggest impact on baseball's surging offensive game.

Ruth entered the Major Leagues at the age of 19 in 1914 as a pitcher for the Boston Red Sox, and he had incredible success on the mound as a left-handed pitcher. After pitching in four games and posting a 2-1 record in 1914, he won 18, 23, and 24 games from 1915 through 1917. In 1917, he threw 35 complete games and had a 2.01 ERA. Ruth also had a 3-0 mark with a 0.87 ERA in three World Series starts. Having the success he had on the mound made the idea of his changing positions seem ludicrous. But there was just something different about Ruth when he hit. Instead of employing the "hit them where they aren't" approach that prevailed, Ruth brought another approach to hitting, which was more along the lines of "hit them where they can't possibly get them." Ruth would grab the heaviest bat and take a mighty cut at the ball, putting every ounce of his being into the swing. Some would laugh when he missed, others would marvel at his effort. When he connected, the balls he hit would clear the fences by great distances and those who watched gawked in awe as if watching a physical anomaly. Nobody had ever approached hitting in Ruth's way. While he might have struck out more than what the era tolerated, the rewards were great. Fans began to clamor to see him hit, which did not go unnoticed by the Red Sox management, who opted to have him play in the outfield on days when he didn't pitch. In 1918, Ruth pitched in just 20 games and won 13 while also hitting 11 home runs. He followed with 29 home runs in 1919 when he pitched in 17 games and won 9. The home run total established a new record, exceeding Gavvy Cravath's record of 24 that was set in 1915. Many years had seen single-digit home run leaders like Wally Pipp, whose nine home runs led the American League in 1917.

After the 1919 season, Red Sox owner Harry Frazee sold Ruth to the Yankees in what would become the most ballyhooed move in sports history. Ruth responded with 54 home runs in 1920 and followed with 59 in 1921.

Suddenly the Yankees slugger had created an entirely new brand of baseball. In the past, leads might have been crafted cautiously with a single, a stolen base, and a well-placed grounder to the right side of the infield to advance the runner to third base from where he could score on a ground ball or a fly out. Ruth brought an all or nothing style of instant gratification. Runs could be scored in bunches in a raucous and unpredictable fashion that brought ballparks alive.

Ruth became the biggest star in the game by hitting home runs. Success brought imitation, so other hitters began to follow Ruth's approach, which seemed to be the future while John McGraw's put-the-ball-in-play method quickly became the past.

Julian Curtiss, president of A.G. Spalding & Company noted: "Ever since Babe Ruth became the center of the baseball spotlight through his home run efforts, it was only natural that the other players would try and duplicate his performances. In the old days when the hit-and-run and the sacrifice had so much to do with the result of many close games, and the pitchers had so many liberties, home runs were scarce. But now the players go up to the plate, not choking the bat in an effort to place their hits, but they take a glance at the stands or fence, get a toe hold and swing."

Curtiss also pointed out that following Ruth prompted hitters to move away from using the once popular choke bat, which had thick handles and was designed with the idea that a hitter would use the bat to place his hits. Looking to hit home runs, players gravitated toward longer bats with thin handles that could be whipped through the strike zone.

Curtiss summed up his disclaimer about the existence of a lively ball with the following:

The so-called lively ball is a myth. I have read much about it, have been asked often if there was any change in its make, and many other questions pertaining to the present day baseball. But I wish to make it very clear that there is no change, has been no change and will be no change in the manufacture of the Spalding regulation baseball, unless such a request comes from the baseball officials, and I do not anticipate such a request. We have been making baseballs for the National League for fifty years and the Spalding standard of a half-century ago is the Spalding standard of the present. I want to repeat that there is no so-called lively ball, and that if the players played as they did in the old days, the lively ball charge would die.

Home runs were in baseball to stay and Ruth remained the model for all players to follow. Other players such as Rogers Hornsby, George Sisler, and Al Simmons began to successfully emulate Ruth, combining batting average with power, and their efforts fueled an offense in the 1920s the likes of which baseball had never seen.

CHAPTER SEVEN

Catalina Island, Spring Training, and $80,000 Per Year

St. Catalina Island seemed more like a hidden paradise than a site for a baseball club to prepare for the season, but the island served as the locale for the Cubs' spring training in 1930.

William Wrigley Jr. purchased part interest in the Cubs in 1916 and gradually increased his portion, enabled to do so through the good fortune of his chewing gum empire, which prospered greatly during World War I while other companies in different industries fell by the wayside due to wartime restrictions. Liquid and loaded, Wrigley discovered that the fortunes of the owner of St. Catalina Island were in dire straits, making the island available for purchase in 1919. Wrigley quickly pulled the trigger and bought it for $3 million. He saw the potential for the island, making him a pioneer in parlaying the lure of a Major League team combined with warm weather to attract vacationing customers from the Midwest looking to thaw out during the cold of winter. By the spring of 1921, Wrigley had become the club's principal owner and moving the club to St. Catalina to conduct spring training operations became one of his first orders of business. Not only would the move benefit the ballclub, it would also benefit Wrigley's development of what would turn into a vacation destination with an exotic flare.

Catalina stood just off the California coast adjacent to Los Angeles, a 25-minute ride by ferry. A tile factory and silver mine were located on the island as was the town of Avalon, which Wrigley brought to life. The Cubs owner installed the infrastructure, which included sewers and streetlights, and he built a grand hotel named the St. Catherine's. Wrigley spared no expense, adding a golf course and a bird sanctuary to the surroundings. Avalon also had a dance hall, touted as the world's largest, and the Avalon Grand Casino. Despite all the development, the charm of the island remained intact.

Automobiles were not permitted on Catalina, so when the Cubs stepped off the ferry that taxied them to the island, they were picked up by a wagon pulled by two horses and were carted to the team hotel, the St. Catherine's.

Pitchers, catchers, and rookies were the early arrivals to camp around mid-February. About a week later the rest of the team would report.

Practices and games took place in Avalon on a practice field and a diamond that replicated the dimensions of Chicago's Wrigley Field. But rather than skyscrapers, foliage encased the diamond, including many eucalyptus trees. The players' clubhouse looked down on the field from its location above at Wrigley's mountainside country club.

During the early days of camp, the Cubs went through twice-a-day workouts. Visitors arrived at the island daily to watch the workouts and later in camp, to watch the games, which were free of charge. The overwhelming portion of games played were intra-squad affairs, but the Cubs would occasionally host a team from the outside, such as the Pacific Coast League's Los Angeles Angels, who were also owned by Wrigley, or on several occasions the New York Giants. But most of the team's exhibition schedule took place once they traveled back to the mainland, where they would play games at Wrigley Field in Los Angeles. Playing games in Los Angeles, a city located in a state without Major League Baseball at the time, added glamour to the spring and gave the Cubs a certain cachet. After a week or so of games, the Cubs would play their way back across the country—earning money from the gates they played for, finishing in Chicago before the start of the season.

The disappointment of the 1929 World Series remained fresh in Wrigley's mind when the Cubs reported to Catalina in 1930. Wrigley continued to hold Joe McCarthy responsible for the Series as well as for other mistakes, like his miscalculation in the case of Lefty O'Doul.

O'Doul had been a sensational minor league pitcher before injuring his arm and converting to the outfield. William Wrigley had seen O'Doul playing for Salt Lake and he had been so enamored with him that he told the Salt Lake owner Bill Lane that he wanted to buy him for the Cubs. Lane had told Wrigley he could have O'Doul for $15,000 and Wrigley had responded, "Wrap him up."

Despite Wrigley's personally signing O'Doul, McCarthy did not consider O'Doul for his team, and he ended up being shipped to Hollywood of the Pacific Coast League. From there O'Doul joined the Philadelphia Phillies and won the National League batting crown in 1929 with a .398 average.

After the Cubs lost the World Series, Wrigley suddenly felt like McCarthy's lack of Major League experience hurt him, so Wrigley and Bill Veeck decided they needed to become more involved in the team's affairs, which resulted in the hiring of former Major League catcher Ray Schalk to McCarthy's staff. McCarthy rebuffed the move by never allowing Schalk to become privy to any moves or strategies he might make. The Cubs manager could read the writing on the wall. He told sportswriter Warren Brown that no matter what the Cubs did, he would be fired at some point during the 1930 season. Brown liked McCarthy and felt him to be an honorable man as well as the best manager in baseball. After McCarthy talked to Brown in confidence, Brown met with Colonel Jacob Ruppert, the owner of the Yankees. The Yankees had hired Bob Shawkey to manage the team in 1930 after Miller Huggins's death at the end of the 1929 season. At their meeting, Ruppert told Brown that he would eventually like to hire McCarthy to manage the Yankees. But no such move would take place prior to the 1930 season.

McCarthy didn't let his precarious position worry him. Instead he worried about Hack Wilson.

The Cubs skipper knew better than most that if the Cubs were going to win their second consecutive pennant, the top slugger in the National League had to be on board. He could not be concerned about the events of the previous year's World Series. Knowing Wilson as he did, McCarthy likely realized Wilson would never truly get over the humiliation of what had happened if he got off to a bad start and the national spotlight refocused on him. If he had too much time to brood over the catcalls of "Sunny Boy" that were sure to follow everywhere he went, Wilson might slide into a dark place from which he could never escape. Wilson's status as a functional alcoholic brought an uncontrollable element to the puzzle; alcohol could accelerate any troubling situation the slugger might face. McCarthy's job was to head off any such bumps in the road before they became major obstacles. A happy Wilson meant a confident Wilson, which translated to a big bat and a lot of Cubs victories.

Any worries McCarthy had about Wilson's state of mind were quickly dispelled early in spring training. Sunny Boy's self-deprecating humor showed he had put the 1929 World Series behind him. Wilson took batting practice during his first spring workout, and predictably, did not exactly create magic with his swings. He then made his way out to center field underneath a brilliant sun bearing down on the island. He teased with his teammates that the weather had been concocted as a means to embarrass him. Building on that theme, a fan offered Wilson an oversized pair of sunglasses, to which Wilson managed to keep his wits by noting that he should have been so fortunate to have a similar pair the previous October. On another occasion Wilson asked the waiter at the dining room of the St. Catherine's hotel if he could dim the lights so he wouldn't misjudge his soup.

McCarthy hit Wilson countless outfield fungos during the spring. One day a youngster began to pester McCarthy for a baseball while he hit balls to Wilson. McCarthy spoke to the youngster. "You see that fat fella out there in the outfield?" The youngster nodded that he did. "Well, you just stand behind him, and you'll get more balls than you know what to do with."

Farther east, Babe Ruth's contract saga played out.

The Yankee slugger's contract that had paid him $70,000 per year for three years had expired, leaving Ruth looking for a new deal. Recognized as the best player in baseball, who also happened to be the game's biggest drawing card due to his colorful personality and the way he played the game, Ruth wanted to be paid accordingly. By the time he departed New York for St. Petersburg, Florida, where the Yankees conducted their spring training operations, he had already revealed his hand. He wanted a three-year contract that would pay him $85,000 a year.

Understanding that the negotiating had just begun, Ruppert made an initial offer of $70,000 for one season. Ruth listened to the offer and smiled, knowing that the process would have to play out and likely would not play out quickly.

When both sides parted, Ruth noted: "I have given 16 years of what I think has been pretty fair service to baseball. And I think I am entitled to a break. Every time the signing of a new contract has come up I have asked for more money and signed for less than I asked for. But this is one time I am going to get what I want or there will be no signing."

The Yankees had acquired Ruth from the Red Sox for the sum of $100,000. When they acquired him, he had one year remaining on a contract that would pay him $10,000 for the 1920 season. After he hit 54 home runs to establish a new Major League record, the Yankees doubled his salary in 1921. Ruth then signed a five-year deal that paid him $52,000 per season.

Ruth had hit 46 home runs in 1929, despite playing in just 135 games, giving him 516 career home runs. He wielded those home runs as a bargaining tool as he did with his overall good physical condition. He weighed in at 225 pounds—his lightest playing weight in more than six years—which he reached by going on an extended hunting trip along with plenty of bowling.

Ruth's salary drive captivated the nation as reports of the negotiation dominated sports pages during the early part of 1930. Even noted satirist Will Rogers weighed in on the situation in a letter to the *New York Times* in which he wrote: "They offered Babe Ruth the same salary that Mr. Hoover gets. Babe claims he should have more. He can't appoint a commission to go up and knock the home runs. He has to do it all himself."

Once Ruth reached Florida he told reporters he would continue to stay in shape with daily rounds of golf. True to his word, he immediately made his way to the golf course with his wife. Unless his contract situation was quickly resolved, Ruth planned to remain in St. Petersburg briefly before heading from the west coast of Florida to Miami in the state's southeast corner.

The Yankees finally sent Ruth an offer of two years at $75,000 per year. Upon receiving the offer, Ruth sent letters to the New York newspapers detailing his finances. According to the documents, Ruth could retire and still make $25,000 per year for the remainder of his life. Thus, if the Yankees wanted to play hardball, he was prepared to play hardball in return. In his letter, Ruth stated:

"If the Yankees reject my request for an increase (less than 20 percent) I will remain idle which, at my age, means retirement from baseball. I mean organized baseball. A few years ago I could not take this attitude. I would be obligated to sign at any terms for the same reason that 95 percent of all players have to sign—bread and butter. Every holdout in baseball history had to sign because he had no money in the bank.

"Well, there is enough bread and butter in our home even if I never touch another baseball in my life. Without receiving 5 cents from the Yankees during 1930 I am assured an income of $25,000 from established dividends and royalties. I have saved exactly $150,000 in less than three years, which pays me every three months."

The letter finished by stating the many offers Ruth had away from the Major Leagues, which included vaudeville, the circus, and independent baseball.

Players of this era had virtually no leverage in contract negotiations—even Ruth—because they were all bound to their clubs due to the "reserve clause," a standard provision in every player's contract. Under the reserve clause, players were obligated to remain with the club that basically owned them as long as they wanted to re-sign them. Players not happy with whatever contract was offered them had no recourse other than to return the contract and threaten to not play. If the player went through with his threat, he would not be allowed to play for another team. If Ruth and the Yankees could not come to an agreement, the Babe had no recourse other than to hold out and refuse to play. Free agency would not come to baseball until the 1970s.

Throughout the early part of spring, Ruth's exploits continued to be a daily national story. When he played a round of golf at the Belleair Country Club in Belleair, Florida, on February 4, the report of his round included a description of how he had navigated the 534-yard 11th, hitting a driver 325 yards before using a 4-iron to reach the green on his second shot.

Ruth went quail hunting with several friends, including teammates George Pipgras, Benny Bengough, and Johnny Nee, on February 13 in an area outside of St. Petersburg and a rattlesnake struck at Ruth. But just before the snake could bite Ruth, one of the group's dogs leapt in front of the snake and got bitten. Ruth then fired his gun to kill the snake. Pipgras treated the dog with an anti-snake bite serum.

Ruth served as a ring judge for a local fight on February 18, he went on a fishing trip along the Crystal River on February 24, and on February 27 he attended a heavyweight fight in Miami between

Jack Sharkey and Englishman Phil Scott that Sharkey won by a knockout when Scott was disqualified.

On March 1, Ruth made his first appearance at the Yankees' practice field, but he did not put on a uniform, though he did entertain the crowd and he talked with his teammates while they took batting practice. Ruth remained unsigned on March 3, but the itch to take part in practice finally got to the slugger and he worked out with the team. During that workout, he managed to incur an injury when he took part in an intra-squad game and spiked himself sliding into third base.

Finally, on March 8, Ruth and the Yankees came to terms on a two-year deal that would pay him $80,000 per year.

"I have nothing much to say," said Ruth after signing the deal. "I am glad I don't have to talk or think about money for a while now. I hope we have a great year, and, as I told the Colonel, I'm going to try to hit a home run for every thousand dollars the club lays on the line."

Herbert Hoover, the thirty-first President of the United States, made a salary of $75,000, which prompted Ruth's famous retort when asked about making a higher salary than the president: "Why not? I had a better year than he did."

Players were already trying to emulate Ruth's power, but the salary paid to the Sultan of Swat proved to be added incentive for any player who even dreamed of being a slugger. Joe Vila of the *New York Sun* wrote: "The players, keeping in mind Babe Ruth's $80,000 contract, are doing their level best to knock the ball over the fences."

The Cubs' camp, meanwhile, was miles away from Ruth. Most clubs would conduct spring training in the future in Arizona and Florida, in which they operated within reasonable distance of other clubs, allowing the teams to play one another in exhibition games. Nevertheless, the Cubs went about their business as usual in 1930.

It was typical in the early days of spring training for a new phenom to pitch batting practice. George Bell took the mound during a morning drill to face seasoned Cubs hitters like Wilson, Rogers

Hornsby, Cliff Heathcote, Lester Bell, and Woody English, and the kid, described as "loose jointed," left them cussing under their breath. Such a scene had played out countless times during every spring training camp for every major league club: a youngster arrives to camp when pitchers are ahead of hitters, as far as getting ready for the season, and proceeds to put his best stuff on display. In Bell's case, that meant a sinker that left the powerhouse lineup pounding the top of the baseball and driving it with great frustration into the dirt. The hitters became even more frustrated because their bodies were sore from activity and their hands were blistered from hitting after months of not swinging a bat. Some of the players were fighting to lose weight, including Charlie Grimm, who wore a rubber shirt in hopes of sweating off the extra pounds. Wilson did not fashion one of the rubber shirts; surprisingly he reported to camp 11 pounds lighter than he had the previous season.

Hornsby boldly told reporters that the Cubs should repeat as National League champions, which he based primarily on the fact the Cubs had the same team that had mauled their opponents the season before, and that the other teams in the National League had done little to improve their clubs over the winter.

Hornsby's right heel brought more concern to McCarthy than Wilson's mental state. The veteran second baseman's recovery from the offseason surgery wasn't supposed to be a concern, but it ranked high on McCarthy's worry list as Hornsby continued to be bothered by pain.

While McCarthy had concerns about Hornsby's health, the Cubs manager felt optimistic about Gabby Hartnett. The veteran catcher had played in just 25 games in 1929 due to a sore right arm. But Hartnett felt as though he had a new throwing arm in the spring of 1930. He felt so good that he begged McCarthy to let him make throws to second base during batting practice, a request denied by McCarthy. The Cubs' chances of making another run at a National League pennant would be greatly enhanced with Hartnett behind the plate. So McCarthy took the conservative approach, while hoping upon hope that what he was seeing from Hartnett was not some cruel baseball mirage.

McCarthy kept his thoughts about the Cubs' batting order secret, leading to much speculation from the press. Initially McCarthy tinkered with Kiki Cuyler leading off and Woody English hitting second, followed by the Cubs' "Murderer's Row"—Hornsby, Wilson, and Riggs Stephenson.

Since the Cubs would not play exhibition games against other teams until they went to Los Angeles later in the spring, McCarthy divided the squad into two teams, "The Regulars" and "The Goofs," so they could play against each other.

Nights saw the Cubs stay mostly among themselves, playing pinochle and poker, and talking baseball. Occasionally there would be team activities such as a dancing contest held at the casino. Trainer Andy Lotshaw and pitcher Hank Grampp tied in the waltz contest, but Lotshaw won the $10 first prize. Other memorable moments from the evening included pitcher Lefty Moss winning the one-step competition and pitcher Bill McAfee winning the foxtrot.

After the Cubs spent a weekend playing games in Los Angeles against the Angels, McCarthy let his team have a rest on Monday morning. All of the players took advantage of the respite, aside from Grimm, who borrowed Wilson's movie camera and toured the island shooting different scenes. In the department of reading between the lines, the *Chicago Tribune* reported that in the steamy afternoon workout that followed, perspiring was made easy and in that department, "As usual, Hack Wilson and Pat Malone excelled." Excelling at perspiring served sufficiently as code for both having hangovers and having to sweat it out.

Days later during a morning drill on the island, Wilson came up with sore feet, or so he said. He tried selling that prospect by showing up in a heavy rubber shirt under the guise of being able to sweat without having to move his feet. McCarthy didn't buy it and directed

Wilson out to center field. McCarthy hit fungos to Wilson until his uniform was soaked after fifteen minutes. That's when Wilson begged off, insisting that his feet could not take the pounding any longer. This occasion served as one of those times when McCarthy recognized that he needed to pick his battles. And after all, he had extracted his pound of flesh from Wilson before letting him leave.

Hartnett's comeback continued to please the Cubs. In mid March he caught five innings during an exhibition game and made plenty of throws, adding further proof that he would indeed be available for the coming season. As was the case for any manager, when one concern eased, another presented itself. For McCarthy, worries about Hornsby remained a constant while additional anxiety came in his new concern for the state of his starting pitching. The Los Angeles Angels minor league club visited the island on March 12 only to pummel their major league hosts 10–2, leaving McCarthy to scratch his head. The one thing he could feel good about was the team's batting order. With the team playing as the Regulars and the Goofs for games in San Diego and Los Angeles, a batting order had begun to take shape with English leading off followed by Grimm, Hornsby, Wilson, Cuyler, and Stephenson.

The exhibition games on the mainland were rained out and another workout on the island got shortened because of heavy winds. Complaints about the facility came on a daily basis. While Avalon felt like a paradise, the general consensus among the players was that it wasn't the ideal place to get ready for a baseball season. They constantly had to deal with the wind, which they maintained played games with their arms and their legs. In addition, the laid back feeling of the area made it difficult for them to shift gears for hard workouts. McCarthy didn't have to hear the complaints to get the same vibe, which he had felt since first conducting training camp on the island. The less than ideal conditions contributed to the Cubs' decision to leave the island earlier each spring to play a slate of games in Los Angeles and en route back to Chicago.

Just prior to the team heading to the mainland to begin the bulk of their exhibition schedule, McCarthy decided he had finally seen enough of Gabby Hartnett. The normally cautious Cubs manager pronounced that Hartnett's arm indeed looked healed and that he would be counted upon to be a cog in the Cubs' attack. Making life even better for McCarthy was that Hornsby seemed to be moving around better and did not limp when he walked. With concerns about the health of Hartnett and Hornsby subsiding in McCarthy's mind, he was free to worry only about the pitching. As late as March 18, he still needed to fill four spots on his 10-man staff.

Back in Chicago, all of the news focused on Al Capone getting released from a Philadelphia prison. During his 10 months in confinement, the Chicago crime boss lost 20 pounds, had his tonsils removed, and took to wearing gold-rimmed glasses, which he attributed to the strain on his eyes from staring at the bright white prison walls. Coinciding with the anticipation of Capone's release was the news about noted gang collector John "The Billiken" Rito getting fished from the Chicago River after his body—bound by picture wire—had somehow slipped free from the rocks that had weighed it down for approximately two weeks. Known as the primary collector for the North Side liquor syndicate, Rito wore two bullets in his head and a chinchilla overcoat, and he carried a list for more than $3,000 in collections.

Among Capone's initial observations after returning briefly to Chicago before heading south to his luxury compound in South Florida was that the liquor business was not doing as well as it had been. More appealing was the prospect of trying to control various labor unions, which would bring in cash from dues and the fees collected by union members. In addition, there would be the payments extracted from builders and contractors to make sure things ran smoothly. Finally, controlling the unions would build his political power through the voting force of the various unions' constituencies. Clearly when Capone got out of jail he found a climate less conducive to running his business interests than he enjoyed prior to his stint in prison.

Meanwhile, the Cubs finally shipped for the mainland and played their first game in Los Angeles on March 20 against the Portland Beavers of the Pacific Coast League at Wrigley Field. Pitching for the Beavers that day was none other than Carl Mays, who had pitched for the New York Giants the previous season. After two gentle outs in the first, the Cubs put on an impressive display of firepower. Hornsby pounded a homer to left and Wilson followed with a blast over the right field fence. Cuyler grounded back to Mays, but the veteran left-hander threw wild to first. Stephenson followed with a home run to left. But the game did nothing to alleviate McCarthy's pitching woes as the Beavers came back to take a 7–6 win in 11 innings.

Later that week, the Angels jumped on Malone, further suggesting that the coming season could be a train wreck. If the Cubs were going to win games in 1930, it appeared as though they were going to have to slug away to do so. Fortunately for the Cubs, they had the lineup to make a go of it. Wilson bailed out Malone with two homers, a double, and a single to lead the Cubs to a 5–4 win.

Disgruntled about the state of his pitching, McCarthy changed his tack by scheduling his starters for plenty of duty against the Pirates during a four-game weekend series in Los Angeles. Prior to McCarthy's decision to use Charlie Root, Malone, Carlson, Guy Bush, and Sheriff Blake, he had planned on letting the group take a slower path of preparation toward the regular season.

Further reminders that the offense would have to guide the way were delivered when the Pirates throttled Blake and the Cubs 15–10 in the first exhibition. Wilson continued to be steady with four singles in the loss. In the second game of the series, Bush took the loss in a 9–8 Pirates win. Malone finally gave the Cubs a solid pitching effort and even though they lost the third game of the series to the Pirates 5–4, it took extra innings to do so. Seeing one of his best pitchers perform up to expectations allowed McCarthy an opportunity to finally exhale. But the moment was short-lived, as Hornsby could be seen after the game walking on his toes to avoid letting his heel touch the ground. The Cubs second baseman insisted that he would be fine by the start of the season. While Hornsby might have been confident he would be healthy, others, such as McCarthy, were not.

Root, whom McCarthy had scheduled to be his Opening Day starter against the Cardinals, started the final game of the series against the Pirates and lasted just three innings. Part of his problem stemmed from Pirates pitcher Erv Brame hitting him on the right forearm with a fastball, prompting a parade of expletives to be hurled Brame's way. Upon reaching first base, Root continued to yell at Brame. Gus Suhr finally heard enough and decided to weigh in on the matter, which prompted Root to tell the Pirates rookie first baseman to keep his mouth shut or else he could expect to be dusted off in his next trip to the plate. Suhr countered by telling Root that if that occurred, he would make a trip to the mound and teach Root a lesson. A battle of toughness ensued and Root prevailed. When Suhr hit, Root twice threw pitches in the vicinity of his head and twice Suhr fell to the ground like a collapsed card table. To make sure his message had not been misconstrued, Root then dusted Jim Mosolf, the hitter who followed Suhr.

By the time Root left the game, the Pirates had scored seven times. McCarthy went from the despair of watching Root get bashed to feeling relief after Bush entered the game and pitched six scoreless innings as the Cubs won 13–7.

McCarthy had never seen his offense look better, but the high octane that seemed to pump through every offense raised eyebrows throughout baseball. The scores in spring training games were up everywhere, as were home runs. Just as suddenly, every pitcher in the game seemed to have gone in the tank. Something just wasn't right.

Baseball players understood they were entertainers in 1930, which Hartnett proved by being a good sport when he agreed to try to catch baseballs dropped from a blimp some 800 feet high above Wrigley Field. Perhaps Hartnett thought the request to have him try to haul in a dozen balls was an April Fools joke, but he didn't back down when baseballs began to rain from the sky. Before the highly entertaining exercise ran its course, he managed to catch two balls while winning some new fans who enjoyed the manner in which he scrambled after the balls.

Hartnett's act played before yet another spring loss for the Cubs on April 1 when the Angels won 13–12. After using most of his veterans against the Pirates, McCarthy used a host of rookies in the contest, which not only saw bad pitching from the youngsters, but also poor baserunning by the team's veterans. Wilson had walked in the first and got picked off at second while daydreaming. Wilson gamely tried to remain safe, wildly pumping his legs in a rundown. Believing that Wilson might hold off the defense long enough, Cuyler took off for second base. An instant later Wilson was tagged out and a throw to second caught Cuyler for a double play.

Blake managed to shut down the Angels the following day, but what had been widely speculated for most of the spring season finally came to fruition when the pain in Hornsby's heel prevented him from playing. Despite having just one of their regular infielders in the game with English, the Cubs managed to win 10–2.

Hornsby went to visit a local doctor, who initially told him that the pain likely came from his favoring the heel. By walking on his toes, he had inadvertently strained the tendons in the area. But when x-rays were taken, the doctor reported that the growth on his heel was returning. Stubborn as always, Hornsby delivered his own diagnosis by noting that he would likely just need a few days off. Floating amid all the anxiety created by Hornsby's discouraging news was the possibility of his having to have a second operation to clean up his heel, which would force him to miss a significant portion of the season if not the entire season. A second x-ray was planned when the team hit St. Louis for the season opener on April 15. If at that point Hornsby's heel showed no improvement, the operation would likely be prescribed.

Rather than wait until the team hit St. Louis, Hornsby made a trip to Chicago on April 4. William Veeck strongly suggested Hornsby make the trip despite Hornsby's insistence that no second operation would be needed. The orders from the top did not sit well with Hornsby, as that day he had visited a bone specialist, who had told him of the strained tendons and that his injury had shown improvement. Hornsby then went to McCarthy and asked to play in that day's game. Hornsby had procured a doughnut-shaped pad he felt would allow him to put weight on his heel without aggravating the sore spot. His request to play fell on deaf ears. McCarthy insisted Hornsby follow Veeck's orders. The Cubs manager continued to be skeptical of Hornsby's condition.

Wilson continued to hit like nobody else on the team. Otherwise, the club continued to resemble a sinking ship. On April 5, the Cubs reached a low point for what had been a low spring when the Hollywood All-Stars trounced the likes of Malone, Moss, and Bud Teachout. Making matters worse, the team lost the services of Grimm. The Cubs first baseman had felt sharp pain in his side for several days. To the best of Grimm's recollection, he had hurt himself in a freak manner, either bumping the area on his side or doing it while sneezing. The pain prompted Grimm to visit an x-ray technician, and the negative revealed a cracked rib. Rest would be the only way Grimm could get better, so McCarthy scratched him from the lineup, at least until the opener.

On April 6, the Cubs finished off their time on the West Coast by drubbing Hollywood 20–5. Cubs hitters pounded out 25 hits during the contest, which included a parting home run by Wilson. Despite the terrible state of the team's pitching, along with the injuries, the Cubs managed to win 11 of the 20 exhibition games they played.

If McCarthy was worried about his club at the end of spring training, he did not let on to reporters. He believed his team had simply remained in the same place too long and had played the same opponents too often, which allowed boredom to enter the equation. He surmised that once they began to play a regular Major League schedule everything would fall into place for the defending National League champions.

After getting his heel examined in Chicago, Hornsby got the go-ahead to play in the opener, so he went ahead to St. Louis to rest until the team arrived for their first game of the season.

Tempering Hornsby's good news was the news that Les Bell, whom the Cubs had planned on using at third base after acquiring him prior to the season, was doubtful for the opener. Bell had nursed a sore arm all spring. He had tried rest, but when he returned his arm remained tired, leaving the prognosis that Bell would need an extended rest to have any chance of recovering. Without Bell, Clarence Blair was earmarked to play third base. Blair had played well throughout spring training, so the news about Bell, though bad, had not been devastating.

After two days of riding the train, the Cubs arrived in Kansas City to finish out their exhibition season. Grimm returned, taking part in a workout at Kansas City's Muehleback Field after getting heavily taped around his torso to try and hold his ribs together. The Cubs beat up the American Association's Kansas City Blues 16–1, fueling McCarthy with hope that his team was peaking at the right time. They followed with a 6–1 win the next day and finished off the series with an 8–7 win that saw Hornsby play—and favor his heel after running out a base hit—while Wilson led the way with four RBIs.

Away from the diamond, a New York scientist predicted that man would reach the moon by 2050, the U.S. Congress voted to appropriate $300 million for road construction, rioting continued in India in support of the fight against British rule over the Indian subcontinent, and director Josef von Sternberg brought Marlene Dietrich to the United States via the darkly erotic film *The Blue Angel.*

Prior to the opening day of the Major League season, Kenesaw Mountain Landis wrote the following letter to fans that ran in newspapers throughout the country:

Baseball and the millions who enjoy clean, fast games should have a great season this year.

The experts pick the Athletics to repeat in the American league and the Cubs to win again in the National, but they may be fooled. All the clubs have strengthened their forces considerably and I look for a hard fast race in each league right down to the finish. They look as open as a beggar's hand.

Given any kind of reasonable consideration by the weather man, who has been forcing a lot of postponed games each spring for several years with his supply of rain and cold blasts, both major and minor leagues should have successful seasons.

I hope every game is an extra inning game and that the best teams win the pennants.

Most of the pundits picked the Cubs to repeat. Irving Vaughn of the *Chicago Tribune* wrote of the selection: "They have strengthened, whereas the other teams classed as contenders appear to have stood still. The real worry for Chicagoans is not about their rivals. To win the second flag McCarthy needs only the luck that will permit him to dodge serious injuries. Let him have the services of his regulars from start to finish and the rest of the league may see nothing more than the Cubs' heels."

Entering the season, National League president John Heydler spoke about the state of the game and pointed out how it was flourishing with team payrolls of $200,000 to $300,000 as compared to the payrolls of 20 years prior that ran from $85,000 to $125,000. In addition, he spoke about the stadiums that were built of steel and concrete rather than the wood frame structures of previous years. Yet he touted that the price of a grandstand ticket remained "two bits"—which translated to a great value, particularly in the pressing economic times.

Even though Hornsby was questionable, the Cubs were said to have the five "best flingers" in the league, according to the *Chicago Tribune*. On top of that, the countless catching problems were put to rest by Hartnett's return.

All in all, the Cubs looked in good shape to repeat as National League champions.

Chapter Eight

RBIs and the Table Setters

HOME RUNS—AND NOT RUNS BATTED IN—DROVE THE IMAGINA-
tions of fans and players alike in 1930. Babe Ruth's home run record
of 60, which he had set in 1927, was regarded as the mark for any
slugger to chase.

Every slugger hoped to make an assault on Ruth's home run
record. RBIs were merely the green beans next to the juicy porter-
house. Home runs were something tangible that one could watch
and admire. RBIs were for the number crunchers.

While the RBI or the idea thereof was believed to have come
into existence around 1879 through the diligence of Henry Chad-
wick, a baseball writer from that era, the RBI would not be recognized officially by Major League Baseball until many years later. The
RBI's journey toward recognition contained several obstacles along
the way.

In 1891, a movement suggested accounts of a game should contain the number of runs each hitter had driven in during the course
of the game. However, the American Association and the National
League both chose to ignore keeping an accounting of RBIs and
the statistic was absent from box scores through the early part of the
20th century.

As the game of baseball continued to evolve, more and more
devoted followers sought additional statistics to quantify what had

happened in the game along with the relative value of the players who competed. Such interest likely played a role in recognizing the RBI.

Ernest J. Lanigan is credited for reviving the RBI through efforts that began in 1907. Lanigan worked at the *New York Press* covering baseball and proposed to his editor that RBI data would enhance the paper's coverage of the sport. Given the popularity of the game and the fact the fans seemed to want as much data as the papers would give them, Lanigan's proposal was embraced by his employers. Beginning in 1907, Lanigan compiled RBI figures for both leagues and continued to do so through 1919 even though he moved from the *Press* to several different newspapers before ending up with the *New York Sun*.

In 1920, the RBI became an official statistic for the Major Leagues as a directive was issued noting that summaries for games would include the number of runs batted in by each hitter. However, the rules governing the awarding of an RBI during certain situations brought a lot of confusion, which of course led to many mistakes.

The accountings for Major League games from the early part of the 20th century were already notoriously error-filled. Sportswriters often served as the official scorers at the games, and simply stated, some of them had no business serving in such a capacity given their level of competency. Others, who *were* qualified, were not immune from errors due to the fact that the figures transferred from the accounting kept during the game to the official box score were prone to human error during the copying process, which was done by hand.

On top of that, rarely were the official box scores scrutinized or double-checked for accuracy. Many of those discrepancies could later be found in the newspaper accountings from the day. Most big league cities had several newspapers covering the teams and the various newspapers often compiled their own box scores. For example, in some cases the official scorer might have ruled an error on a play that one of the newspapers called a base hit.

So as the Major Leagues moved into the 1930 season, the RBI entered its 11th official season. Thus, the statistic that offered some tangible reflection of how a hitter fared in the clutch continued to evolve while struggling to gain acceptance for its importance.

Had the RBI been more popular in 1930, baseball fans along with those who covered the game might have compared Hack Wilson more favorably to Ruth. Alas, the only true measuring stick in the minds of most was the home run. And where any talk of the home run was concerned, Ruth remained king. He hit the most home runs, he hit the longest home runs, and he performed with a sense of style. When Wilson was compared to Ruth, he normally came up short, even though his numbers seemed to gain on the great slugger every season. The following words, written by New York sports columnist Joe Williams, typified the comparisons between Ruth and Wilson, shedding light on the perceptions of the two: "There are a lot of people who would rather watch Babe Ruth hit a long fly than see Hack Wilson smack the ball over the garden wall. One is an artist, the other is a plumber."

A major difference between the home run and the RBI was that a home run could be accomplished during any given trip to the plate. Of course, an RBI could be accomplished in any given trip to the plate, as well, since batters were awarded an RBI on a home run. However, for the most part, if a hitter was going to drive in a lot of runs, he needed to have a lot of runners on base when he hit, or table setters.

The Cubs of 1930 entered the season with a bevy of players who were likely to be found on base most times when Wilson stepped to the plate.

Rogers Hornsby had been a major producer in 1929, but based on his spring training—which indicated he might not be healthy enough to play on an everyday basis—he could not be counted on to be one of the guys getting on base in front of Wilson.

If Hornsby was available to play, the lineup would see Woody English, Clarence "Footsie" Blair—who appeared to be a solid fill-in for Lester Bell at third—and Hornsby followed by Wilson and Riggs Stephenson. However, the prospect of that lineup being in place for many games seemed unlikely given the status of Hornsby's cranky heel.

On days when Hornsby wasn't available, Blair would shift to second base, English would move to third base, and either Doc Farrell or Clyde Beck would play shortstop.

Blair would lead off in the lineup without Hornsby, and he would be followed by English—or they would flip-flop in the order with English first, then Kiki Cuyler, Wilson, and Stephenson, a formidable group that presented a lot of problems for opposing pitchers.

Cuyler had attended West Point during World War I. When he returned home afterward, he took a job at the Buick plant in Flint, Michigan. His baseball ability helped facilitate a move to work for Chevrolet so he could play on the company's team in the Detroit Industrial League. The quality of play in the league attracted many scouts and Cuyler's skills were evident. Not only could he hit, he could run and throw. Being a standout in a high-quality league led to a professional contract, and by 1921 he found himself in the Major Leagues with the Pittsburgh Pirates where he became a legitimate star.

During the 1925 season, Cuyler hit .357 with 18 home runs and 102 RBIs, and he led the National League in triples with 26, which allowed him to finish second in the Most Valuable Player voting to Hornsby. In addition, his work helped lead the Pirates to the World Series that season, where they met the Washington Senators.

Cuyler distinguished himself in Game 7. Walter Johnson pitched for the Senators and already had picked up wins in Game 1 and 4, with the latter being a 4–0 shutout. In the eighth inning of Game 7, Johnson was on the mound and the Senators led 7–6 when Cuyler went to the plate with two outs and the bases loaded. Cuyler drove a ball to right-center field and everybody scored, giving Cuyler an inside-the-park home run. Eventually, the umpires ruled that Cuyler's hit had gotten caught in a rolled-up tarp at the base of the wall thereby making his hit a ground-rule double. Despite the ruling, Cuyler's hit had given the Pirates a 9–7 lead. When the Senators went quietly in the top of the ninth, the Pirates were world champions and Cuyler had elevated his status with Pirates fans to an even higher level.

Cuyler probably would have finished his career with the Pirates had Donnie Bush not become the manager. Bush wanted Cuyler to change from hitting third in the order to second, where Max Carey had served for years before getting traded.

In addition to being superstitious, Cuyler didn't like the move because his skills differed from Carey's. Both were fast and used their speed to steal many bases, but while Carey employed the old school style of hitting that included bunting and bat control, Cuyler never got cheated on a swing and he slashed hits with power to all fields. He also struck out more than the conventional second hitter.

Cuyler also drew Bush's ire when he did not slide going into second base on a double play. The ploy managed to keep the second baseman from making the relay to first, in fact he bobbled the ball, but he recovered in time to tag out Cuyler, who was not on the base. The first-year manager barked at Cuyler about not sliding, pointing out that he would have been safe had he slid. Cuyler finished the season on the bench, a move Bush would not have been able to pull off had Pirates owner Barney Dreyfuss not been frustrated with Cuyler as well. Cuyler had gotten the best of Dreyfuss by gaining a higher salary for the 1927 season than he wanted to pay. That coupled with the Pirates' recent acquisition of Lloyd Waner to join his brother Paul in the outfield likely spelled the end of Cuyler's days with Pittsburgh. Dreyfuss's Pirates would have had one of the best outfields in baseball history with Cuyler and the two Waners, but he also worried about the cost associated with such a trio. Labeling Cuyler as a disciplinary problem served as the perfect ploy to pacify the fans, who clamored for an explanation as to why he was benched. Cuyler's plight in Pittsburgh turned into the Cubs' good fortune, since it triggered a trade that sent him to the Cubs for Pete Scott and Sparky Adams in November of 1927. Pirates fans had been mystified as to why Cuyler had been benched in the first place. When he was traded, many wondered if his skills had simply eroded at the age of 29.

Cuyler put his critics to rest once he reached Chicago. Not only did he continue to play well under Joe McCarthy, he played as well as he ever had. After having a down year in 1928 when he hit 17 home runs and drove in 79 while playing in 133 games, he shot to .360 in 1929 while scoring 111 runs and leading the National League with 43 stolen bases.

Cuyler had distinctive looks accented by hazel eyes and a head of curly hair, giving him an appearance of innocence. He enjoyed great popularity among his teammates, who were said to admire him for the way he conducted himself as the consummate gentleman away from the field; he did not drink or smoke. Adding to Cuyler's popularity with his teammates, who called him "Cuy," was the way he played the game. When Cuyler was on the field, he displayed a great competitiveness and zeal. If Cuyler was on base when Wilson hit the ball to the deep reaches of Wrigley Field, a run was more than likely going to be minted on the scoreboard.

English joined the Cubs in 1927 at the age of 21. He had been a standout shortstop for the American Association's Toledo Mud Hens, prompting the Cubs to purchase him for $50,000. The money turned out to be well spent as English took over at shortstop and did not miss a beat. Though he stood at just 5'10", English possessed large hands, which helped him field his position.

English hit from the right side and proved to be the perfect complement for the power hitters hitting behind him, as his game was getting on base by drawing a walk or through making contact and slapping the ball in all directions. In 1929, English hit .276 and scored 131 runs.

Blair hailed from Oklahoma and came up with the Cubs as a 28-year-old rookie in 1929 and hit .319 in 26 games. He hit left-handed, which made him an oddity in the predominantly right-handed hitting Cubs lineup.

Stephenson hailed from Akron, Alabama. Prior to beginning his professional baseball career, he played football and baseball at the University of Alabama. On the gridiron, he lined up at quarterback. While playing the position during a game in 1920, he faded back to pass and got hammered by two tacklers, severely damaging his right shoulder. That injury brought an end to his days playing quarterback and created a weakness for him as a second baseman, particularly when trying to turn double plays. Still, his hitting made scouts look the other way. Rather than finish at Alabama, he opted to sign with the Cleveland Indians, and he made his Major League debut on April 13, 1921.

Stephenson's play in the field continued to haunt him once he reached the Major Leagues, but he did manage to hit .330 with 17 doubles as a rookie. The Indians looked for a position to hide him in the field and moved him to third base in 1922 where he showed improvement, committing 11 errors while playing 34 games at third, 25 at second, and 3 in the outfield. His offense continued to shine as he hit .339 with 24 doubles. In the coming years, Stephenson would continue to change positions and continue to hit, maintaining his status as the Indians' resident dilemma: If they played him they had to cope with his poor defense, and if they didn't they had to compensate for not having his offense. After Stephenson hit a career high .371 in 1924, he played in just 19 games in 1925 before the Indians decided they wanted to make him a full-time outfielder. Only they didn't want him to learn the position at the Major League level, so they sent him to Kansas City of the American Association to master the conversion.

Stephenson then became another of McCarthy's celebrated acquisitions. The Cubs manager knew all about Stephenson and had always been enamored of his hitting. Cleveland did not bring Stephenson back to the Major Leagues even though he had hit .337, indicating to McCarthy that the Indians had lost interest in him. McCarthy inquired if Stephenson was available, and when he discovered he was, he made a deal with Cleveland to acquire him prior to the 1926 season.

Stephenson did not play every day with the Cubs, but he found a spot in left field and he continued to hit, posting a .338 average in 82 games. Finally in 1927, Stephenson became a full-time player for the first time, hitting .344 with a .415 on-base percentage while playing in 152 games.

By 1929, Stephenson had become a critical component of the Cubs' attack. Not only did he hit .362 with a .445 on-base percentage, he had 17 home runs and 110 RBIs.

If Wilson was going to be driving home runners in 1930, he needed pitchers to respect the hitter behind him enough to not pitch around him every time he stepped to the plate. With Stephenson hitting fifth in the lineup, Wilson appeared to have the protection he needed.

Chapter Nine

Beginning of the Season

During a workout in St. Louis prior to the Cubs' season opener, Rogers Hornsby continued to show signs of a bum heel while Charlie Grimm looked fine after missing a week due to a cracked rib.

Joe McCarthy addressed his team, telling them that the previous season meant nothing and that what they did from Opening Day forward would define them.

Sheriff Blake got the Opening Day start. The hard-throwing West Virginia native had been denied a chance to pitch during the World Series. In the aftermath of that slight, Blake told McCarthy how disappointed he had been. Some felt that the start was McCarthy's way of making things right with Blake.

Though the pitching staff as a whole had been less than superlative during spring training, Blake had shown well, as had Hal Carlson, making the pair appear to be the strongest links in the rotation.

After the workout concluded, McCarthy announced the following lineup for the inaugural game of 1930:

Woody English, shortstop

Clarence Blair, third base

Rogers Hornsby, second base

Hack Wilson, center field

Kiki Cuyler, right field

Riggs Stephenson, left field

Charlie Grimm, first base

Gabby Hartnett, catcher

Sheriff Blake, pitcher

Opening Day on April 15 at St. Louis's Sportsman's Park brought out a crowd of approximately 35,000 to see the hometown Cardinals play the defending National League champion Cubs.

Flint Rhem drew the starting assignment for the Cardinals. The right-hander owned a reputation as a bad boy due to his after-hours work performed on barstools. Many of those hours came at the side of Grover Cleveland Alexander. One oft-repeated anecdote cited Cardinals owner Sam Breadon being upset with Rhem for staying out late. Rhem did not deny the charges, but he had a hero's explanation. He was simply taking care of Alexander. Boldly, Rhem told the club's owner that since everybody on the team had an obligation to keep Alexander out of the sauce, he had acted responsibly after finding Alexander with a quart bottle of booze in front of him. In order to prevent Alexander from killing the bottle himself, Rhem did the deed for him.

Of course, as many players who have played the game time and again proved, if you had talent, you were allowed plenty of color. Rhem first came up with the Cardinals in 1924. He won twenty games in 1926, but he found himself out of the Major Leagues for the length of the 1929 season, which he spent pitching for the Houston Buffaloes of the Texas League and the Minneapolis Millers of the American Association. Rhem had successfully navigated spring training with the Cardinals in 1930, so he looked to his opportunity against the Cubs as the beginning of what he hoped to be a successful comeback story.

Cubs hitters were hardly sympathetic to Rhem's cause. All spring long they had battered opposing pitchers, so the regular season wasn't the time to start swinging at air. In the first inning, they began making the solid contact that had earned them the name of "Murderer's Row." Unfortunately for the Cubs, and Wilson, Hornsby's heel ended up costing them a run. Hornsby singled in his first at-bat and then Wilson followed by thumping a double to right field that landed a foot inside the line. Hornsby tried to score from first base and given his reduced speed, everyone in the ballpark could see there would be a close play at the plate. Hornsby continued to baby his heel by trying to score standing up when he should have slid, resulting in the the Rajah getting tagged out, costing the Cubs a run and Wilson his first RBI of the season.

Wilson never was the sort to worry about missed opportunities. He simply went out and created more. After the botched opportunity in the first, he didn't have to wait long for another. Wilson again faced Rhem in his next at-bat, which came in the third with Blair in scoring position just 90 feet away. The situation called for a fly ball distant enough to score Blair. Wilson delivered on cue and Blair tagged up and scored easily to push the Cubs' lead to 4–1. Wilson had his first RBI of the season.

Blake validated McCarthy's faith by showing well through six innings while the Cubs built a 5–1 lead. But when Blake covered the plate in the fourth, he somehow managed to tweak a muscle in his right leg. The leg didn't begin to really bother him until the seventh. That's when the Cubs' pitching began to bring back memories of spring training. Guy Bush took over for Blake and allowed five runs to score before Pat Malone mercifully entered the game to record the final two outs of the ninth inning to preserve a 9–8 Cubs win.

After the Cubs dropped their second game of the season, a 13–3 loss to the Cardinals on May 16, McCarthy penciled in a lineup for their third game that did not include Hornsby or Grimm, as both had aggravated their previous injuries. Grimm appeared more likely to find his way back to the lineup than Hornsby, whose heel injury appeared as though it would linger for a prolonged period of time.

English led off followed by Blair and Cuyler with Wilson batting cleanup and Stephenson hitting fifth. Malone pitched masterfully, allowing no runs in the game that rain cut short to six innings, giving the Cubs a 3–0 win. By the end of the 1930 season, holding any team to no runs would look like a Herculean effort.

Bill Hallahan's performance in the fourth game of the season proved even more impressive than Malone's, but it was an odd gem.

"Wild Bill" Hallahan's methods had kept him on a perpetual shuttle between St. Louis and the minor leagues. In 1925, Hallahan won one game and lost four in his first season as a starting pitcher. Included in his performance were 32 walks in 57 innings while striking out 28.

Pitching in the Texas League for the Cardinals' affiliate, Houston, Hallahan began to get a handle on his powerful left arm, winning 23 games and losing 12. That season he walked 149 while striking out 244, giving him the appearance of being effectively wild.

He returned to St. Louis in 1929 and went 4-4 on the season, walking 60 and striking out 52.

Hallahan's pitching on April 18 led an 11–1 Cardinals win in which the hard-throwing Cardinals left-hander held the Cubs to two hits, which stemmed primarily from his being effectively wild. Nobody wearing a Cubs uniform felt too comfortable in the batter's box for fear of taking one off the chin. At the end of the day, Hallahan had the oddest of pitching lines: 11 strikeouts—Wilson struck out twice—along with 9 walks. In addition to not having their pitching exactly up to speed, the Cubs knew they wouldn't exactly be sneaking up on anybody. On most days they could expect the other team to play their best, hoping to show up the defending National League champions.

The Cubs left St. Louis in the midst of a batting slump, which carried over into their opening game of a three-game series in Cincinnati against the Reds.

Hack Wilson in relaxed pose. When Wilson wasn't camped out on a barstool—or suffering the aftereffects from having sat on a barstool too long—he cut the figure of a pretty nifty ballplayer.

Hack Wilson in the outfield. Note that he is wearing sunglasses in this photograph. Wilson neglected to wear sunglasses in the 1929 World Series. He came away with the nickname "Sunny Boy" after losing two balls in the sun to cost the Cubs a game and earn a goat label.

Joe McCarthy was a brilliant manager and did wonders with the Cubs prior to his leaving the team at the end of the 1930 season. McCarthy was one of Hack Wilson's biggest supporters and knew how to get the best out of the Cubs slugger.

Pat Malone was Hack Wilson's hard-drinking, hard-throwing running mate. Like Wilson, he knew his way around a bottle of whiskey, and many of those bottles were shared with Wilson. Malone was one of the Cubs' best pitchers and could usually be found alongside Wilson any time trouble occurred.

Hal Carlson became one of manager Joe McCarthy's shrewd pick-ups. The right-hander performed well for the Cubs before reaching a tragic end.

Rogers Hornsby shown wearing the uniform of the St. Louis Cardinals. As player/manager Hornsby led the Cardinals to a World Series championship. The future Hall of Famer had great skills as a player, but he proved to be a toxic influence on the Cubs.

Hack Wilson and Rogers Hornsby appear to be talking hitting in this photograph. Hornsby did not care for Wilson's hard-drinking ways and ultimately played a role in Wilson's demise. Having both sluggers in the lineup gave the Cubs a formidable offense.

The "Great Shires" had a lot of talent on the baseball field, but he had far greater skills as a promoter. Prior to the 1930 season, Shires saw dollars on the horizon, prompting him to challenge Hack Wilson to a boxing match. Unfortunately for Shires (or perhaps fortunately for the man's health), the match never came to fruition.

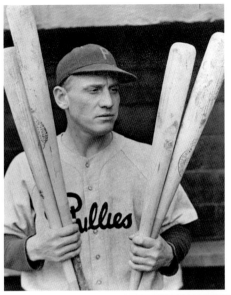

Phillies slugger Chuck Klein entered the 1930 season as the reigning National League home run champion. Klein had a similar background to Hack Wilson's. He worked in a steel mill and played semi-pro baseball en route to the Major Leagues. He would win four home run titles.

Lou Gehrig and Babe Ruth were polar opposites in personality, but they brought a similar destruction to the baseball while batting in the middle of a formidable New York Yankees lineup.

Babe Ruth is shown here displaying one of his many faces. Hack Wilson was recognized as the most productive hitter in baseball in 1930, but Ruth remained the king of baseball. Ruth introduced the long ball to the Major Leagues, changing the face of the game forever.

When Hack Wilson stood in the batter's box, opposing pitchers knew they were facing trouble. Here's a good look at what opposing hurlers saw when he was at the top of his game. Wilson looks relaxed, strong, and confident.

Hack Wilson never got cheated on a swing. In this photograph, the essence of Wilson's powerful swing is put on display. When Wilson's bat made contact with the baseball, the force of the swing usually translated to its traveling a long distance.

Hack Wilson had a playful, almost childlike quality about him. In this photograph we see Wilson clear-eyed, wearing a smile, and in his most-relaxed state. Wilson was said to be such a generous man that he would literally give someone the shirt off his back.

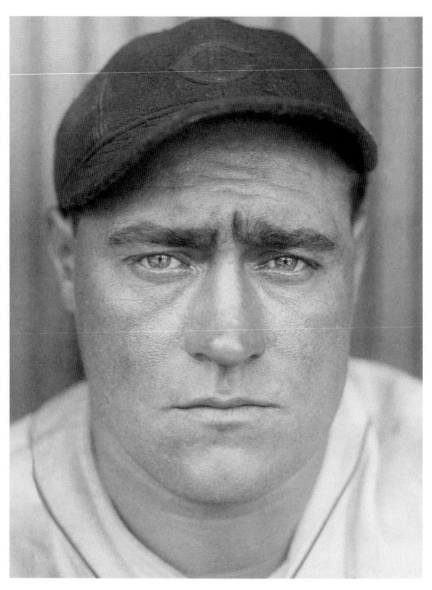

The somber Hack Wilson. Though he brought many of his personal problems upon himself, Wilson had a sad life, which seems to be reflected in this photograph.

Wilson had a bulls-eye on him once he stepped on the field in Cincinnati. Reds fans had not forgotten the episode at the Cin- cinnati train station and booed him accordingly. Cries of "Sunny Boy"—and worse—were directed at Wilson, but he got the best of them on that afternoon by keeping the Cubs in the game with, of all things, his glove. The Reds hitters teed off on Charlie Root, constantly sending drives to the deepest part of the outfield. Fortunately for the Cubs, Redland Field had a far more spacious outfield than Wrigley Field, so many of the drives hit off of Root that would have found the bleachers at Wrigley became outs. Wilson flagged down several of the drives, resembling a man with a little extra motivation while making the catches with taunts ringing in his ears.

Despite Wilson's heroics with his glove, the Cubs lost 2–1, thanks to a triple play the Reds pulled off in the third inning. Root singled to lead off the third and English walked to bring Blair to the plate. Hoping to move the runners into scoring position for Cuyler and Wilson, McCarthy gave Blair the bunt sign. He made contact, but the Reds pitcher, Benny Frey, pounced off the mound to catch the ball in the air. Frey threw to Tony Cuccinello at third base, who tagged Root for the second out before throwing to shortstop Hod Ford, who tagged out English to complete the triple play.

In addition to the misfortune of hitting into the triple play, the Cubs had a call go against them when Wilson tried to score on a double steal. Home plate umpire Cy Pfirman called him out much to the delight of the Reds fans, many of whom had paid the price of admission for the sole purpose of razzing Wilson.

Pete Donohue gave Reds fans more of what they wanted to see the next day when he started, further rekindling the train station episode since Donohue had been one of the Reds players Wilson had pummeled. That situation allowed Irving Vaughn of the *Chicago Daily News* to have some fun in his account of the Cubs' 4–3 win when he described a base hit by Wilson in the third inning as follows: "Wilson punched a slow bounder back at Donohue who had been punched before by Hack. The thought of it made the big Texan jumpy and he failed to waylay the ball."

Resistance to Al Capone's takeover attempt with the unions was met with force on April 20 when three of his henchmen were gunned down inside a South Side speakeasy on South Wells Street. According to the police, the three men had been part of a master plan to force out union leaders so the Capone regime could control the unions. The police further believed that the lone gunman had acted in response to the constant threats brought about by Capone's men.

In the midst of all the violence, Chicago prepared for the 1933 World's Fair, prompting a good will tour through the Southwest to drum up interest and support for what would be a monumental event. Among the participants in the tour was Charles S. Peterson, Chicago's city treasurer, who made news when addressing a commentary that had been written in the *Tulsa Tribune* entitled "Cowardly Chicago." The piece read in part:

> *Chicago is the sickest city in America. Chicago is disgustingly stupid. Chicago talks boastfully of a great fair in 1933. Chicago can't create a great fair. Chicago isn't big enough to arrest and protect Chicago's own society from the vicious operations of one little Al Capone. Chicago collectively is a municipal coward that no longer deserves the respect of a civilized world.*
>
> *The Chicago Club, the University Club, the Union League Club and the Hamilton Club of Chicago swell up with pouter pigeon's pride over their memberships of strong men. They are pigmies. Little men, very, very, little men, who collectively can't cope with one little Capone. Shameless, incompetent, cowardly Chicago.*

Peterson told a Tulsa audience that alcohol cost Chicago approximately $30 million a year. He broke down the costs as half being for the actual liquor and the rest going to bribery and payments to hired assassins. However, he managed to find a silver lining in the city's situation in spite of the facts:

But even with that vast expenditure, we are not the crime capital of the United States. The census bureau ranks us as thirty-ninth in murder rates and that is surely a modest standing for a city of 4,000,000 people. Furthermore, we haven't missed those done away with very badly. Although I am not convinced that Prohibition is not a good thing, these facts must be faced.

Meanwhile, six games into the season, Wilson found himself with just four hits, a .190 batting average, no home runs, and just one RBI. It was time for him to face those facts, and he surely did. In the seventh game, played on April 21, he homered in the first inning off Archie Campbell. The blast did not just sneak out of the ballpark but rather looped long and far over Redland Field's center field wall for an estimated 425 feet. At that time only Babe Herman, Ethan Allen, and Babe Ruth—in an exhibition game—had reached the territory achieved by Wilson that day. Wilson's blow came with two aboard, moving his RBI total to four for the season.

Carlson's mound work served up another positive note for the Cubs as the veteran right-hander pitched a complete-game five-hitter in which he allowed just one run in the Cubs' 9–1 win.

The Cubs returned to Wrigley Field for their home opener against the Cardinals on April 22, where a crowd of 38,000 fought chilly temperatures to cheer enthusiastically for their team, the defending National League champions. Outside Wrigley Field the morning of the game felt vibrant. Kiosks were set up selling various souvenirs, young boys hawked newspapers, and the soothing smells associated with the ballpark permeated the air as the El train rattled past. And, finally for Wilson, he had the chance to play in front of a crowd that loved him. Or would they? Had winning changed the loveable nature of Cubs fans to the point where they remembered the slugger more for his World Series gaffes than for his immense body of work dating from the moment he first put on a Cubs uniform?

Personifying the generous nature of Cubs fans, the crowd embraced Wilson with cheers from the moment he peeked out of the home dugout. Whether or not the fans understood the psychology of handling the Cubs slugger as well as the team's manager did, the effects of their cheers were as needed for Wilson as McCarthy's positive words. Gaining approval of those who mattered to him fueled Wilson, taking him to places he might not have otherwise reached had he not been properly motivated.

For the second time in less than a week, the Cubs had to face Hallahan. And once again he proved to be a tough customer, holding Chicago scoreless for the first six innings before Wilson stepped to the plate with two runners aboard in the seventh. Wilson rubbed a handful of dirt together, wiping his hands on his uniform and the back of his neck. He then stepped into the batter's box before taking a huge cut and missing for strike one. Hallahan then blew a fastball through the strike zone that Wilson watched for strike two. Not rattled in the least, Wilson collected himself and took a huge rip at Hallahan's third pitch. This time he connected, depositing the baseball into the left field stands for a three-run homer. The home crowd loved Wilson and rewarded his effort with a raucous ovation. While a lot of things seemed in flux with their club, Cubs fans knew they could count on Wilson to come through. His blast proved to be the only blemish on Hallahan's line as the Cardinals' lefty posted another complete-game victory in the Cardinals' 8–3 win over the Cubs. And once again he had done so in similar high-wire fashion with nine strikeouts and seven walks.

Wilson did not get any hits the following day, but a good thing happened for Wilson's and the Cubs' future chances during the summer. During the midst of a third-inning rally, the Cardinals elected to intentionally walk Wilson to face Stephenson hitting in the fifth spot. If the Cardinals' maneuver worked—if Stephenson failed to come through—the Cubs could expect to see Wilson walked by other teams. Stephenson proved, as he had many times in the past, that pitching to him did not offer an opposing pitcher a much better option by drilling a single through the middle to score two. The Cubs went on to score five in the inning en route to a 6–5 win.

Wilson faced an interesting defensive alignment against the Cardinals. Second baseman Frankie Frisch began lining himself up on the outfield grass at least 10 feet behind the infield clay whenever Wilson stepped to the plate. In no way did Frisch disrespect Wilson's speed. His positioning had more to do with his respect for the way Wilson hit the ball to the opposite field. His wicked shots to the right side came off the bat like balls pulled to the other side of the infield by other hitters. Frisch reasoned that the balls Wilson hit arrived so fast that he had more than ample time to field the ball and throw him out at first no matter how fast Wilson ran.

Hornsby's heel continued to be a problem. While the pain could at times be manageable, the heel simply refused to improve, which prevented him from returning to regular duty. Questions about whether he needed to have another operation to clean things up remained constant. However, to give in to the pain would have been in contrast to everything Hornsby stood for, so he grimaced and limped when he played, but he refused to undergo surgery that might end his season. Though he did not play regularly, he did not totally disappear from the lineup. When he played in April, he came through with some big hits, including a pinch-hit double against the Reds on April 25. Though Hornsby got lifted for a pinch runner, Dan Taylor, who subsequently got picked off, Hornsby's double seemed to ignite a Cubs' rally that fueled a 6–5 win. Wilson hit his third home run of the season during that same game, while driving in two runs.

Interest in the fortunes of the Cubs and the White Sox had never been greater than in 1930. Both of Chicago's Major League teams seemed to appreciate the adoration and treated the public accordingly. Both Cubs and White Sox players participated in a series of baseball clinics sponsored by the *Chicago Tribune*.

Since the White Sox began the season at home, they conducted the first clinics of the season. The Cubs followed on April 26 with a clinic that drew 5,500 boys to Wrigley Field for a session advertised as a catching clinic by Hartnett, but one supported by his teammates and his manager.

Given the formal nature of the era, the kids showed up wearing collared shirts with ties, newsboy caps, many wearing knickers, and all looking as though they wanted to be well groomed for the occasion. Despite the polish, the theme of baseball ranked highly on each of the young boy's minds as evidenced by the equipment they brought along: gloves, shin guards, chest protectors, bats, and balls. The scene personified the innocence of the era with Hartnett receiving cheers from the boys the moment he showed his face.

Wilson, Grimm, Clyde Beck, English, Blair, Lon Warneke, McCarthy, and third base coach Jimmy Burke accompanied Hartnett and were treated with equal appreciation by the boys.

Meanwhile, understanding the popularity of both teams, the *Tribune* created a special telephone line so fans could call to find out the scores of either team on any given day.

In the early part of the season, Wilson's work in the field had pretty much allowed the Chicago fans to forget "Sunny Boy." But Wilson still played in Wrigley Field, where the winds could present for outfielders the kinds of problems familiar to sailboat captains. One minute the wind could blow one way and seconds later it could be blowing in another direction, or it could be swirling. And that did not even take into account the midday sun that often accompanied such winds. If you were a marked man with the glove such as Wilson, Wrigley Field's outfield simply wasn't the best place to ply one's trade. At some point during the 1930 season, Wilson was going to remind Cubs fans of "Sunny Boy." The question wasn't whether Wilson would blow a play in the field; the question was when. The answer came on April 26 when the Cubs put forth a poor effort in a 9–5 loss to the visiting Pirates.

Adam Comorosky hit a line drive straight at Wilson in center field. Initially, Wilson appeared content to field the ball on the first bounce. But just after easing up, he suddenly seemed to change his mind and began to accelerate. Something had told Wilson at the last instant that he could make the catch. But he didn't. Nor did he stop the ball, which hit the grass and shot past him. Before the ball could be retrieved and thrown to the infield, Comorosky stood on second base with a double and the Pirates scored their third run to take a 4–0 lead. In the fourth, Wilson let George Grantham's fly ball sail right through his hands, which triggered a two-run inning for the Pirates, who took a 6–0 lead. The crowd did not turn en masse on Wilson, but for the first time that season, he did hear a few boos and a few of the familiar "Sunny Boy" taunts.

Wilson hit a solo home run off Pittsburgh's Percy Jones in the seventh inning of a 5–2 Cubs win over the Pirates on April 30 to end the season's first month on a high note. But his numbers were hardly awe inspiring. In 16 games, he had 11 RBIs, which put him on pace for 100 RBIs, a number most players would gladly settle for, but a number that would be a disappointment based on Wilson's 159 the previous season. In addition, Wilson finished April with just four home runs. To the general public, this number served as the litmus test for sluggers. Some had been bold enough to forecast that Wilson could challenge *the* record that mattered most, Babe Ruth's single-season home run mark of 60. Based on his start, Wilson would have to hit 56 home runs in the Cubs' remaining 138 games to catch the king. And due to Ruth's omnipotent status, Wilson would surely have to break the mark by more than a couple of home runs to truly surpass the Yankees slugger. Any chances of that happening appeared remote given the manner in which he had gotten out of the gate.

Wilson's April numbers were mediocre, which some of his teammates attributed to his historically being a slow starter.

Various accounts have teammates noting that Wilson had always been slow to get going because he had a difficult time getting into shape. However, though the body language or manner of his play might have given the impression that he was a slow starter, the numbers from his previous Aprils told a different story. In 1929, Wilson hit .340 with 3 home runs and 15 RBIs in 11 games; in 1928 he hit 3 home runs with 10 RBIs in 13 games; in 1927 he hit 3 home runs with 15 RBIs and hit .296 in 14 games; and in 1926, Wilson had 2 home runs with 23 RBIs and hit .345 in 16 games. Thus, Wilson's start in 1930, though not disastrous, was his worst since becoming an everyday Major Leaguer in 1926. Had split statistics showing such breakdowns been more prevalent in 1930, Wilson's performance likely would have been scrutinized like hitters' performances would be decades later. Fortunately for Wilson, baseball number crunching was still in its primitive stages. Hitters from Wilson's era weren't constantly reminded of their inadequacies by stat-heads, which would have added anxiety to every at-bat.

Though Wilson's April had been less than dazzling, Ruth and Lou Gehrig were far from lighting the baseball world on fire. Gehrig, who had accrued 175 RBIs in 1927, had 3 home runs and 7 RBIs and Ruth had 2 home runs and 11 RBIs.

Wilson's month served as a reflection of the Cubs' overall month. The defending National League champions went 8-8 in April. Given the way the Cubs had played, 8-8 almost looked like a gift. Having failed to play a brand of baseball anywhere near that of the 1929 team, the Cubs felt encouraged to have a .500 record.

Even though three of the game's most acclaimed sluggers were not producing at their normal rates, the rest of baseball was exploding offensively, adding new fuel to the fire that baseball had tinkered with the ball. Those screaming the loudest only had to cite what happened on April 29, 1930, when 123 runs were scored in just seven games. Brooklyn and New York led the way that day in a 19–15 slugfest that saw the teams combine for 41 hits. Ironically, Wilson did not have an RBI that day.

Denials about the livelier ball continued, but those within the game were not buying it. John McGraw, who had watched a lot of baseball as a player and a manager, had no doubt: "I don't care what the manufacturers of the ball . . . say," McGraw noted. "It's lively, and every sensible baseball man knows it. Why, most of the pitchers are scared to death when they are sent to the mound. The home run slugging has taken the heart out of them."

Noted umpire Bill Klem also weighed in on the subject when he said baseball needed to change the ball because it was making a joke out of the game. Woody English spoke of the 1930 season in a *Baseball Digest* interview in October of 1994 and he noted: "The ball was live, but not as lively as it is today."

CHAPTER TEN

May

DESPITE HIS TEPID APRIL AND THE LINGERING CLOUD OF THE 1929 World Series loss, Hack Wilson remained the most visible sports figure in Chicago. To many fans he remained a beloved figure. Typifying that sentiment, the following letter appeared in the *Chicago Tribune* on May 2 under the headline, PRO HACK:

> *Chicago, April 26. It gives me a pain in the neck to go and see the Cubs play when some so-called Cubs fans go out there not to root for the Cubs, but to boo Hack Wilson. It seems just too bad for one of the poor Cub players if they pull a boner. Why is it that some people do not look at the good the players do for the Cubs, but all eyes are on them when an error is made? We are still strong for Hack, and I am glad to see that the booing does not seem to annoy him at all. Why don't the people forget about what happened last year and notice what Hack is doing for the team this year?*
> *—Mr. and Mrs. Herb Hoerr*

Once May began, neither Wilson nor the Cubs would have to be defended.

A Ladies Day crowd of 33,000 packed Wrigley Field on May 2 to watch the first game of the new month, which the Cubs won 11–8 over the Phillies. That win would turn out to be their second consecutive win of a streak that would stretch to eight games before it had run its course.

The Cubs had been marketing pioneers with Ladies Day, but the problems associated with the May 2 game prompted the organization to change the manner in which they conducted the promotion. Rather than simply opening the gates and letting all ladies flood into the ballpark, the Cubs hoped to restore some semblance of order with a new policy that capped the number of freebies at 20,000. For future dates the ladies would have to pick up their tickets at the box office; those tickets were limited to two free ducats per customer. Though the new procedure brought an inconvenience to the ladies, all of the 20,000 tickets were claimed two days prior to the next Ladies Day on May 9.

Continuing with their community service project working with the White Sox and the *Chicago Tribune*, the Cubs sent out Rogers Hornsby to conduct a baseball clinic on hitting and playing the infield on May 3.

Hornsby had many despicable traits, but above all else, he played the game at a level few had ever reached. Plus, the man knew the intricacies of the game, making him a natural for such a clinic if he participated without an attitude. To his credit, he did just that. He liked to talk baseball and having a captive and admiring crowd fed his ego.

A crowd of 6,000 showed for the clinic that also saw Charlie Grimm, Woody English, Herman Jones, and Ray Schalk participate. Hornsby quickly got to work putting on a demonstration about playing the infield in which he displayed how an infielder made throws to first without changing the position of his body; he also demonstrated the double play. He then provided the kids with their biggest thrill of the day when he picked up a bat and told his audience that he would hit the ball over the fence. On the first pitch the Rajah did exactly as he said he would, hitting the ball the opposite way into the right field stands.

Later the kids began to chant, "We want Hack!" and "We want Kiki!" When Wilson and Cuyler finally stepped out of the Cubs' dugout, a roar went up. Hornsby graciously continued the clinic until begging off by telling the kids he needed to make a dentist appointment.

The Cubs then went out and beat the Phillies 1–0 to take their third consecutive win. After winning their fourth consecutive game on May 4, the Cubs' game against Brooklyn on May 5 got rained out after one inning. The bad weather deprived the Cubs of a 2–0 lead and Wilson of an RBI single, since a rainout was an unofficial game. Nobody could control the rain, but the weather seemed to have worked against the Cubs, who hoped to get a win against the Dodgers before having to face Arthur "Dazzy" Vance. In addition to being one of the great characters of his era, the hard-throwing right-hander always seemed to present problems for the Cubs. Twice during his career "The Dazzler" had struck out 15 Cubs in a single start. Though Vance's best years were behind him by 1930, his body of work and competitiveness never made the prospect of facing him pleasurable.

From 1922 to 1928, Vance led the National League in ERA three times, wins twice, and strikeouts for seven consecutive seasons. In 1924 he put together his best individual season when he led the league in wins with 28, strikeouts with 262, and ERA with a mark of 2.16 to claim the pitching Triple Crown. For his efforts he won the first-ever National League Most Valuable Player award, edging out Rogers Hornsby, who hit .424 that season. On September 24 of that season, Vance distinguished himself in the second inning of a 6–5 win over the Cubs by striking out three batters while using just nine pitches. By doing so, Vance became the seventh pitcher in Major League history to achieve the feat.

On July 23, 1929, Vance went up against the Cubs in Brooklyn at a time when Wilson was red hot after hitting in 27 consecutive games. Vance enjoyed smiling on the mound, which gave the hitters the impression that he knew something they did not.

Seemingly he did on that day, particularly when it came to retiring Wilson, whom he struck out four times. At no point in any of his at-bats did Wilson appear to have a clue about hitting the veteran. Vance's smile broadened after each of the strikeouts, further aggravating Wilson.

So when Vance started against the Cubs on May 6, 1930, most conceded the game to the Dodgers before a pitch had been thrown. Even after English tripled to open the Cubs' first, Vance appeared to be totally in control. He struck out Cliff Heathcote on three pitches and Hornsby managed only a pop out to first to bring up Wilson. Even he had to be thinking the odds were against him doing anything against Vance, who seemed to own him.

Vance's success fueled his cockiness, while his size—6'2", 200 pounds—fueled his fastball. He intimidated hitters. Vance cut a cocksure figure on the mound and he smiled broadly, exuding confidence as Wilson made his way to the plate with two outs. To those in the stands who were aware of Wilson's frustrations against Vance, Wilson's walk to the plate appeared to be a stroll to the gallows. Not only had Vance struck out Wilson four times in one game, he had struck him out in six consecutive plate appearances.

Finally, Wilson stepped into the batter's box, going through his ritual dirt bath in before readying for the pitch. After watching a ball sail past, Wilson swung at Vance's second pitch and held nothing back, almost corkscrewing himself into the ground in a comical fashion that drew laughter from the crowd. Wilson lacked grace of movement to begin with, so when he did let go, the results could be embarrassing. Vance's smile remained intact even after throwing his third pitch outside to put the count at 2-1. He then delivered another fastball that Wilson went for, and once again the Cubs slugger fell to the ground swinging at the offering. Laughter mixed with a smattering of boos drifted across the field. Frustrated, Wilson got to his feet, dusted himself off, and dug in with a look of determination etched on his face as he readied for Vance's fifth pitch.

Once again, Wilson saw a pitch he liked and again he took a mighty cut. Only this time wood met horsehide and produced a magnificent drive that arched over the center field wall and rattled off the scoreboard. Wilson did not hide the pleasure he derived from finally doing something against Vance. He seemed to be dancing as he floated around the bases. When Wilson's right foot touched down on home plate, he turned toward Vance and grinned.

Vance lasted just six innings as the Cubs took a 3–1 win thanks to Wilson's blast. His home run also moved his hitting streak to 10 games.

A day after hitting the home run against Vance, Wilson drove in four runs against Brooklyn in a 9–5 Cubs win. The following day he hit his sixth home run of the season to help seal a 7–4 win over Brooklyn to give the Cubs their seventh consecutive win. Wilson then had three hits and two RBIs in a 6–5 win over the Giants on May 9 at Wrigley Field to push the streak to eight.

Hornsby's status continued to be day-to-day, which didn't keep Joe McCarthy from using him to his advantage. Take the May 9 game for example. The Cubs trailed 5–3 in the eighth inning with Riggs Stephenson up to bat pinch hitting for second baseman Clyde Beck when McCarthy sent Hornsby to the on-deck circle as if he were about to pinch-hit for the pitcher, Hal Carlson.

Hornsby waved around a handful of bats as if limbering up to hit while Giants manager John McGraw considered the situation. Did he want to pitch to Stephenson—a good hitter—or Hornsby, a future Hall of Famer? McGraw understood that Hornsby could be a decoy, but he had no choice but to take the bait. McGraw instructed his pitcher to pitch to Stephenson rather than walk him. Stephenson proceeded to double home two runs to tie the score. Hornsby then returned to the bench and Carlson hit for himself, stroking an RBI single to score Stephenson and give the Cubs a 6–5 lead. Miraculously, Carlson went the distance, allowing just 5 runs despite allowing 14 hits on the afternoon to pick up the win.

May 9 turned out to be an eventful day for the Cubs, since in addition to winning the game, Pat Malone had his day in court and justice prevailed—Chicago justice that is. Thanks to some of Malone's shenanigans, he had to appear before Judge Joseph L. McCarthy, who ruled over a South State Street court. The Cubs right-hander faced charges of disorderly conduct and attempting to defraud.

Malone had been at Frolics Cafe and according to the manager of the inn, Herman Friffin, Malone had called for the check, but after being presented with the bill, he had refused to pay.

What followed reaffirmed how smitten Chicago had grown with their Cubs and how much the public as a whole had lost their perspective. Through their immense popularity, Cubs players had seemingly been issued a license to steal. Malone and the judge ended up going into his chambers for a private meeting. That meeting concluded with Malone posing for photographs with the judge before he was released after paying the delinquent bill of $35.40.

"Justice" served, the Cubs would try to extend their winning streak to nine games on May 10, but before the game, Wilson and Cuyler put on an outfield clinic with more than 6,000 kids showing up at Wrigley Field, as did a contingent from the visiting New York Giants.

Wilson might not have cut the figure of a baseball professor while addressing the kids, but he did manage to open some mouths and widen some eyes when he demonstrated how to hit a baseball with power by slashing three balls over the fence. With the ballpark not even a quarter full, each of Wilson's hits resulted in a dramatic echo that resonated throughout the grounds.

Later that day the Cubs' eight-game winning streak was snapped, but Wilson could not be blamed for the 9–4 loss.

After hitting a home run off Joe Genewich in the first inning, Wilson added a single and drove in two to extend his hitting streak to 14 games. But the Giants pounded Malone, who started and allowed three earned runs in two and two-thirds innings. During the eight-game winning streak, Wilson had turned his season around by hitting three home runs and driving home 12 while raising his average to .353. From May 4 through May 10 in a span covering six games, Wilson drove home 14 runs.

May 10 brought a huge boost to Chicago's ever-growing reputation as a cultural center as the Adler Planetarium & Astronomy Museum opened in Grant Park, giving Chicago the first planetarium built in the United States. Philanthropist Max Adler, who founded and built the structure, addressed his audience that day at the dedication, telling them:

The popular conception of the universe is too meager; the planets and the stars are too far removed from general knowledge. In our reflections, we dwell too little upon the concept that the world and all human endeavors within it are governed by established order and too infrequently upon the truth that under the heavens everything is interrelated, even as each of us to the other.

Heady stuff, but the stars weren't quite aligned for the Cubs on May 12. The wind at Wrigley Field blew out toward Lake Michigan that day making for a game in which the Cubs would show heart and firepower but come up short. After falling behind 14–0 to the Giants, the Cubs scored one in the fifth, three in the sixth, five in the seventh—on four home runs, including Wilson's eighth—one in the eighth and two in the ninth before losing 14–12. Larry Benton surrendered all of the Cubs' home runs and still managed to get credit for the win. The Cubs' third consecutive loss dropped them into second place by a half a game as they changed places in the standings with the Giants.

Needing someone to step forward to stop the team's bleeding, the Cubs found their doctor in Wilson on May 13 against the Braves. In the third inning he faced right-hander Ben Cantwell with two aboard. He took two pitches then powered his ninth homer of the season over the right field fence to put the Cubs up 7–0. Wilson's homer extended his hitting streak to 17 games and the Cubs hung on to win 9–8 in a wind-blown affair at Wrigley Field.

Further east, Captain Roscoe Turner, one of America's swash-buckling aviators of the era, made big news on the same day.

Turner had convinced Earl B. Gilmore, who was the head of Gilmore Oil, to buy him an airplane that he would fly to glorify Gilmore products. Playing off the company's trademark symbol, a lion's head, Turner procured a five-month-old lion cub, which he planned to bring along with him as a mascot while he performed dramatic aerial feats.

The idea caught on immediately, bringing about "The Gilmore Lion," a cream-colored Lockheed with red-and-gold trim. Every-body knew that behind the wheel of the Gilmore Lion was the flam-boyant Turner along with his lion cub, and both were fitted with parachutes. He made national news on May 13, 1930, when he tried to break a transcontinental record set by Charles Lindbergh.

Unfortunately for Turner, Gilmore oil, and the lion cub, Turner came up a little short of the mark when the plane ran out of gas before reaching Roosevelt Field on Long Island. Turner did not strike anyone as a person who would give up easily, and two weeks after coming up short, Turner set a new east-west record by flying from Roosevelt Field to Los Angeles's Grand Central Airport in 18 hours, 42 minutes, and 54 seconds.

Discoveries and testing limits were a big part of the Depression era, one that desperately embraced advances to distract Americans from economic woes. Included in those discoveries were those of the universe. Scientists had discovered a ninth planet in March, and in May that planet came to be known as Pluto.

On May 15, Wilson continued his torrid month with a double and two RBIs against the Braves. Unfortunately for the Cubs, the season still resembled a slow-pitch softball league and the Braves managed to outslug Wilson and the Cubs 10–8. Wilson extended his hitting streak to 18 games and by driving home 2, he pulled into a tie with Philadelphia's Chuck Klein for the top spot among National League hitters for RBIs with 27. The day's perception of the statistic? The battle for the top spot as the league's top run producer received absolutely no recognition. The Cubs then lost three of four games at St. Louis and the first game of a four-game series at Pittsburgh. Wilson had two home runs and three RBIs in the Cubs' only win, which came in the second game of the St. Louis series. The game had been scheduled for May 17, but got rained out and rescheduled as the first game of a May 18 doubleheader. The Cubs' 9–6 win ended the Cardinals nine-game winning streak.

Wilson made an impression on Cardinals third baseman Sparky Adams, who spoke about the slugger's penchant for hitting the ball.

"Hack could hit a ball with his eyes shut, and he could hit it a long way," Adams said. "I have a mark on my shins yet. We played in to catch the man going home and he hit a line drive right at me. The grass was wet and it skidded and hit right on my shin. I didn't say nothin'. I picked the ball up and threw the guy out going home. But hurt? Oh boy!"

Wilson's day established him as the National League leader in RBIs with 30 and extended his hitting streak to 21 games. Two days later, Wilson hit his 11th home run of the season against the Cardinals in St. Louis, giving him a 22-game hitting streak. The following day the Cubs lost to the Pirates 10–3 and Wilson went hitless to snap his impressive run. During the 22-game streak that extended from April 25 to May 20, Wilson had 10 home runs, 28 RBIs, and hit .442 in 77 at-bats.

Hal Carlson started against the Pirates on May 23 and allowed four earned runs on five hits in three innings before McCarthy lifted him after he had been hit on his right hand by a line drive. The Cubs went on to lose 7–6 at Forbes Field; Wilson had two doubles in the game, but no RBIs.

Rain caused the Cubs' May 27 game against the Reds to be cancelled. Hal Carlson had been scheduled to start for the Cubs, but when the game wasn't played, he retired to his residence at Chicago's Carlos Hotel, where many of his teammates also lived. After eating dinner, Carlson sat in the hotel lobby shooting the bull with Kiki Cuyler until after 10 p.m. According to Cuyler, Carlson appeared to feel fine when he told him he had decided to go to bed. But approximately four hours later, Carlson made a call to Eddie Froelich, telling the Cubs' clubhouse boy that he was in great pain. He went on to tell Froelich he did not need to call a doctor because just a year earlier he had endured similar pains. Carlson began to bleed from his mouth shortly after Froelich's arrival. At that point, Froelich called Cuyler, Heathcote, and Stephenson to the room. When Carlson's panicked teammates arrived, he was semi-conscious, prompting them to call team physician Dr. John Davis. Carlson died of a stomach hemorrhage at 3:35 a.m. before they could get him to the Illinois Masonic Hospital, where emergency surgery had been scheduled.

Speculation about Carlson's death—and his health in general—focused on the fact that he had been gassed during the time he spent in France during World War I. The popular Cubs pitcher left behind a wife and four-year-old daughter. The Cubs had to play on May 28, the actual date of Carlson's death, and they defeated the Reds 6–5.

A May 29 game against the Cardinals was postponed until May 30—making for a doubleheader—so players could attend Carlson's funeral. Wilson was noticeably absent from the funeral, which surprised some since Wilson and Carlson had been friends. Wilson cited a family matter for not being able to attend, but most felt the excuse was just his way of coping with death. McCarthy offered a eulogy at the funeral when he said of Carlson: "When you're in one of those games, with first place at stake, Carlson's the pitcher. He can come up with those 1–0 and 2–1 victories. He knows what he's doing out there. He knows how to protect himself."

Having a player die during the season was something few teams in the history of Major League Baseball had experienced. The Cubs were not ready for the emotions Carlson's death would bring, and neither the team nor the National League tried to make any special allowances for those who struggled with losing a friend and teammate. Grief counseling was virtually unheard of in the 1930s. Instead, the team got back to work the day after the funeral with the doubleheader against the Cardinals. Bad news would accompany grief during the doubleheader.

Hornsby started the first game at second base and had two hits in two at-bats. While on base in the third inning after collecting the second of his hits, Hornsby slid into third base, twisting his body in the process so that his left heel would hit the bag first. By doing so, he collided with Cardinals pitcher Sylvester Johnson, who covered third on the play. Hornsby left the field with a broken ankle, making Footsie Blair the team's permanent second baseman. Hornsby's injury brought to mind McCarthy's Fifth Commandment: "When you start to slide, slide. He who changes his mind may have to change a good leg for a bad one."

In the Cubs' final game of May, they trailed the Reds throughout the contest and went to the bottom of the ninth two runs down. But by the time Wilson stepped to the plate in the ninth, the Cubs had tied the score at five and Wilson saw Cuyler standing at second base representing the winning run. Wilson had not enjoyed a good afternoon, and the fans had let him know about their displeasure by raining boos on him after he struck out in his first two at-bats and failed to come through in his next two at-bats.

Such at-bats defined hitters and spurred never-ending debates. Was an RBI simply a matter of percentages? The more times one hit with runners on base, the higher one's RBI total would be. Or were RBI producers the kinds of players who reacted favorably to pressure, rising to the occasion to produce when runners were on base?

Here was Wilson stepping to the plate without a hit in four at-bats and seemingly not having a clue about how to make contact that afternoon. Nevertheless, he appeared eager for his fifth at-bat of the game, knowing that if he could somehow drive a ball into the outfield, the speedy Cuyler could race home with the winning run and the Cubs could end May—a month filled with heartbreak and disaster—on a high note. Jesse Haines had started for the Cardinals and had gone the distance when he faced Wilson. The Cardinals right-hander delivered his first pitch and Wilson hit a ball screaming through the middle of the infield for a single. Cuyler was running on contact and scored easily to give the Cubs a 6–5 win.

Wilson finished a monster month that saw him hit 10 home runs and drive in 33 while hitting .366 in 26 games; for the season he had 14 home runs and 44 RBIs. Wilson's stick work led to a popular ballad that would remain on the tongues of Chicago baseball fans that summer. It went as follows:

Here lies the body of Spike McGlunk,
A brother of our lodge;
Hack Wilson hit one back at him,
And Spike forgot to dodge.

Wilson's teammates enjoyed a good month in May as well. After hitting .306 with a .386 on-base percentage and scoring nine runs in April, Cuyler hit .373 with a .423 OBP and scored 22 runs in May. English hit .274 with an OBP of .392 and nine runs scored in April before improving to a .321 average in May with an OBP of .387 and 26 runs scored. Hornsby had 30 more at-bats in May after hitting .240 with an OBP of .296 and two runs scored in April, and he improved to a .364 average with a .426 OBP and 10 runs scored. With Hornsby's season apparently over, Blair would be taking his place in the batting order, which represented a significant decline in production.

Over in the American League, Babe Ruth and Lou Gehrig both seemed to shift into a higher gear while their manager, Bob Shawkey, had difficulty running the club. Just 37 years old, Shawkey had played for the team and ran hard with Ruth and the rest of the club's carousers. Suddenly he was the manager, so having him try to maintain discipline among his old running mates was a difficult proposition. For Ruth the change from Miller Huggins to Shawkey meant he had free reign. Few of the players obeyed curfews, card games no longer had limits, and Shawkey had no answers. Ruth had wanted the manager's job after Huggins died, lobbying the Yankees' ownership for the position, pointing out how other top players such as Ty Cobb, Tris Speaker, and Hornsby had all successfully managed teams. Yankees owner Jake Ruppert made it clear to Ruth he wanted him as a player and not as a manager. That being the case, Ruth was more than happy to run roughshod over the new regime. Ruth's game did not seem to suffer under the new regime, which was more conducive to his lifestyle.

Ruth hit 13 home runs and drove in 33 during May, giving him 15 home runs and 44 RBIs on the season. He led Wilson in home runs by just one while tying the Cubs slugger for RBIs. Gehrig hit 8 home runs and drove in 35, pushing his totals to 11 home runs and 42 RBIs.

The Cubs finished the month in fourth place with a record of 20-19, four games behind first-place Brooklyn. Meanwhile, Connie Mack's Philadelphia Athletics looked as though they had a good chance of making a return trip to the World Series; the Cubs had some work to do.

CHAPTER ELEVEN

June

NOT HAVING ROGERS HORNSBY DIDN'T SEEM TO BOTHER THE CUBS at the beginning of June when Hack Wilson led a 16–4 rout of the Pirates with 35,000 watching at Wrigley Field. With the victory, the team extended its winning streak to five games.

Wilson doubled in the Cubs' five-run third and then hit his 15th home run of the season in the fourth with two aboard. He added a single in the sixth and finished off his onslaught with a solo home run in the seventh. Wilson's five RBIs on the afternoon moved him to 49 for the season, just 43 games old at this point.

When the club traveled east to play the Boston Braves, Joe McCarthy remained behind to confer with Bill Veeck about possible trades they might make to try and improve the team's offense without Hornsby. Arthur Whitney, the Phillies power-hitting third baseman, was rumored to be the player the Cubs wanted to acquire, but at what cost?

Once the Cubs took the field on June 3 in Boston, they played like a team that didn't need help in any phase of their game or at any position as they took a 15–2 win over the Braves.

Rookie pitcher Bud Teachout performed well, allowing just two runs and pitching a complete game, while Cubs hitters continued to carve up opposing pitchers. Footsie Blair stood out among those most prominent in leading the Cubs' offense. In Hornsby's absence, most of what was being written and said about the Cubs had something to do with Blair's inferior offensive abilities. But he proved to be anything but an offensive liability against the Braves when he stroked three singles and a triple. Though Wilson went hitless, he did manage to accrue one RBI by hitting a sacrifice fly to give him 50 for the season.

Back in Chicago, a new gang war was initiated on June 1 at a dinner party at the Fox Lake Hotel, a resort 50 miles outside of Chicago. The hotel was known to be a favorite hangout for remaining members of "Bugs" Moran's gang. Machine gun wielding assassins riddled hotel guests with bullets, killing three and wounding two others. Among those killed were a member of Al Capone's gang, a member of the Klondike O'Connell gang, and a member of the Druggan Valley gang. The episode brought an end to a gangland truce, perpetuating what felt like a dangerous atmosphere within the city.

The Cubs extended their winning streak to seven with an 18–10 win the following day in a game that saw the Cubs pound out 20 hits. Wilson had two hits and an RBI sandwiched in the lineup between Kiki Cuyler and Riggs Stephenson, who each had five hits and four RBIs for the afternoon.

While the Cubs were away from the Windy City, the Yankees visited the White Sox on June 4 and Babe Ruth homered for a third consecutive day to give him 18 on the season. Even in Chicago, Ruth's effort grabbed the headlines. He maintained a lead over Wilson, who kept pace with the Bambino by hitting his 17th home run on June 5 to lead the Cubs' eighth consecutive win, this one over the Braves 10–7.

Wilson's homer came with one out in the fifth when he hit Bob Smith's first pitch deep into the center field stands to lead a four-run inning. Though portrayed as being impotent without Hornsby, the Cubs' offense scored 43 runs in their three-game sweep of the Braves.

Rolling into Brooklyn the next day to face the Robins, the Cubs' winning streak appeared in jeopardy. They were scheduled to face their old nemesis Dazzy Vance. Though the Cubs had gotten the best of Vance earlier in the season, the veteran hurler still referred to the Cubs as his "meal ticket" and one bump in the road wasn't about to change Vance's sentiment. But Charlie Root started for the Cubs and allowed no runs on two hits. And despite Vance's striking out 10 in six innings of work, the Cubs teed off on him, tallying seven runs—of which five were earned—on 10 hits en route to a 13–0 win. The win marked nine in a row and moved the Cubs within one game of first place, held by the Robins. Wilson's RBI double off Vance put his season tally up to 53.

Beginning with the 16–4 win over the Pirates on June 1, the Cubs scored 72 runs in five games, which prompted record-keepers to peruse old scorebooks to see if they had set a modern record for runs scored in a five-game period. An 88-run total in four games by the Chicago National club in 1876 was discovered, but all agreed that records from that era were unreliable, leaving the Cubs' mark as a modern standard.

Over the course of the five games, the Cubs employed the same lineup, and only Clyde Beck hit less than .333. Charlie Grimm led the offense with .579 average, while Cuyler and Stephenson each hit .458, Gabby Hartnett hit .450, Wilson .440, English .363, Blair .333, and Beck .105.

Run totals were equally as impressive. Cuyler scored 13, Stephenson and English each scored 11 times, Grimm scored 10, and Wilson 9.

On June 7, the Cubs appeared to be full of good fortune and well on their way to their 10th consecutive win and a share of first place. Leading Brooklyn 3–0 with one out in the third, Wilson popped up in foul territory between home plate and first base against Johnny Morrison. Robins first baseman Del Bissonette and the catcher, Al Lopez, each called for the ball before each pulled away, watching the second out fall to the turf and giving Wilson another chance.

Wilson, figuring he was going to be out, had already hustled back to the Cubs' bench to get out of the drizzle that had been constant throughout the game. He gladly ventured back into the foul weather to swing at Morrison's very next pitch and plant the baseball into the left field stands to give the Cubs a 5–0 lead and tie him with Ruth at 18 home runs for the season.

The Cubs held a 9–8 lead after they hit in the seventh. English hit one home run that cleared the fence and another that bounced over the low fence in center field. Wilson and Beck each bounced balls over the left-center field fence, which would be a ground-rule double today, but counted as a home run in 1930. Despite the Cubs' four home runs, opposing player Bill Clark's proved to be the biggest. The Robins pitcher hit a three-run homer in the bottom half of the seventh to lead a 12–9 Brooklyn win that snapped the Cubs' winning streak at nine games. Wilson drove in two in the game to extend his RBI streak to eight games dating back to May 30.

Wilson's RBI streak came to an end the following day when he collected no hits in three at-bats against diminutive Brooklyn right-hander Dolf Luque, who tossed a 6–0 complete-game win over the Cubs. Luque presented an interesting look for Wilson. The native of Havana, Cuba, stood just 5'7". Since Wilson stood just 5'6", he normally had to watch the path of the pitch arrive at a pronounced downward angle. Against Luque, the ball arrived on more of a flat path. In theory, such a path normally makes hitting the ball easier for a hitter. But Wilson wasn't used to seeing the ball arrive in said fashion and struggled against Luque throughout their careers, hitting just .161 with one home run against him.

While the Cubs traveled from Brooklyn to Philadelphia on June 9, a disturbing crime rocked Chicago. Jake Lingle, a well-respected police reporter for the *Chicago Tribune,* took a single shot to his head from a .38 while waiting for the 1:30 p.m. express at the Illinois Central station at Randolph Street. The train would have taken him to the Washington Park racetrack in south suburban Homewood. The bullet sent him forward, and his body lay dead with a cigar still clinched in his teeth and a racing form in his hand. The shooting had taken place in the middle of a crowd that watched as the assailant raced up a stairway before blending into the crowd west of Michigan Avenue.

While the murder of Lingle brought the city its 12th mob hit in 10 days, this one had a different flavor. The other hits had been on other mobsters. Lingle had been a regular citizen and a newspaper reporter at that. Suddenly, a realization that anybody in the city could be the target for a mob hit caused a mild panic along with an outcry to public officials that the crime in the city needed to be cleaned up. The *Chicago Tribune* immediately offered a $25,000 reward for help in finding Lingle's killer.

Meanwhile, the Cubs were away in Philadelphia, beginning a four-game series against the Phillies on June 10. Though only 95 miles separated Philadelphia and New York, travel wasn't the easiest of propositions for a baseball team. Summers were hot, and trains offered little relief. Even getting to the train was tough. From the time a team dressed after the game until it reached the train station to head to its next destination, there was no escaping the heat. Hygiene issues aside, dehydration could be a factor, leaving players with cramps and extremely uncomfortable while being hot and sticky.

Al Lopez chuckled when asked about Hack Wilson and the heat.

"It's not like today," said Lopez in a 1991 interview. "There was nowhere to go to get out of the heat. That summer [of 1930] was particularly hot. Hack always seemed to be sweating whether you saw him in street clothes or his uniform. Of course, some of that he might have brought upon himself."

Lopez did not elaborate, but his meaning was clear. Alcohol often ran out of Wilson's pores from the previous night's activities.

Chuck Klein played for the Phillies and many considered him to be of the same class of slugger as Wilson. Born in Indianapolis, Indiana, Klein also had a background similar to Wilson's. He worked in a steel mill and when he wasn't working he played in a semipro baseball league. Eventually the St. Louis Cardinals signed him to a contract and he began working his way through the Cardinals' vast farm system. During the 1928 season, Klein played for a Cardinals' minor league team in Fort Wayne, Indiana, and he thrived, hitting 26 home runs in his first 88 games. Unfortunately for the Cardinals, Kenesaw Mountain Landis found out that the Cardinals also owned the Dayton, Ohio, club, which presented problems since Fort Wayne and Dayton played in the same league. The commissioner of baseball mandated that the Cardinals sell their Fort Wayne team. Along with that order came the one that really stung: They had to give up the rights to the players on the Fort Wayne team.

The Cardinals had plans for Klein that did not come to fruition due to Landis's ruling. After that, the Yankees were beaten out for Klein's services by the Phillies, who bid more for the slugger. By July of 1928, Klein was in Philadelphia.

Klein played his first Major League game on July 30, 1928, and by the end of the season he had accrued 11 home runs and 34 RBIs in 64 games.

Klein's first of four home run titles came the next season, but it did not come without its share of controversy. By the end of the 1929 season, New York Giants slugger Mel Ott and Klein each sat at the top of the National League leader board with 42 home runs. Coincidently, the Phillies played the Giants in a twin-bill on the final day of the season. In the first game, Klein hit his 43rd home run of the season—establishing a new National League home run record—to take the lead. Phillies pitchers then took over in the second game by walking Ott five times after walking him once in the first game. Ott failed to get a home run in the Giants' final game of the season the following day against the Boston Braves, leaving Klein alone at the top of the leader board.

Entering the June 10, 1930, Phillies-Cubs contest, Klein had 15 home runs and 55 RBIs as compared to 18 and 55 for Wilson, which made the clash of the sluggers an intriguing point of interest for the fans.

Klein won the first battle, hitting his 16th home run and collecting two RBIs in game one of the series while Wilson had a hit with one RBI in two at-bats. And the following day Klein drove in two while Wilson got blanked. Klein went three-for-three in the third game and Wilson had one hit with an RBI. Each player had a hit in the final game of the series and Klein had one RBI. So the talk of Klein being up to the task of overtaking Wilson did not seem to bother the 25-year-old Philadelphia slugger. And why should such talk have bothered him? After all, he held the National League home run record and he reigned as the defending home run king.

Klein accrued eight hits during the series while driving in six—including a three-for-three day on June 12 that saw the Cubs fall to the Phillies 5–3.

That night at Yankee Stadium, Jack Sharkey and Max Schmeling fought for the heavyweight title, which had been vacated by Gene Tunney in 1928. The infamous fight saw Sharkey dominate, but throw a low, crippling left below the belt that sent Schmeling to the canvas. In the aftermath of the confusion that followed, Schmeling was declared the winner and the new heavyweight champion by way of a foul, which had not previously happened in professional boxing. The sports world was humming.

On June 7, the Yankees played for the first time after two days off and Ruth homered for the fourth consecutive game, hitting his 19th of the season in a game in St. Louis against the Browns.

In Cleveland on June 15, the Yankees played the first-place Indians in front of an overflow crowd of 33,828. Because the crowd spilled out onto the outfield, special ground rules had to be put in place, which helped to facilitate nine doubles in the game won by the Yankees in a 17–10 route.

Ruth and Gehrig led the way with Gehrig hitting 2 home runs and Ruth his 21st of the season to knock the Indians out of first place. No special mention was made about Gehrig driving in 7 runs during the game, giving him 66 RBIs for the season. At that same juncture, Wilson had just 60 RBIs. So while everybody focused on Wilson and Ruth battling it out for home run superiority of baseball, all of baseball was missing a great race between Wilson and Gehrig to see who would become the RBI king.

The longer the season went on, the more games came in with double-digit scores, prompting newspapers and fans to begin taking notice of what was happening to the national pastime.

The *Chicago Tribune* ran a regular column, "In the Wake of the News," that answered letters from readers. Here's a sample of what was on the minds of many during the 1930 season from a letter that appeared in the paper on June 20, 1930.

Dear Wake:

About these big league baseball games with scores like race horse odds, 15-2, 11-1, etc., I don't blame any ball player for trying to equal Babe Ruth's or Hack Wilson's home run record. Nor do I blame any team for fighting to win. But how about the fans, who think home runs are due to lightning balls and short fences, and that baseball is losing its science? Won't they begin to stay at home on Sundays, day of biggest crowds, and get the score over the radio?

I don't say make it a pitchers' battle, but certainly cut down these ridiculously large scores so the contests may become more interesting. They changed the official golf ball, making it lighter and larger, so it would not carry so far. Now what about changing the official baseball the same way, or else take out some of the rubber core?

A.T.L.

"The Wake" answered the letter with the following reply:

Despite denials of manufacturers that the official baseball has been made livelier, home runs certainly are more numerous than they once were. In fact, home runs are common instead of being events, as once. The Wake feels much of the strategy of our national sport has been sacrificed in the process. When any batting rally, punctuated by home runs, may yield a half dozen markers, there is less incentive to steal bases, to bunt sacrifices, and to struggle for the one run which in the past often has decided keen battles. We sympathize with the plaint of Helper A.T.L.

On June 21, the Cubs conducted a ceremony commemorating their 1929 league championship season. Prior to the doubleheader against the Braves, Cubs players paraded the bunting around the field before watching it get raised with a stiff northeast breeze blowing. A crowd of 42,000 swelled its collective chest while remembering with great pride the Cubs' 1929 pennant-winning season. Seeing the pennant hoisted and the positive feelings created by the grand ceremony made the idea of the Cubs winning another pennant in 1930 seem possible. That possibility seemed even more real when the Cubs went out and played like champions that afternoon, winning both games by the score of 5–4, taking the first game in 12 innings.

Wilson had three hits in the first game, including his 20th home run of the season, a two-run shot off right-hander Bob Smith. He continued to lead the team offensively while McCarthy seemingly came up with one right decision after the next, never letting the team fall apart despite the setbacks of losing Hornsby to injury, Hal Carlson's death, and the constant worries brought about by Wilson's and Pat Malone's drinking, though Malone brought about more problems during the 1930 season than his running mate, Wilson.

Cubs fans continued to embrace Wilson, the flawed hero who could hit baseballs to all corners of the ballpark with authority, go out on a bender in the surrounding neighborhoods afterward, then be back at the ballpark to run through the same cycle again the following day.

The *Chicago Tribune* had another column that ran daily entitled, "The Inquiring Reporter," in which a reporter asked a question of five people picked off the street. Their responses were put in the following day's paper. On June 22, the following question was asked: "Which player is doing the most to keep the Cubs in the pennant race?"

The answer given by Miss Marie Kellner, of 6611 Oshkosh Avenue, gave an indication of how beloved a figure Wilson had become when she said:

Hack Wilson is my choice and how that boy has been clouting that ball and doing superhuman fielding stunts! His all around work this year has been marvelous and the poor sports who were razzing Hack are as quiet as lambs now. He is running Babe Ruth a merry race for home run honors, and I bet he beats him out, too.

On June 23, the Cubs hosted the Phillies, bringing about another chance to contrast the National League's top two sluggers in Wilson and Klein.

Klein arrived at Wrigley Field carrying 19 home runs and 73 RBIs on his ledger; Wilson stood at 21 home runs and 67 RBIs. Of course, the comparisons favored Wilson since he was leading the reigning home run champion in four baggers; the RBIs were simply garnish for the main course.

Wilson clearly bettered Klein the first game of the series when he had two singles, a double, a triple, and a home run, which meant he hit for the cycle, the quirky feat difficult for any hitter to achieve. Wilson's five hits and five RBIs gave him 22 home runs and 72 RBIs for the season while leading a 24-hit Cubs attack that fueled a 21–8 win over the Phillies.

In the second game of the series played on June 24, a foul ball hit by Wilson went into the grandstands at Wrigley and caused an interesting situation. A young man, Arthur Porto, who was 17 at the time, caught the foul ball. When an usher went to retrieve the ball, Porto refused even when the usher, who worked for the Cubs, informed Porto that the Cubs' policy was to reclaim baseballs hit into the stands. Eventually Porto and three of his friends got into a fight with the usher, which led to their arrest. Subsequently they were hauled into the courthouse in Chicago on disorderly conduct charges, but a Judge Allegretti ruled the ball belonged to Porto and all four of the youths were discharged.

In the final game of the three-game series against the Phillies, Gabby Hartnett had a game-winning single in the bottom of the ninth to give the Cubs a 13–12 win and a sweep of the series. For the day, Hartnett had two home runs, two singles, and he drove in six runs.

Hartnett's play continued to remind McCarthy and the Cubs' faithful of what they had missed without having Hartnett available for most of the 1929 season. After Hartnett's big day against the Phillies, he had a .328 batting average with 17 home runs and 50 RBIs. He had been with the Cubs since 1922 mostly serving as a backup for Bob O'Farrell. Then a freak accident occurred. Like a lot of catchers, O'Farrell favored an old mask. In his particular case, the protective caging over his face had suffered many dents from baseballs hitting his mask over the years. In 1924, a foul ball ripped through his face mask and fractured his skull. He recovered from the accident, but the time away afforded the Cubs the opportunity to see Hartnett, who responded to his chance by hitting .299 with 16 home runs and 67 RBIs in 111 games. The Cubs were convinced Hartnett could do the job, which prompted the team to trade O'Farrell to the Cardinals in 1925. Hartnett brought another dangerous bat to an already lethal Cubs offense. In 1925 he had finished second in the league in home runs with 25, but he was often injured. When he first joined the Cubs,

Hartnett maintained his composure and had a quiet, understated manner that did not include much extra conversation. Thus, his teammates gave him the nickname "Gabby." Eventually he loosened up and became one of the team's biggest characters.

During the three-game series with the Phillies, Klein collected five hits in 13 trips to the plate and had two RBIs while Wilson had eight hits in 16 at-bats with a home run and six RBIs.

Al Capone had often attended Cubs games, but was not around much in 1930. With the increased gangland warfare, he decided to remain primarily at his Miami compound. Bill Veeck Jr. once humorously alluded to the fact that he didn't have to see Capone to know he was in the ballpark. He only had to look at the box office take and if he saw a $100 bill, he knew Capone and his entourage were somewhere in the house. Capone normally sat next to the field and was accorded celebrity treatment, which meant talking to the players on many occasions.

By late in June, the reward money offered by the *Chicago Tribune* and other sources for information leading to the arrest of Lingle's killer had reached $55,725. Questions about Lingle also began to arise once his finances were examined and revealed a $60,000 a year income, yet he made just $65 per week as a newspaper man. Most put two and two together to draw the conclusion that he had worked as a middleman between politicians, mobsters, and the police. One of the biggest surprises to come from the entire episode was that the *Tribune* had never questioned his finances even though he owned a house on the West Side, where his wife and two children lived, while he often stayed in a room on the 27th floor of the Stevens Hotel, one of Chicago's finest hotels, and had a weekend house in Long Beach, Indiana.

The investigation of Lingle would be ongoing, with the reports striking a daily chord of fear for Chicago citizens. Following Wilson's exploits offered a lighter fare for Chicagoans to consume.

Despite Wilson's achievements, Ruth continued to capture most of the notice nationally. After hitting two home runs on June

25 in the second game of the Yankees' doubleheader against the Browns, Ruth had 26 home runs for the season, putting him 8 days and 2 home runs ahead of his record-setting year of 1927 when he recorded 60. During the 1927 season, he did not hit his 26th home run until July 3, and on June 25, 1927, he had just 24.

On June 30, Ruth hit his 30th home run of the season off Tommy Thomas in a 15–4 Yankees win over the White Sox at Yankee Stadium, putting him 15 games ahead of his 1927 pace while leaving the rest of the hitters in the Major Leagues in his immense wake.

In June, Wilson hit eight home runs and drove in 29 while hitting .361, putting him at 22 home runs for the season with 73 RBIs. Wilson and Wally Berger of the Braves were tied for the National League home run lead and they ranked second in the majors trailing Ruth by eight. Gehrig had 20 and Klein finished June with 19 home runs and 78 RBIs for the season.

Wilson's success did not change the perception of the slugger. Many still considered him the same person, a wayward soul headed in the wrong direction on a one-way street. Any irregularities or sluggish behavior by Wilson were normally attributed to his having seen the sun come up through a bottle of gin, and normally such foregone conclusions were accurate. Wilson's response to those inquiring as to how he could hit with a hangover: "I see three balls and swing at the middle one."

With a hangover or sober as a judge, Wilson led the Cubs to a 20-7 mark in June, which put the team back in the pennant hunt. During the month, the Cubs scored 218 runs for an average of 8.1 runs per game. Huge numbers, but many games were being played in 1930 in which 8.1 runs were not enough to win.

Chapter Twelve

July

Despite their many hardships, the Cubs found themselves in first place on July 1, a position many attributed to McCarthy's work calling the shots. Admirers of the Cubs manager could be found as far away as Minnesota, where *Minneapolis Tribune* writer George Barton wrote: "Joe McCarthy once more is proving to the baseball world that he is one of the greatest managers of modern times." Barton went on to call McCarthy a leader of men and a master strategist. Based on the job McCarthy had done for most of the season, such praise was well deserved.

Wilson entered July in the midst of a relative cold spell. Though he had collected seven hits in six games, he did not drive in a run during the Cubs' final six games of June. Of course, during that same stretch, Cuyler, batting in front of Wilson in the third spot in the order, had 13 RBIs, including five against the Phillies on June 25 when he hit a double and a home run. So even if Wilson did get hits, Cuyler had already cleaned off the bases. Heading into July, Cuyler—not Wilson—led the Cubs in RBIs with 74.

Wilson connected for his 23rd home run off Freddie Fitzsimmons in his first at-bat in the Cubs' 7–5 loss July 1 against the Giants. The following day he drove in two. Then, after going without an RBI in the first game of a July 4 doubleheader at Pittsburgh that the Cubs won 10–1, he drove in the Cubs' lone run in the second game with a sacrifice fly in a 5–1 loss. That RBI put Wilson's season total at 77 while Cuyler moved to 81.

Newspapers made a big deal about the importance of the Cubs getting into first place on Independence Day. If they had swept the Fourth of July doubleheader against the Pirates, they could have moved past Brooklyn into first place. The Cubs' doubleheader split combined with the Robins' split with the Giants left the Cubs in second place by percentage points. In the morning, Brooklyn led the Cubs in winning percentage, .6069 to .6056, and at the end of the day that difference had been reduced to .6029 to .6027.

In an odd statistic, Brooklyn stood in first place, five games ahead of the third-place Giants, whereas the Cubs were in second place, but ahead of the Giants by five and a half games.

The Cubs no longer needed their slide rules the next day when they bombed the Pirates 12–3 to move back into first place as the Robins lost to the Giants 11–3. Wilson had three singles and three RBIs on the day.

Wilson managed a single RBI in each game of the Cubs' July 6 doubleheader loss to the Reds to give him 82 RBIs with 78 games left in the season. He would not record another RBI until 10 days later and was said to have "miseries" in his stomach. The mysterious problem was attributed to the hot weather, but the problem likely originated elsewhere.

During the interim, the Cubs lost six of seven, including a loss at Cincinnati on July 9 that saw the Reds catch the Cubs sleeping with a squeeze play. Starting a runner from third base and having the hitter place a bunt had once been a staple of any offensive attack, but with the changing face of baseball's offense, the play seemed a forgotten art. So when the Reds employed the play in the bottom of the 10th, they did so successfully and the Cubs looked as if they had never seen the good ol' squeeze. The Reds won 4–3.

While the Cubs were in Cincinnati, the *Cincinnati Enquirer* got the whiff of a rumor that Rogers Hornsby was done with Chicago regardless of whether his injured ankle and heel improved. McCarthy would not discuss Hornsby with reporters, but he did indicate that he felt a big story regarding Hornsby would play out before the season was complete.

The *Chicago Tribune* contacted Hornsby, who had returned to his home in Anglum, Missouri, while he healed. When told about the rumors circulating about his future, the Rajah told the *Tribune* that his ankle and heel were feeling fine and about the rumors: "There's nothing to it. Somebody was hard up for a story when he wrote that piece. I shall be back in Chicago July 10 for another examination of my injured ankle and I expect to be able to work out a few days later. I hope to be in the lineup not later than August 1."

William Veeck also addressed the rumors by telling the *Tribune*: "There's nothing to it. We haven't reached the point where we are trying to get rid of .375 hitters."

If the squeeze-play loss wasn't enough, what happened in the Cubs' next road stop at Boston personified the meaning of hard luck.

The Cubs had lost to the Braves 2–1 in the first game of a Sunday afternoon doubleheader on July 13 and were trailing 3–0 heading into the ninth inning of the second game when they began to get their offense going by erupting for four runs in the ninth. Unfortunately the runs did not count because of the Massachusetts Sports Law, which had been passed in 1929. Accordingly, the game in Boston could not continue past 6 p.m.

Ed Burns of the *Chicago Tribune* wrote: "[Lieutenant] McCluskey of the Commonwealth stepped in under the Sunday law which makes it wicked for ball fans to enjoy themselves after 6 p.m."

The end of the game had seen the Braves put on a stalling act until the clock ran out, which made the official game result retroactive back to the eighth inning when the Braves led 3–0. The reversal gave the home team a sweep.

What happened had been set into place a year and a half earlier at the end of a long fight between both Boston baseball teams, the

Braves and the Red Sox, with Boston lawmakers finally agreeing to allow games to be played on Sundays under the condition that they only took place between the hours of 2:05 p.m. and 6 p.m. Despite the rigid constraints, both teams scheduled doubleheaders that tested the time limits. Up until the July 13 Braves-Cubs fiasco, the only games that had to be called had clearly defined winners. Most felt a game with an outcome like the July 13 contest was inevitable, given the rule. In that fateful ninth inning, Wilson had snapped a string of 20 at-bats without a hit as he ignited the meaningless four-run Cubs rally.

The Cubs protested the game based on the Braves' stalling antics, and in addition, McCarthy cited umpire Ernie Quigley telling him the inning could be finished under the law as long as it began prior to 5:40 p.m. McCarthy thought the best solution would be to re-play the game. Three days later, National League president John Heydler refused to allow Chicago's protest.

Meanwhile, Hornsby returned to Chicago on July 14. The plan for his return called for him to work out at Wrigley Field before joining the team in Philadelphia on July 24. Veeck wielded this news like a saber to defend the club against rumors regarding Hornsby, as he told reporters: "It is improbable that Hornsby will be available for regular service when he reports to manager McCarthy a week from Thursday. But we expect him to take over his old job at second base by August 1. This ought to end rumors that his days with the Cubs are over."

Wilson's six-game RBI drought finally ended on July 16 when he drove in two runs against the Robins in the first game of a doubleheader in Brooklyn. That first game proved memorable because someone wearing a Cubs uniform other than Wilson charged the stands.

Del Bissonette of the Dodgers tried for an inside-the-park home run and knocked himself out when he hit his head on home plate while sliding. The crowd at Ebbets Field held Cubs catcher Gabby Hartnett responsible for Bissonette being injured and they tried to pelt him with bottles, which prompted Hartnett to try to go into the stands before being restrained by teammates.

Wilson hit his 25th home run of the season—a solo shot July 18 at Brooklyn, ending a homerless drought that dated back to July 6. The next day Dazzy Vance started for the Robins and he again took his lumps against the team that he had hitherto dominated. Making matters worse for Vance, Wilson, the hitter he had always owned, hit his 26th home run of the season into the right field stands in the sixth inning. When Vance stood on the mound in the eighth, he looked at the on-deck circle where Wilson wildly swung three bats around readying to take his swings. Wilson clearly was enjoying himself, smiling out at Vance, who no longer seemed to be his nemesis. Normally unflappable, Vance opted to throw in the towel. He stuffed his mitt into the pocket of his pants and headed to the dugout to end his outing in a 5–4 Cubs win.

Wilson's two homers in a 6–0 win over the Giants on July 21 gave him home runs in four consecutive games and put the Cubs back atop the National League standings. Both of his home runs found the right field stands at the Polo Grounds, his 29th topping his 28th for distance. Given Wilson's penchant for hitting with power to right field, the Polo Grounds served him well, since the right field foul pole stood just 257 feet from home plate. That fact often made Giants fans wonder out loud what might have been had their manager, McGraw, hung on to Wilson and allowed him to play his game.

With the Cubs still on the road, Hornsby worked out at Wrigley Field and he picked up where he left off, playing all the angles, shaping the thoughts of William Wrigley Jr. by bending the team owner's ears at every opportunity with opinions about why the club could not shake free from the other teams in the National League.

Behind the scenes the players did not like the Rajah, and his relationship with McCarthy deteriorated daily. Amid all of the talk about Hornsby being a despised character on the team and the rumors that he might be traded were rumors that his gambling had gotten him in trouble with Judge Kenesaw Mountain Landis. Hornsby addressed allegations in the *Chicago Tribune*.

"I can't understand why they call me a troublemaker," said Hornsby upon his return to Wrigley Field to work out prior to rejoining the club in Philadelphia. "So far with the Cubs I haven't had an argument with Manager McCarthy or any player. No one realizes more than I do that I was far off form during the early season with my sore heel. I tried hard, but I couldn't field well, and with the strength gone from my right foot, I had a tough time hitting. I'm not worried. I'm just puzzled, that's all."

Years later the belief that Hornsby had been in trouble was validated within the papers of Leslie O'Connor, who served as Landis's chief assistant. Hornsby had issued a statement on July 17, 1930, written on stationery with a "Chicago National League Ball Club" letterhead that was addressed to Landis. It read as follows:

I wish to inform you that I do not in the future intend to have anything to do with gamblers, bookmakers, horse races or bets, etc. I also wish you to know that I do not play cards or shoot craps; and intend on taking no part in any of these enterprises.

The Cubs played day baseball like all of the other teams in the Major Leagues in 1930, and they would continue to do so long after their opponents added lighting systems to their stadiums to accommodate night baseball. Ironically, at Wrigley Field in Los Angeles, which was built by William Wrigley Jr., a night game was played on July 22, 1925—the first such sundown event—as the Los Angeles Angels of the Pacific Coast League played the Hollywood Stars. Cincinnati hosted the Major Leagues' first night game in 1935; the Cubs did not have official night baseball at Chicago's Wrigley Field until 1988.

Wilson's legend for being able to burn the candle at both ends continued to grow in 1930. Bill Veeck Jr. walked into the clubhouse on July 26 to find the team trainer, Andy Lotshaw, working to sober up Wilson, who sat inside a large tub.

"In the tub with Hack was a fifty-pound cake of ice," Veeck Jr. said. "Well, what would you do if a fifty-pound cake of ice jumped into your bathtub with you? You'd try to jump out, right? That was precisely what Hack was trying to do. Enthusiastically, but not successfully. Every time Hack's head would bob up, Andy would shove it back down under the water and the cake of ice would come bobbing up. It was a fascinating sight, watching them bob in perfect rhythm, first Hack's head, then the ice, then Hack's head, then the ice."

Veeck Jr. remembered the date because Wilson hit three home runs that afternoon in a 16–2 win over the Phillies. Not since Cap Anson did it in 1884 had a Cubs player hit three home runs in a game.

Nobody ever doubted that Veeck witnessed the scene he described, but years later some felt he had gotten the date wrong. Whether what Veeck had seen happened on the day Wilson hit three home runs could be debated, but Wilson's antics that day at the Baker Bowl in Philadelphia had to be enjoyed.

If Wilson had been nursing a hangover, he recovered quickly. While fans filed into the ballpark that day, they were treated to Wilson enjoying the music of a Moose Lodge band. So joyous was the Cubs slugger that he marched in rhythm up and down the third base line with his bat over his shoulder, seemingly without a care in the world. Wilson's prolonged dance show went on until just prior to the first pitch when he returned to the Cubs' dugout accompanied by laughter and applause from the Philadelphia fans, who appreciated his good nature and the entertainment value of his actions.

When Wilson hit in the first inning, he stepped to the plate and went through his usual ritual, grabbing a handful of dirt, rubbing his hands together, then dusting the back of his red neck and his already soaked uniform with the dirt. Digging in, he stared out at Phillies pitcher Phil Collins, seriousness etched in his expression. The Phillies right-hander fell behind 2-0 in the count before Wilson swung at the third pitch, driving the baseball deep over the right field fence. Upon making contact, Wilson's face lit up with a smile, which he maintained while scooting around the bases.

Wilson mirrored his first-inning performance in the second, again driving one of Collins' offerings over the right field fence and joyfully rounding the bases. He capped off his performance with his third home run of the game in the eighth inning, yet another blast to right field, a blow that dwarfed the previous two. When the last of his three home runs landed, he had 32 home runs on the season and his 5 RBIs moved his total to 98 in just 95 games.

Another odd moment in an odd season of twists and turns occurred during the Cubs' game against the Reds in Cincinnati on July 27. The Cubs trailed 2–1 after five innings, but appeared on the brink of breaking the game open in the sixth inning after Woody English led off the inning with a leadoff triple against Reds right-hander Larry Benton. Kiki Cuyler then hit a single to send home English and tie the score at 2. Wilson followed with a double off the right field screen at Redland Field. The drive scored Cuyler, giving the Cubs a 3–2 lead and Wilson his 99th RBI of the season. Benton uncorked a wild pitch that allowed Wilson to move to third and Danny Taylor drew a walk. Dan Howley had seen enough and the Reds manager called for right-hander Ken Ash to enter the game to face Charlie Grimm.

With the pulse of a big inning pumping, Grimm swung at Ash's first pitch and hit a routine grounder to the right side of the infield. Hod Ford pounced on the ball and looked to third. Wilson had made his break for home before heading back to the base. Ford alertly threw to third baseman Tony Cuccinello and the Reds had Wilson caught in a rundown between home and third.

"I'll never forget how Wilson looked when he got caught," said Cuccinello in a 1991 interview. "He wasn't panicked; it was like his survival instincts took over. He had those big shoulders and barrel chest with those stumpy legs. He got those things chopping and dirt was flying everywhere."

Cuccinello ran Wilson briefly toward home then tossed to Clyde Sukeforth. The Reds catcher tagged out Wilson then quickly viewed what action, if any, remained on the bases. It didn't take long to surmise the Cubs had gotten themselves in trouble as Taylor and Grimm both stood on second. Grimm instinctively headed back to first and was out on a toss from Sukeforth to first baseman Joe Stripp. Taylor tried to advance to third during the Grimm putout, but was retired on a Stripp-to-Cuccinello throw to complete the unusual triple play.

Triple plays are not a normal occurrence during a baseball game, so the fact the Reds had turned two in the same season—against the same team—was unusual. Cuccinello and Ford were involved in both for the Reds.

"Strange thing," Cuccinello said. "That was my rookie season. Never saw anything like that after that and I played in a lot of games. Two triple plays in the same season, against the same team, isn't that something?"

Ash had needed just one pitch to get the triple play. In the bottom half of the sixth, he got lifted for a pinch hitter. The Reds scored four runs and then held on to take a 6–5 win. So Ash got three outs and earned a win by throwing just one pitch. Talk about economy.

Wilson surpassed the 100 RBI mark during a doubleheader against the Reds the following day when he went two-for-eight with three RBIs—but he should have been credited with four. Not until years later would baseball historians come to the conclusion that Wilson had been shorted an RBI that had been erroneously awarded to Grimm that day. Later it would be suggested that possibly during that same season, Wilson was shorted another RBI in a game against the Reds. The story originated from Reds catcher Clyde Sukeforth, who reported that he had been sitting in the bullpen during a game against the Cubs and Wilson had connected, sending a deep drive against the screen and causing the ball to bounce back onto the field. The umpires were not able to see that the ball had cleared the fence and, since they had not seen the ball clear the fence, they ruled it in play, thereby taking away a home run and an RBI from Wilson. Sukeforth noted: "Of course, we weren't going to say anything."

Sukeforth's account would be discounted once the 1930 season was carefully scrutinized. He had played catcher for the Reds in eight of the team's 11 games against the Cubs played at Redland Field in 1930. None of the three remaining games in which Sukeforth sat out appeared to offer evidence that backed Sukeforth's claim.

Wilson finished the month with a two-run homer against the Reds on July 29 to give him 33 home runs and 104 RBIs, completing a month that saw him hit 11 home runs and drive in 31 while hitting .330.

Chuck Klein had a monster month too, hitting 10 home runs while hitting .433 and driving in 38 runs. The Philadelphia slugger still trailed Wilson in home runs with 29, but he led Wilson in RBIs at the end of July by 12.

Babe Ruth hit only 6 home runs in July while driving in 25 and hitting .307, giving him a Major League–leading 36 home runs—and 104 RBIs. Lou Gehrig had a huge month by hitting 12 home runs and driving in 49 while hitting .375 to give him 33 home runs and a Major League–leading 134 RBIs—which seemed to be of no interest to fans or the media in comparison to the home run competition.

Through July, Wilson definitely was having one of the best seasons of any hitter in the game. But he trailed Gehrig's RBI total by a whopping 30, and had not yet differentiated himself from the pack.

Chapter Thirteen

August

Not only were baseball's offensive numbers up by August 1930, but so were temperatures. Heat consumed America.

Record highs smothered the country and Chicago sat in the core of the heat wave, leading to heat-related deaths, including that of a vegetable peddler, who died of sunstroke on the doorstep of a customer while making a delivery. No relief came once the sun went down due to the "urban heat island effect."

Early in the nineteenth century, English chemist and meteorologist Luke Howard identified the reasons why a metropolitan area had warmer temperatures than the surrounding rural areas, and his conclusion came to be known as the urban heat island effect. A large population center like Chicago personified this phenomenon, which brings even more dramatic temperature differences at night than during the day. Contributing factors to this effect include the alteration of the land by big city development. Heat is retained in the materials used for that development.

Traffic at the railroad terminals reflected the effects of the higher temperatures in the city as thousands of Chicago citizens flocked to the trains in hopes of being taken anywhere that might bring them relief from the heat. Others who could not flee the city were left to seek more simplistic methods for cooling off such as the municipal beaches, wading pools, and natatoriums, which brought additional deaths through drowning.

Lack of rain contributed to the heat and brought on drought conditions. A derivative of any drought is the danger of wildfires. Indeed, fires burned many pastures, which brought a distinct decrease in butter and cream production.

On the North Side of Chicago, the Cubs played on despite the sweltering heat, wearing flannel uniforms, made from wool or a wool-cotton blend. Not until the 1940s when the textile industry came up with new inventions did uniforms change to a wool-and-cotton blend that was considerably cooler and of lighter weight than what teams wore in 1930.

One can only imagine how the combination of the heat, wearing a heavy uniform, carrying excess belly fat, and nightly boozing affected Hack Wilson. No doubt his uniform bore the brunt of the alcohol-spiked sweat he produced. Yet Wilson seemed to be unaffected by the temperature.

A week before the first home stand in August began, the Cubs continued to try to find a way to deal with Ladies Day. Throughout the season they had admitted women for free at the expense of male customers willing to part with their money to enter the games. Thus, for the August 1 Ladies Day, the Cubs advertised the fact that 17,500 tickets would be issued through the mail. The Cubs' offices were immediately flooded with 35,000 requests.

While the Cubs struggled to get a handle on the best way to conduct Ladies Day, they were clearly ahead of their time with their progressive approach, which included broadcasting their games over the radio for free. Other Major League teams felt like such freebies were detriments, giving away the product. Instead, the Cubs were giving away a little and getting back in the form of a demand for Cubs tickets. Exposing the women to the games—17,500 attended home games every Friday for free—made them want to go to other games. In addition, those listening to games on the radio wanted to go to Wrigley Field and see the team play.

The Ladies Day crowd roared with delight as the Cubs took a 4–0 lead. But the Pirates took a 5–4 lead in the top of the third. In the second inning, Wilson struck out with runners in scoring position and he did the same after the Cubs had tied the score at 5. Finally, he came up to bat in the sixth with two outs and the Pirates leading 6–5. Kiki Cuyler stood on first and Footsie Blair on third when Wilson ripped a triple to put the Cubs up 7–6. They came away 10–7 winners.

On August 2, the Pirates bombed the Cubs 14–8 in a game that saw Wilson hit his 34th home run of the season, leaving him 10 home runs short of breaking Chuck Klein's National League record of 43. Feeling good about that fact, he brashly told reporters to send out a call to all of his Elks and Moose and Eagles of the Country to let them know that, "Brother Lewis Robert Wilson personally guarantees that this season he will set a new home run record for the National League."

At that point, the Cubs had 53 games remaining on the schedule and Wilson had averaged a home run every 11 times to the plate. Estimating that he would get another 209 at-bats, he executed the simple math equation.

"I have found after careful research that 11 goes into 209 exactly 19 times, which proves that I will make 19 more homers," Wilson said. "Any schoolboy knows that 19 added to 34 makes 53, which will make me beat Chuck Klein's record of 43 by 10 home runs.

"I couldn't hardly believe it myself until I compiled the figures. But figures don't lie, and that's the reason I've had no reluctance coming out with this announcement to my several lodges."

Wilson had entered August the previous year with 30 home runs, but only managed nine for the remainder of the season, making some wonder if his math took his late season history into account. However, the experts pointed to the fact that the Cubs would play

28 games at Wrigley Field in August and just three on the road. All of the cards were in place for a big month for Wilson.

On August 3, Wilson homered for the second straight day to break a 4–4 tie and he drove in two on the day to give him 109 RBIs, but the Pirates put together an eight-run rally in the eighth en route to a 12–8 win.

The Cubs traveled to St. Louis to begin a three-game road trip on August 5 and Wilson led a 5–4 win by hitting his 36th home run of the season, giving him a home run in three consecutive games. Wilson's homer—a two-run shot—came in the sixth just at the right time as the Cubs trailed 4–0 and needed a lift. They ended up rallying to score three in the ninth to take the win.

"Sunny Boy" cries came out of the closet the following day when Cardinals pinch hitter George Watkins hit a line drive to deep center field in the seventh inning. Wilson moved to his left and appeared to have the ball in his sights when he ducked at the last instant after losing the ball in the sun. The ball hit off the center field wall while Wilson scurried to retrieve it. By the time he got the ball back to the infield, Watkins had a two-run, inside-the-park home run and the Cardinals had a 4–3 win. Wilson made up for his miscue the following day when he drove home the winning run in a 6–5 Cubs victory that gave Chicago a series win in St. Louis before heading back to the Windy City, where they would spend the rest of the month playing games at Wrigley Field.

Babe Ruth hit his 41st home run on August 5, employing what appeared to be a golf swing when he connected on a low fastball delivered by Washington's Irving Hadley. His blast came during the first game of a doubleheader against the Senators, putting him 13 games ahead of the pace he had set in 1927 while establishing his single-season home run record of 60. Making the blast even more special was the epic nature of the hit, which arched high over the center field wall until reaching its final destination approximately 450 feet away from home plate. The ball was the first to ever reach the little block of bleachers at the base of the scoreboard in Yankee Stadium's center field.

While Ruth continued to be ahead of his record-setting pace, most figured he would establish a new record if he didn't break down under Bob Shawkey's velvet hand of non-discipline. But something was different; the thrill of the home run had diminished. Back when Ruth first came onto the scene, he was the only act in town. Nobody else hit the ball over the fence, much less out of sight, which he seemed to do on many occasions. In doing so, he brought a circus element to the game. Nobody went to the restroom or concession stands when Ruth stepped to the plate for fear they might miss some Herculean feat never seen before. By 1930, it seemed everybody in baseball had developed into a slugger. Ruth had challengers to his throne in the American League in the form of Jimmie Foxx of the Philadelphia Athletics and his own teammate, Lou Gehrig, while Wilson and Chuck Klein were making noise in the National League. Though Ruth remained the most popular player in the game, he no longer was the only man who possessed the secret of fire.

On August 8, the Cubs were in second place, three and a half games behind the first place Robins. Meanwhile, the Cardinals were 12 games out of first floundering in fourth place with a record of 53–52.

Heading into the Cubs' August 8 contest against the Robins, Wilson had accrued 23 RBIs in his previous 13 games. He attempted to play in that day's game, but he could not due to heat exhaustion and stomach pains. Of course, just as Wilson had executed the math to forecast the number of home runs he would finish with for the season, most fans did the math regarding his stomach problems and every-thing added up to the brown bottle flu rather than heat exhaustion.

Waite Hoyt, who would later be a teammate of Wilson, spoke of the general perception about Wilson.

"He managed to thrust himself on the public consciousness as a guy who didn't take care of himself," Hoyt said. "And the impression was correct. He was a very irresponsible type of fellow, especially in the latter days. He would have been better off if he knew his limitations."

Hoyt cited Wilson's use of home remedies for hangovers, such as drinking a quart of milk prior to a game thinking that would counterbalance the booze he drank the previous night.

While chaos brewed in Wilson's body, Ladies Day continued to bring chaos to Wrigley. On August 8, the Cubs' box office received 60,000 requests for the 17,500 free tickets that would be given away for the August 15 game against the Robins. And this was after the Cubs had once again changed the manner of distribution by limiting the number of tickets per request to one.

Beginning on August 5, Chicago started to feel some relief from the heat when three thundershowers drenched the city, reducing the temperature to 90 degrees. Typifying the damned if it does rain and damned if doesn't situation that engulfed the city were two deaths during the thunderstorms. Lightning struck and killed a bricklayer finishing a new chimney for a church, and lightning also killed a housewife, who was electrocuted while standing underneath a tree that was struck on the trunk.

Days later more rain followed, bringing more relief from the heat in addition to another electrocution, this time a golfer, and the disruption of a sailboat race on Lake Michigan that saw several sailboats overturned. Fortunately, the Coast Guard rescued the sailors from drowning in the rough waters.

As if to celebrate the passing of the heat wave, even if for only a brief period, and his return to the lineup, Wilson picked up where he left off with seven RBIs in an August 10 doubleheader against the Braves to move his total to 121. He hit two home runs in the first game—both to right field—and added another in the second with a rare homer to left to give him 39 for the season, which tied Wilson's career best and left him five short of breaking Chuck Klein's National League record. Of far more importance to the baseball world, Wilson's homers kept him on pace to reach Ruth's season record.

On August 12, the Cubs began a four-game series against the second-place Robins. The Cubs entered the series with a .596 winning percentage compared to the Robins at .595. The clubs were well matched: Cubs hitters had a composite .311 average and the Robins were at .309, while both teams had a .971 fielding average.

The first game on August 12 went to the Cubs, 3–2 in 11 innings. At the end of the contest, a 59-year-old man, Harry Pumplan of Chicago, could not handle the excitement of the extra inning affair and died while sitting in the upper right field stands at Wrigley Field watching Woody English score the winning run in the 11th. According to the Cubs team physician, Dr. James Davis, Pumplan suffered a heart attack due to the thrill of the game's finish.

Dazzy Vance started for the Robins and had been so eager to have a good outing that he resorted to wearing an undershirt that had what amounted to a flapping sleeve, which served as a distraction to hitters. The ploy did not work as Vance took his third loss to the Cubs in 27 days.

The Robins rebounded the following day, beating the Cubs 15–5 in a game that featured Wilson hitting his 40th homer of the season to establish a new career best.

The Cubs finished off the series with a 4–3 win in 10 innings with 42,000 watching on Ladies Day, giving the Cubs a ledger that showed three wins in four tries against the Robins, which extended the Cubs' lead in the standings to two games over the second-place Robins.

The Phillies came to town on August 16 and the Cubs took the first game of their doubleheader 10–9. Wilson hit his 41st home run in the first game, which saw the Phillies overcome an 8–2 deficit to take a 9–8 lead. The Cubs then came from behind to take the win. In the second game the Phillies took a 3–0 lead into the ninth, but the Cubs came back to tie the game and send it into extra innings. After 11 innings the game was called due to darkness.

Two days later on August 18, Wilson clouted his 42nd home run and he also had three singles, driving in four runs for the day. Afterward, Wilson again addressed his lodge brothers as he had earlier in the season, this time telling them that the next day he would surpass Klein's home run record. For him to do so, he would have to hit two home runs in a doubleheader against the Phillies at Wrigley Field. Part of Wilson's cocksure attitude stemmed from the fact that Phil Collins was scheduled to start for the Phillies and the last time he faced Collins, Wilson tagged him for home runs in the first and second innings.

Wilson did not break the record the following day, but he did hit his 43rd home run of the season in the seventh inning off left-hander Les Sweetland in a 9–8 loss to the Phillies in the first game of a doubleheader. Wilson drove a ball to the opposite field and when the ball landed deep in the right field stands, he had tied the record set by Klein, who tipped his cap to Wilson as he rounded the bases.

The second game of the doubleheader resulted in a 6–6 tie after 16 innings. Rogers Hornsby made an appearance as a pinch hitter, which was his first appearance since breaking his ankle.

At the end of July, Connie Mack forecast that the Cubs would return to the World Series to be the Athletics' opponent in a Fall Classic rematch. McCarthy shared that same belief on August 19 when he told reporters that he felt his Cubs could be back in the World Series "if our pitching holds up."

Wilson made an appearance at the annual picnic at Lincoln for the orphans and "old folks" from 500 institutions in Cook County. Dressed in a skimmer and a coat and tie, Wilson was swarmed by the orphans as they carried baseballs, paper, and pens hoping to get an autograph from the Chicago icon. Wilson, though not an orphan himself, seemed to have great empathy for the youngsters given his upbringing. He went to great lengths to do anything he could to entertain them.

After making the appearance, Wilson played in the final game of the Cubs-Phillies series, which the Phillies won 10–8 in large part because McCarthy saved his top starters for the four-game series against the second-place Giants that began on August 21. The Giants beat the Cubs 13–6 in the first game, but the Cubs came back to win three in a row to take a five-game lead over the Giants. Wilson did not hit a home run in the series, but he had six RBIs to help the Cubs score 25 runs in the four games. After the final game of the Giants' series, Wilson again made a prediction, this time that he would break Klein's record the following day in the first game of a two-game series against the Pirates.

Ironically, everybody focused on the prospect of Wilson establishing a new home run record while he continued to drive in runs in obscurity. From August 13 through August 23, Wilson had 23 RBIs and at least one RBI in seven straight games.

In addition, over 23 days he had driven home 40 with six games remaining in the month of August.

True to his word, Wilson took care of the National League home run record in the Cubs' first game against the Pirates on August 26. The blast put Wilson ahead of Ruth's pace from 1927 when the Bambino did not hit his 44th home run until September 2.

Wilson is said to have called his record-setting home run. The story begins with another mistake in the outfield.

In the top of the seventh, Lloyd Waner hit a line drive to center field. With his first movement, Wilson fell down and the ball went past him for an inside-the-park home run. Any fielding problems by Wilson were magnified given his past, so embarrassed and upset, he returned to the bench and spoke to Cubs starting pitcher, Sheriff Blake:

"Sheriff, it seems like things always happen to you that never have happened before. That belly buster couldn't have occurred behind any other pitcher. But for your sake and for the pride of West Virginia I'm going to get that homer back with a legitimate homer. And in this very inning."

Blake hailed from the state of West Virginia, and though Wilson didn't originate in West Virginia, he called the state home and felt a kinship with West Virginians.

In the seventh inning, Wilson connected off left-hander Larry French. Appropriately, the record-setting blast landed in the right field stands. In addition to the home run, Wilson drove in four runs in the Cubs' 7–5 win, which expanded their lead in the standings to five and a half games. Wilson drove in three runs the next day during a 10–8 loss to the Pirates. Despite the loss, the Cubs maintained their lead. With four days remaining in August, the Cubs appeared to have finally packed away all their bad luck and seemed well on their way to claiming their second consecutive National League pennant.

The Cardinals arrived in Chicago on August 28 for a three-game series against the Cubs and game one turned into a marathon. The Cubs trailed 5–0 in the seventh with Burleigh Grimes pitching for the Cardinals when the Cubs put on a display of their power and heart by tying the score with three in the seventh—chasing Grimes—and then two in the eighth. After a scoreless ninth, five scoreless frames followed until the 15th inning when the Cardinals scored two in the top half of the inning and the Cubs answered with two in the bottom half to keep the game going. Four more scoreless frames ensued before Andy High singled to drive home Taylor Douthit in the top of the 20th inning. High tried to stretch the single into a double and was tagged out at second for the final out of the inning, but Douthit's run had already scored, giving the Cardinals an 8–7 lead that the Cubs could not overcome. Wilson did not get a hit or drive in a run in seven at-bats, striking out three times and taking a swing in the seventh in which he hurt himself. But he managed to remain in the game for the final 13 innings. The 20-inning affair lasted just 4 hours and 10 minutes. By winning, the Cardinals won their ninth consecutive game to move within five and a half games of the lead. Suddenly the Cardinals were recognized as a legitimate contender along with the Robins and Giants.

The pain in Wilson's left side intensified after the game, prompting him to pay a visit to a doctor and resulting in his exclusion from the lineup the next day. Without Wilson in the lineup, the Cubs bounced back against the Cardinals with a 9–8 win in 13 innings. The Cubs slugger's pain was gone after a day off and he returned to the lineup with a bang on August 30 when the Cubs beat the Cardinals 16–4. The *Chicago Tribune* dismissed the win as "not being the big news of the afternoon." It seemed that being in first place and winning paled in comparison to Wilson hitting two home runs to give him 46 for the season. He had passed Ruth as the Major Leagues' top home run hitter.

In doing so, Wilson found himself a week ahead of Ruth's record-setting pace in 1927. On page one of the *Tribune's* sports section, a photo ran of Wilson connecting for the historic blast.

Wilson hit his 45th home run in his first at-bat that 30th day of August, depositing the baseball deep into the center field stands for a three-run homer. In the fourth he hit his 46th into the stands in left-center field.

In Ruth's record-setting season he did not reach 46 until September 6. On that day he hit three home runs during a doubleheader at Boston to put him at 47. He then went on a tear. After Labor Day of 1927, he hit 13 home runs in the final 24 days of the season. Wilson had 27 games remaining in which to hit 15 home runs, which would give him 61 for the season to establish a new single-season home run mark.

The Cubs lost the final game of their series with the Cardinals on August 31 when Bill Hallahan shut them down with his typically absurd—but effective—method of pitching in which he seemed to always walk a hitter or strike him out. Wilson struck out once and walked three times against Hallahan as the Cardinals left-hander allowed four hits, walked eight, and struck out twelve to lead an 8–3 Cardinals win. The *Chicago Tribune* heralded the day as "an off day in the home run business" in the caption below a series of photos of Wilson.

The loss to the Cardinals gave the Cubs a 19-10 record in August and an overall record of 77-51, which was good for a five-game lead in the standings over the second-place Giants with 26 games remaining in the season. But was the lead big enough? After playing 26 of 29 games at home during August, the Cubs faced a September schedule that included just 5 of 26 games at Wrigley Field.

Looking at the final tally for August, Wilson hit 13 home runs and drove in an incredible 53 runs, giving him 46 home runs and 157 RBIs heading into the final month of the season. (Note: Philadelphia's Sam Thompson set the National League record for RBIs in a month with 61 in 1894. Wilson's 53 ranks as the National League's modern record; Joe DiMaggio shares the record as he had 53 in 1939 for the Yankees.)

Lou Gehrig finished August with 4 home runs and 14 RBIs, giving him 37 home runs and 148 RBIs. Ruth hit 8 home runs and drove in 25, putting him at 43 home runs and 129 RBIs. And Klein had just 2 home runs and 25 RBIs, leaving him at 31 home runs and 141 RBIs.

To that point in the season, the Cubs had overcome a great deal. Hal Carlson had died, Hornsby had missed most of the season, and they had not gotten what they thought they would be getting from Les Bell, whom the Cubs had been counting on for big things in 1930. Bell had played in just 48 games entering September. Still, the Cubs led the National League heading into the final month of the season. Despite that lead, all that the Cubs had overcome, and the fact that Wilson was having the best offensive season in baseball—due in part to the manner in which McCarthy handled the slugger—rumors of McCarthy's job being in jeopardy began to circulate, fed largely by the manner in which Cubs' management began to react to McCarthy's requests. During his tenure with the Cubs, when McCarthy had requested that the team pick up a player, the Cubs' management normally acquiesced. But when McCarthy asked that pitcher Ed Baecht get brought up from the Los Angeles club, which Wrigley owned, that request was denied on the basis that Wrigley wanted to keep the Los Angeles club together.

Hornsby played in four games in August, but did not get any hits in three official at-bats. He did draw a walk. Hornsby's presence grew increasingly unsettling and only served to fan the flames of rumors about McCarthy. Despised by his teammates, Hornsby could often be seen talking to William Wrigley or Bill Veeck, in essence, filling the ears of Cubs management with his opinions. McCarthy did not admit to any concerns about his job security, but there is no doubt he felt as though his premonition about being fired would come to fruition. McCarthy was too intelligent not to recognize the writing on the wall. Meanwhile, Wilson went about his business with childlike naiveté, blissfully swinging his bat without a care in the world. Had he known what was brewing in the background and how that would profoundly affect his future, Wilson might not have been able to get out of bed.

CHAPTER FOURTEEN

September

SEPTEMBER DID NOT BEGIN WELL FOR THE CUBS. THE GOOD FORTUNE they had enjoyed in August evaporated due primarily to the demise of the pitching staff. Sheriff Blake's back bothered him, Charlie Root's arm hung like a limp noodle, and Guy Bush suddenly could not get anybody out. Pat Malone stood out as the team's only remaining effective pitcher.

Beginning the month in Cincinnati, the Cubs were held to three hits in the opening game of a doubleheader they lost to the Reds 5–0. In the second game, the Reds scored twice with two outs in the ninth to take a 2–1 win. On seven occasions since July 6, the Reds had reversed their fortunes with comeback wins against the Cubs. This time their work left the Cubs with a four-game lead over the Giants, four and a half games over the Cardinals, and five over the Robins.

After Wilson's incredible August, which ranks as one of the top months accomplished by any player in Major League history, he attracted the national spotlight like never before.

Babe Ruth returned to the Yankees' lineup on September 1 after missing two games with a wrenched back. Meanwhile, the New York press acknowledged the battle being won by Wilson, but minimized the battle's significance. John Kieran of the *New York Times* wrote in his "Sports of the Times" column:

Hack is short and stubby, almost as wide as he is high. His build is a handicap and yet he shows amazing speed and unflagging industry in the field. He has plenty of color and fighting spirit. If he leads the home-run hitters for the season, that will be another feather in his cap. But if a man expects to attract attention for home-run hitting these days, he will have to hit them two at a time. Overproduction has ruined more than one popular industry. Big oil companies sometimes join forces to cut down on production. Perhaps the baseball sluggers will have to meet the same problem in the same way.

Some reports suggested that Rogers Hornsby had played his last game. Hornsby renounced any such suggestion. He continued to tell reporters that he was ready to play second base if called upon and that McCarthy simply had to put him in the lineup. Some interpreted Hornsby's remarks as the veteran proposing that McCarthy had somehow been holding him back. The tension between the two became palpable among the Cubs, though it was not aired for public consumption.

The Cubs defeated the Reds 8–2 in the final game of their series on September 2, and then headed for the train that would take them to Pittsburgh for a five-game series. The mood ran light while waiting for the train to depart. Cubs players began their annual ritual of destroying the straw hats they had fashioned all summer. This particular team custom called for the players to destroy all of the straw hats after recording their first win in September. Everybody took part in the exercise except for Wilson.

Baseball players have always been superstitious, so Wilson's decision irritated some of his teammates. He was bucking the tradition of destroying the skimmers, and that meant Wilson was courting the possibility of creating bad luck. On the other hand, Wilson was having the best season in baseball, thus, he did not want to change anything, putting him in an odd position: Be a creature of habit or be a good teammate? In the end, logic prevailed. If he continued to play like he had played all season, he would be the best teammate he could be. So he paid homage to the odd world of superstition that so often guided Major Leaguers. He parted his hair the same, he stuck to the same routines, and he wasn't about to change the fashion that had worked for him all season by ditching his straw hat. When asked about his decision to continue with the straw hat, Wilson grew testy with reporters almost to the point of getting physical.

Thus, the rest of the team converted to felt fedoras while Wilson clung to his straw hat, and Hack said he would continue to do so until the pennant race had been decided, though he suggested that he might relent after hitting his 50th home run.

On September 3, Wilson had three hits and drove in his first run of the new month. But the Pirates defeated the Cubs 9–6 at Forbes Field to reduce the Cubs' lead over the second place Giants to three and a half games.

Cubs fans weren't about to give up on their team, even though they had lost four of five games. Telegrams flooded the visiting clubhouse at Forbes Field prior to the next game. All of the wires contained encouraging messages to keep up the fight. The Cubs responded by taking a 10–7 win over the Pirates; Gabby Hartnett hit two home runs to lead the way. By winning, the Cubs increased their lead back to four and a half games and kept alive the hopes of the team and the city.

Babe Ruth hit his 45th home run of the season on September 5 to move to within 1 home run of Wilson for the Major League lead. Earlier that day, Ruth had opened a new haberdashery on the corner of Broadway and 52nd in Manhattan, Babe Ruth's Shop for Men, Inc. The anticipation for the store's opening served as a demonstration of what a lightning rod Ruth continued to be. More than 600 people awaited Ruth's arrival and when he showed, he did not disappoint. He chirped with the crowd and signed autographs while fitting his guests Lou Gehrig, Notre Dame football coach Knute Rockne, Bob Shawkey, and well-known broadcaster Graham McNamee for hats.

Ruth's 45th home run was his first since August 17. Wilson had not homered since August 30 and could feel Ruth breathing down his neck. Whoever won the home run title reigned as king. Wilson wanted the crown. Being king would enable Wilson to step outside his 5'6" frame and his brute image to make more money than he had ever imagined, but more important, achieving said status would bring acceptance, which he had fought to achieve his entire life. He had battled Ruth all summer and now that the summer began to draw to a close, there was no way Wilson would give in to the Sultan of Swat. So he continued to do what he did best by swinging away.

Wilson answered Ruth on September 6 with three hits in six at-bats, including his 47th home run and four RBIs as the Cubs defeated the Pirates 19–14. Wilson's home run came in the ninth off rookie right-hander Andy Bednar during an inning that saw the Cubs score six runs to pad their lead. Number 47 gave him a two home run cushion over Ruth and the RBIs moved him to 162, surpassing his record of 159. The newspapers even noted the personal best, which was unusual given the lack of attention accorded RBIs.

While the Cubs were claiming victory in Pittsburgh, six teams met with baseball commissioner Judge Kenesaw Mountain Landis to review what could be done to prepare for the World Series, how the shares and proceeds would be divvied up, and other details. Joining the Cubs at the meeting were representatives from the Cardinals, the Giants, and the Robins from the National League and the Philadelphia Athletics and Washington Senators from the American League.

Even though the Cubs remained in first place, the rumors that McCarthy would be fired at the end of the season persisted. On September 7, when the Cubs and Pirates shifted to Wrigley Field for one game, McCarthy publicly addressed the rumors.

"I have heard reports that I will be dropped, but it's news to me," McCarthy said. "My contract expires January 1 and I have had no discussion with club officials about renewing it. There will be time enough to talk about that after we win the National League championship.

"Of course, every old timer in baseball knows that a player or manager can be dropped like a hot potato, but I am not concerned about my future. The club always has treated me right."

Even though Hornsby's shadow remained clearly visible behind the scenes, McCarthy also dismissed the idea that the Cubs were not together in the clubhouse.

"I have had no trouble with Rogers Hornsby or any other member of the club," McCarthy said. "Hornsby always has taken orders like everyone else. That's all a manager can expect."

William Veeck confirmed that they had not talked to McCarthy about his 1931 contract when the Cubs president said, "There will be no discussion of McCarthy's contract until the season is finished. We have only two objectives: First, to win the National League championship and secondly, to win the World Series."

That same day, Hornsby approached McCarthy after playing three consecutive days and told the Cubs manager he thought it would be best if he did not start based on the condition of his legs. A reporter heard the conversation and after Hornsby walked out of hearing range, McCarthy told the reporter: "I'm glad you were here to hear that, because in a couple of days I'll be reading stories that I kept him on the bench to embarrass him."

Capping the eventful day, the Pirates tallied six runs in the final three innings to beat the Cubs 9–7 with 35,000 watching at Wrigley Field. Meanwhile, the Cardinals won twice to move to within two and a half games of the lead. What had once felt like an insurmountable lead for the Cubs suddenly felt like shaky ground.

Two days later on September 9, the Cubs began a series in Brooklyn and the Robins proceeded to dismantle Chicago with a

3–0 win in the opener followed by wins of 6–0 and 2–1 on successive days. After the third loss, which took place on September 11, the Cubs' lead over the Cardinals had dwindled to a half game. At the other end of the spectrum, the Cardinals had won nine of their last ten games.

Suddenly everybody on the Cubs seemed to be in a slump. Hitters were missing their pitches and pitchers were not putting the ball where they wanted, and the results could be seen in the lack of offensive production and the potent attacks of the Cubs' opposition. Only Wilson seemed to be oblivious to the bad run. He had three hits against the Robins including his 48th home run of the season, which came off of Dazzy Vance in the seventh inning of the September 11 contest.

That same day, Joe Hauser of the International League's Baltimore Orioles hit his 60th home run of the season against Jersey City and Ruth hit his 46th against the Tigers in Detroit. Back in the minors in 1930, Hauser played for the Orioles and regained his hitting touch. He would finish the season with a then-professional record 63 home runs in one season while playing in the cozy confines of Oriole Park.

The Cubs went from Brooklyn to Philadelphia, where they tried to regroup against the last-place Phillies. They showed some signs of getting back on their feet by beating the Phillies 17–4 on September 12. Wilson put forth a heroic effort with five hits in five at-bats, two doubles, two singles, a walk, four runs, and six RBIs, and he hit his 49th home run of the season, which came when he rode a pitch over the right field wall in the second inning.

The contest with the Phillies brought quite a contrast from the Cubs' previous three games. They had 20 hits in nine innings against Philadelphia; they had 15 in three games—only five in each game—during the Brooklyn series. During each of five innings in the game against the Phillies, the Cubs scored more runs than they did the entire series against the Robins.

Cubs fans remained a loyal breed and they followed their team's fortunes the best they could. Impromptu makeshift scoreboards sprang up on at least a dozen street corners throughout the city of Chicago to watch the results of the Cubs-Phillies contest as the scoreboard operators hustled to update the results. One such scoreboard operated in the second story window of an office building at State and Washington. Men and women alike jostled for position to watch as the game progressed. At State and Lake, the scoreboard had an advertisement for 100 percent wool suits that were priced to sell, which the store attributed to cutting out the middleman. Store employees operated the scoreboard, hustling about to make sure they had the right scorecard to illustrate every single play and not just what happened in each half inning.

When Wilson's homer was posted, the State and Washington crowd greeted the news with loud cheers. In Hack Wilson they had their hero. He had become Chicago's slugger, a Midwestern trump over Babe Ruth. Chicago usually played second fiddle to New York, so having a slugger of its very own, a behemoth who outperformed New York's Bambino, meant everything to the region. If the Cubs were going to win the pennant, Wilson would lead the way, carrying Chicago's team on his broad shoulders with whiskey on his breath and destruction of the baseball on his mind.

On September 12, Hornsby met with Bill Veeck to discuss what the Cubs could do to end their September slide and what they might do in 1931; Veeck did not meet with McCarthy, which spoke volumes in the department of foreshadowing.

Typical of the era, the players were looking for ways to cash in after the season. Many such plans hinged on the Cubs' fortunes. If they won the pennant and went to the World Series, opportunities would be plentiful for everyone. If they didn't manage to finish on top, they understood any such opportunities would likely dry up. Since the Cubs had not locked up the pennant, all of the postseason gravy remained on hold. Affected most were the Cubs' most popular players, Wilson and Hornsby, along with McCarthy, who had pending literary and vaudeville plans that could not become finalized until the season was decided. All three had multiple deals on the table when and if the Cubs managed to win the National League pennant.

One such deal had backfired the previous season after Charlie Grimm, Kiki Cuyler, and Cliff Heathcote arranged a trio featuring a banjo, ukulele, funny anecdotes, and singing. An advertisement for the act had been shown at a movie theater during the World Series shortly after the Cubs had gotten blitzed by the Athletics. The advertisement was jeered.

Wilson served as an interesting study on the extra-income front. He had found great frustration the previous season and had sworn off any kind of deals because he felt he had been wronged. He had signed a syndicated deal to share his thoughts with a publication, only to have that publication renege on the arrangement, which had left him baffled because he had a contract. Apparently that contract included escape language for the publisher, which allowed them to sack the whole thing if they so desired.

Up-front money of $500 helped Wilson forget the previous year, money he received to have a ghostwriter pen his thoughts—and the good part was Wilson didn't even have to talk to the writer if he did not wish to do so.

Any possibilities for postseason gravy for the Cubs appeared to be slipping away on September 13 when they lost to the Phillies 7–5; Wilson continued to hit by collecting three hits in four at-bats, but he did not drive in a run. Meanwhile, the Cardinals defeated the Braves 8–2 in Boston to assume control of the National League. Making the loss tougher to swallow for William Wrigley Jr. was the fact that pinch hitter Lefty O'Doul hit a two-run homer in the eighth to break a 5–5 deadlock. O'Doul lived eternally as the player Wrigley had wanted and, in his mind, he had been denied by McCarthy.

The following day, the Robins moved into first place by defeating the Reds 8–3 to record their tenth consecutive win, thereby giving them a half a game lead over the Cardinals and a game lead over the Cubs.

Most of the Cubs sat around a hotel lobby in Philadelphia on that Sunday afternoon in a foul mood considering their fall to third place after losing 10 of 14 games. However, the Cubs had not lost hope and they still believed they could win the pennant. Those hopes appeared more remote given their circumstances. On the optimistic side, if the Cubs could manage to win 9 of 13—against the Giants, Braves, Reds, and Phillies—Brooklyn had to win 8 of 11 and the Cardinals 10 out of 13 to beat out Chicago.

That same day, applications for World Series tickets became available for Cubs fans. Tickets could be purchased for Games 3, 4, and 5 in the National League city—scheduled for October 4, 5, and 6—through mail orders that included a certified check, money order, or bank draft. In return, the person making the order would receive strips of tickets for each of the three games. Box seats cost $6.50, which included tax; grandstand tickets were $5.50. If the Cubs did not make the World Series, all money would be returned by mail.

After not playing on Sunday, the Cubs had trouble handling O'Doul in the first game of their September 15 doubleheader against the Phillies. He homered off Bud Teachout with one out in the bottom of the ninth to lead the Phillies to a 12–11 win. Had Wilson not taken matters into his own hands, the whole day would have been lost in the devastation of the first-game's loss. Wilson hit his 50th home run off Phil Collins in the sixth inning of the second game to help the Cubs win 6–4. While Wilson's home run gave him a four home run lead over Ruth, the split put the Cubs one and a half games behind the Robins and a half a game behind the Cardinals.

In the aftermath of the doubleheader split and the ascent of the Robins and Cardinals to the top of the standings, the response to

World Series tickets in Chicago was lukewarm. Just 1,200 orders for World Series tickets were received on the first day they were available. Certainly a wait-and-see attitude prevailed for skeptical Cubs fans.

Hornsby's voice continued to spew negatives to Wrigley about McCarthy, who could obviously feel the vibe of impending doom for his stint as Cubs manager. Despite the negativity, McCarthy remained in control and did not engage in verbal exchanges in the press with Hornsby. Clearly, everybody around the situation knew that the pair did not have a good relationship and most could read the tea leaves for who would win between Hornsby and McCarthy.

Bad luck intervened for the Cubs on September 16 when they met the Giants at the Polo Grounds and found themselves facing 27-year-old left-hander Carl Hubbell, who was just hitting his stride en route to what would become a Hall of Fame career. Employing a devastating screwball, the man who would come to be known as "King Carl" threw a three-hit, complete-game shutout against the Cubs, striking out 10, including Wilson twice; Wilson had one of the Cubs' hits. After the loss, the Cubs remained one and a half games out.

Prior to the Cubs' game against the Giants on September 17, Cubs players sat around the clubhouse talking about Flint Rhem's bizarre story, no doubt shaking their heads with amusement at a tale that would have made Aesop proud.

After disappearing for two days, the Cardinals' pitcher spun a tale about being kidnapped by Brooklyn fans, who kept him locked up in a hotel while forcing him to drink large amounts of alcohol to keep him subdued. Needless to say, Rhem's credibility—and his taste for alcohol—made the story tough to swallow.

Later that afternoon, Wilson drove in four, moving him to 176 RBIs for the season, to set a new record. While a significant mark, Wilson's accomplishment was hardly noticed. In the *Tribune*, the third item of a notebook column read as follows:

Hack Wilson's name appears in the record books many times, but usually his accomplishments are qualified, mostly by something Babe Ruth has done. But the record set today has no strings on it. No other major league player ever has batted in 176 runs in one season.

He also hit 2 home runs, giving him 52 for the season, leaving him 8 shy of Ruth's record. Both homers went to right field and they put him six ahead of Ruth for the season. Wilson's offense came at the right time, leading a 5–2 win.

McCarthy could feel the Cubs' pennant chances growing slimmer and slimmer every day. Looking for any possible maneuver to help his team gain an advantage, McCarthy hustled his team to the train station following the game to make the five and a half hour trip between New York and Boston. By doing so the team could have a decent night's sleep in a hotel bed rather than sleeping in the beds on the train.

Explanations for why the Cubs had not again run away with the National League pennant began to surface. Among the more amusing came the news that Hornsby had purchased two peacocks for $150 during spring training from William Wrigley's exotic bird farm. After making his purchase, Hornsby sent the birds to his home near St. Louis, where one of them had died over the summer. According to superstitions that prevailed at the time, having peacocks in the backyard or having the tail feathers of the bird in a vase were invitations for disaster. Thus, the Cubs' season had been jinxed from the beginning.

The Athletics clinched the American League pennant on September 18. Upon learning the news of the Athletics taking the pennant, William Veeck offered his congratulations to Connie Mack, who had been among the Athletics' contingent who had expressed a desire to again play the Cubs in the Fall Classic.

"Nothing would please us more than to meet the Athletics again in World Series competition," Veeck said. "We haven't forgotten 1929 and we are anxious to even up."

The Cubs took a 5–4 win over the Braves on September 19, but the Cardinals were on a roll and continued to win as well, leaving the Cubs two and a half games out of first place, tied with Brooklyn for second place. At this same juncture, Irving Vaughn of the *Chicago Tribune* interviewed Wrigley, and the Cubs owner spoke frankly about a number of topics.

Wrigley noted that he felt the Cubs' departure from Chicago to begin their road trip in Cincinnati had been the beginning of the end. He noted that the physical condition of the team bothered him and that he had observed that the players were getting by on "sheer nerve."

Vaughn suggested to the Cubs owner that the team's situation had come from the accumulation of a number of factors such as Hornsby's lack of playing time, Hal Carlson's death, Guy Bush's bad arm, Les Bell's physical troubles, along with other problems. Wrigley told the reporter, "You've hit the nail squarely on the head."

"The setbacks wore them down gradually, finally to a point where they had to surrender," Wrigley said. "Their own ill luck got them mentally. I could see it in their eyes during the recent series at Philadelphia. They weren't the same spirited men I had watched tear the opposition to pieces during the long home series in August."

Wrigley also spoke of an episode that took place at the Baker Bowl in Philadelphia when he sat among the fans during the Cubs–Phillies series from September 12 through September 15. Phillies fans had recognized Wrigley and began to good-naturedly tease him about his team and the fact that the Phillies had O'Doul on their roster and the Cubs did not. Furthermore, the fans had told Wrigley that he should have felt some relief because not having O'Doul ensured they would not win the National League pennant and therefore they would not again lose to the Athletics. Wrigley summarized that encounter by saying, "I know now how an umpire feels. They made me think I was friendless. And Philadelphia is my home town."

Wrigley noted that their comments about O'Doul had hit a "tender spot" since during his time in baseball he had bought just one player without consulting his experts, and that player had been O'Doul.

"Well, the world knows that we didn't keep O'Doul and now he turns up and just about beats us out of a pennant," Wrigley said. "Anyway, my buy was a good one. I still refer to him as 'My Mr. O'Doul.'"

McCarthy had accomplished many great things with the Cubs, including making shrewd personnel moves. Unfortunately for McCarthy, O'Doul remained a blind spot for Wrigley, who could not see past the fact that McCarthy had not been on his side of the fence with the player.

Wrigley's interview with Vaughn was candid, but he would not discuss the rumors about the status of McCarthy's job as manager of the team.

"I've heard them for several weeks, but I can't reply to them," Wrigley said. "I am a great admirer of McCarthy and as I said before the team, injuries considered, did the best it could. I will not say McCarthy will be manager next year. Neither will I say he will not be offered a new contract.

"We have no way of knowing what McCarthy might demand in the way of salary. He might ask $100,000 a year. Or maybe McCarthy might not want the job any longer. He might feel that by failing to win a pennant he had placed me in an embarrassing position. Why don't you go down and ask Bill Veeck about it? Whatever he says or does, I will second. I regard Veeck's baseball judgment as perfect. He's running the job."

Prior to the Cubs' 3–2 loss to the Robins on September 20, McCarthy would not address any of Wrigley's comments that had appeared in the *Chicago Tribune*.

He allowed that he had not discussed contract matters with either "Wrigley or Mr. Veeck," so he felt it inappropriate to "discuss anything pertaining to the future management of the Cubs."McCarthy also stated that his contract did not expire until January 1, 1931, and that he was confident that the future would "take care of itself." Those observing McCarthy's reactions noted how calm McCarthy seemed despite his precarious situation.

Though they had not yet been eliminated, thoughts of the offseason were prevalent in the Cubs' clubhouse. In that vein, Pat Malone thought of his good buddy, Wilson. In talking to a reporter for the *Chicago Tribune*, Malone revealed his elaborate plans for the offseason and what he planned to do for Wilson. Malone was well aware Wilson belonged to the Moose Lodge in Martinsburg. Having visited Wilson at his home there, Malone knew Wilson had a fine den. Thus, the Cubs pitcher figured he would head to Canada after the season, bag a moose, and surprise his friend with the moose's mounted head in what he felt would be a grand gesture.

However, there were several flaws in Malone's logic, which no doubt could have been distorted by the spirits that often pumped through his body. For starters, Malone had spent thousands of dollars over the years to buy hunting gear to use while hunting moose, including an inlaid moose horn that he had paid $75 to purchase. But for one reason or the other, he had never killed a moose, nor had he even squeezed off a shot at one. Furthermore, Malone believed the gift would take Wilson by surprise and he would be floored by its magnitude. Yet Wilson revealed his feelings to the *Chicago Tribune* about receiving such a gift. Speaking in the newspaper, Wilson asked the reporter to not "say a word to Pat" because "I wouldn't hurt his feelings for the world." He added that he was "deeply moved by the sentiment which is going to lead him to spend his money and time to brave the hardships entailed in shooting the biggest moose in Canada," noting that only a "real pal" would embark on such an undertaking.

Making the whole episode more comical is the fact that Wilson went on to tell the reporter why the moose head would not work out, which is further detailed in print. Wilson informed all that he had talked over the moose head with his wife and she told him that such an object would not be found in their home. She had told him in no uncertain terms that such an object would be a bigger dust collector than a "six-masted ship" and that such a head would molt and be "as hairy as a mattress factory."

Even though Malone had not even shot the moose yet, Wilson had thought the whole thing through and even went so far as to consider taking the moose head to his lodge for "others to share my joy." Unfortunately the lodge already had four moose heads, leaving Wilson in a quandary as he told the *Tribune*: "I have got to think of some way of getting rid of the damn thing, but don't say a word to Pat, for I wouldn't hurt his feelings for the world."

Also facing the Cubs players if they did not manage to re-route their fortunes and win the National League pennant would be the reality that they would have to play the White Sox in a City Series. Such a prospect did not please many of the Cubs players, who held the view that even though they liked the idea of making some extra cash by playing the White Sox, they looked down on the idea with an air of entitlement while questioning why a National League pennant contender should play an American League team that had finished in seventh place.

McCarthy did not get cranky when asked about his future, even though rumors that he would be replaced by Hornsby were so constant that such a move now appeared a foregone conclusion. However, he did get cranky after the Cubs' September 20 loss. Falling three games behind the Cardinals did not upset McCarthy; what did upset him was catching a nameless player talking to an author. McCarthy felt like the player was leaking stuff privy only to those behind clubhouse doors, so he read the riot act to the player and the author shortly before he went to the movies. Once at the movies, McCarthy found another of his players in the company of an author.

Ruth hit his 47th home run against the White Sox on September 20 and two days later hit two more, only they didn't count since they came in an exhibition game between the Yankees and Buffalo. The Cubs beat the Braves 4–2 on September 21, and still, there was no word on McCarthy's fate.

On September 22, the Cubs defeated the Braves 6–2 in a game that saw Wilson hit his 53rd home run and move to 181 RBIs on the season. With four games remaining, the Cardinals still held a two and a half game lead. The next day, Wrigley Jr., at age 69 and said to be in failing health, invited the press to his mansion on Lake Shore Drive, where he made the following statement after announcing that Joe McCarthy had been fired: "I realize that McCarthy is one of the best managers in baseball. But I must have a winner. I have always wanted a world championship team and I'm not sure that Joseph McCarthy is the man to give me that kind of team."

Most recognized the obvious—that Hornsby had stabbed McCarthy in the back, taking his shots when he could over the course of his two seasons with the team, which began during the 1929 World Series when he told a reporter that the club had used bad scouting reports furnished by Joe Tinker for their first two games against the Athletics. McCarthy also received criticism for allowing his players to continue to be the "toast of the town" following their 1929 season; many felt he should have tightened the reins more to make sure they focused more on baseball. Wilson, of course, had not curtailed his activities away from the diamond and he managed to play just fine.

Rud Rennie of the *New York Herald* concluded that the Cubs wanted some return on the $200,000 they had invested in Hornsby, who at that point appeared headed toward retirement as a player due to the injuries he had suffered through over the course of the 1930 season. Rennie surmised that the Cubs decided Hornsby would remain as the manager and McCarthy would be fired, as he wrote: "Having killed the plain goose that laid the golden eggs, Mr. Wrigley will try a golden goose."

After the Cubs announced their change of managers, the only question that remained was whether McCarthy would finish out the season. In the meantime, Wrigley went to great lengths to let everyone know in what high regard he held McCarthy.

"Joe is taking a manly attitude toward the whole thing," Wrigley said. "He assured me that he wasn't going to complain now after five years in which there never was a cross word between us. He has been in baseball long enough to know that a club has the right to make changes if it sees fit. One thing about Joe is that, win or lose, he never quit trying and I say this because of the booing he was subjected to in some of the recent home games. He didn't deserve that."

In deference to the evidence that suggested otherwise, Veeck maintained that Hornsby had not worked behind the scenes to orchestrate McCarthy's demise.

"In his two years with the club I never heard Hornsby comment on McCarthy's management," Veeck said. "He simply played the game to the best of his ability. He hasn't sought the job. It is being offered to him. It is possible that because of the many rumors flying around for the last month a slight chill may have arisen between the pair, but I have McCarthy's word that when it was a matter of playing the game Hornsby never questioned or balked at orders."

Many players on the team did not share Veeck's view, including Charlie Grimm and Gabby Hartnett, each of whom had enjoyed a good relationship with McCarthy. Evidence suggests that nobody on the Cubs liked the idea of Hornsby managing the team in 1931; there were few doubts this collection of Cubs belonged to McCarthy.

McCarthy continued to maintain his calm demeanor even after the news of his termination broke.

"There has been no specific trouble between the business office and myself," McCarthy said. "The only official criticism I have heard is that I haven't made certain changes. I merely am following a long line of other Cub managers. [Frank] Chance is the only one who lasted as long as I have."

When the team headed back to Chicago by train, McCarthy took a detour through Buffalo as the Cubs did not have another game until September 25. Speculation began to run rampant that McCarthy would succeed Bob Shawkey as the manager of the Yankees. Neither Yankees owner Col. Jacob Ruppert, nor Ed Barrow, the club's secretary, would discuss the matter.

Though the Cubs made it clear they wanted McCarthy to finish out the season, McCarthy informed the team's management on September 25 that he preferred to step down and not finish the season in the post in which he had served for five years. The Cubs issued the following statement: "It is the wish of McCarthy to be relieved immediately and the club has placed Rogers Hornsby in charge."

Classy until the end, McCarthy told reporters that he had "nothing to complain about and nothing to explain."

Though his exodus had a stench to it, McCarthy maintained he held no ill will toward the club as he told reporters: "As proof that our relations were pleasant right to the end I want the world to know that despite my withdrawal I am receiving the second place bonus called for in my contract. They dealt with me in a big way at the start five years ago and concluded in the same way."

At the time of McCarthy's announcement the Cubs had not yet been mathematically eliminated from the pennant race, even though the chances of winning the race were minuscule. Still, they had a chance, a fact that McCarthy reminded the team of during his parting remarks. McCarthy then told the players he had enjoyed his association with them and wished them well. Included in his departure was an awkward moment when he faced Hornsby. McCarthy defused the situation by shaking his hand and offering him congratulations.

Some Cubs fans did not like what had transpired. They remembered where the club had been prior to McCarthy's arrival and worried about a future without Marse Joe. Thus, when Hornsby walked onto the field prior to the Cubs' September 25 game against the

Reds, he received a chorus of boos from the McCarthy contingent. Other Cubs fans, who blamed McCarthy for everything that had gone wrong with the team in 1931, responded with cheers for the new manager.

Wilson had enjoyed a good relationship with McCarthy, who had always looked out for him much like a father would a son. And Wilson had rewarded McCarthy by giving him his best on the field— even if his best occasionally was influenced by how he felt from the previous night's activities. So even though Wilson offered no comment about the team's new manager, everybody knew on whose side of the fence he stood. No doubt, swimming in the back of Wilson's mind there had to be a sense of angst about what the future would bring while playing for Hornsby, given their relationship.

Ruth continued to chase Wilson with little success. On September 25, for the second time that season, Ruth hit a ball that should have been a home run, but instead it ricocheted off Shibe Park's amplifier horns and landed on the field for a ground-rule double. The ball had cleared the right field wall by a dozen feet, but struck one of the horns projecting above the wall and bounced back onto the field. The blast would have been his 48th home run of the season.

In the Cubs' dugout, an awkward situation ensued when Hornsby began to discuss the 1931 season. Wilson's status for the next season became one of the top questions presented to Hornsby, who had always looked down on him for his drinking. That contempt led to rumors that Wilson, despite his huge season, would be on the trading block. Hornsby laughed at the mention of such a scenario, noting: "Don't talk about strengthening a ball club and getting rid of Wilson in the same conversation. There isn't another Hack Wilson in baseball, and his power and color are priceless to the team in my estimation."

Some speculated that if Wilson remained with the team Hornsby would make him a corner outfielder, which likely would have meant moving Kiki Cuyler to center field. Hornsby's opinion about whether Wilson should stay or go was no doubt influenced by the Cubs' front office. To placate fans after Hornsby's announcement as manager, Veeck told reporters that Wilson, Charlie Root, Pat Malone, Cuyler, and Gabby Hartnett would be back with the team in 1931.

The Cubs won their final six games of the season to finish with a record of 90-64, two games behind the Cardinals, who had gone 39-10 from August 8 until the end of the season to claim the National League pennant. Included in the Cardinals' incredible roll to finish the season was a 7-game winning streak and two 5-game winning streaks en route to a 19-4 record in their final 23 games.

Wilson continued to do what he had done all season by hitting like few men in the history of the game had ever managed to do. From September 12 through September 28, Wilson had 27 hits in 67 at-bats, with 8 home runs and 26 RBIs. In other words, he had hit in the clutch when the team needed him most. He hit his 55th and 56th home runs on September 27, drawing raves in the *Chicago Tribune* that teased from the front with the following: "Hack Wilson hits 55th and 56th home runs as Cubs beat Reds, 13-8 at Wrigley Field."

Malone also won his 20th game of the season in the contest. The story did not even mention that Wilson also had four RBIs on the day to move to 189 on the season.

On September 28, 1930, the Reds played the Cubs at Wrigley Field in the final game of the season. Bush got hammered in the top of the second when the Reds got him for six runs. Jesse Petty then allowed three more before the final out of the inning was recorded to give the Reds a 9–0 lead.

The Cubs began their comeback by scoring three in the third, including a bases-loaded walk that Wilson drew from Reds starter Si Johnson to give him 189 RBIs for the season.

Continuing to fight back, the Cubs scored twice in the fifth and three times in the sixth to cut the lead to 9–8. The Reds scored two in the eighth to take an 11–8 lead, but the Cubs answered in the bottom half of the inning with five runs. Wilson drove home one of the runs when he hit a dribbler that just got past Reds pitcher Bennie Frey for an infield hit that allowed English to score, giving Wilson 190 RBIs.

In the *Tribune*, the only mention of Wilson's new mark came under the subheading "Hack Adds to Record" within the write-up about the game. The story went on to ask why 22,000 fans would attend the game since nothing rode on the outcome. It then suggested, "Maybe, though, it was to see if Hack Wilson could make four homers to tie Babe Ruth's all-time record. Hack made nary a homer, but he did lift his major league record for runs batted in to an even 190, fifteen ahead of the former record."

Wilson had accomplished a great feat, but instead of celebrating the accomplishment, he was disappointed to have fallen short of Ruth's single-season home run mark, the only mark that seemed to matter at the time.

Ruth hit his 48th and 49th home runs on September 27, but those would be his final home runs of the season. While he did not lead the Major Leagues in homers for the 1930 season, Ruth did end the season in style by pitching a complete game against the Red Sox on the final day, holding the Red Sox to three runs on 11 hits on September 28 at Fenway Park.

Hornsby managed the club without incident for the final four games of the 1930 season, which came as no surprise. With all the suspicions about how he had landed the job and how he intended to run the club, the last thing Hornsby wanted to do was to rock the boat in the last few games of the year.

Though upset about McCarthy's firing and uneasy about the announcement of Hornsby as his successor, Wilson had played brilliantly for the final month of the season. Warren Brown recounted Wilson sharing with him his feelings about Hornsby: "He [Hack] cherished a very low opinion of one of the members of his club throughout all last year, and very few ever knew about that. Certainly he didn't let it interfere with his playing. On the contrary, it spurred him on to his greatest effort since he entered the National League."

Adding insult to the Cubs' season was the outcome of the Chicago City Series. After the White Sox took the first game 5–1 at Comiskey Park, the Cubs took a two games to one lead in the series with a 12–1 defeat of the White Sox at Wrigley Field. The White Sox then rattled off three straight wins to take the series, which translated to a second place finish in the National League and a second place showing in the Windy City.

CHAPTER 15

1930 in Perspective

THERE WERE THOSE WHO MAINTAINED THAT THE BALL HAD BEEN doctored in 1930, which prompted famed sports journalist Ring Lardner to write an article in the *New Yorker* entitled "Br'er Rabbit Ball." Regardless of whether baseballs were doctored—as many liked to speculate—attendance went through the roof in 1930 despite the early Depression economy.

The St. Louis Cardinals and Philadelphia Athletics played in the World Series and the Athletics repeated as champions thanks to the pitching of Lefty Grove, who won two games and saved a third.

While attendance in the Major Leagues reached 10.5 million in 1930, 16 seasons would pass before that figure would be surpassed. The Depression would take its toll on Major League Baseball. Not since the early 1900s had any Major League team encountered financial problems the likes of which arose after the 1930 season. Particularly hard hit were Major League franchises in cities with two teams.

When all the smoke cleared from the 1930 season, the results accomplished offensively were astonishing.

To put the season into proper perspective, consider the fact that the Cardinals sent outfielder George Aloys "Showboat" Fisher to the minor leagues after 254 at-bats. Why should that be significant? Well, Fisher was hitting .374 at the time with eight homers and 61 RBIs. Eighty years later he would have become a very rich man by accruing those numbers. But he did not set foot in the Major Leagues again until 1931.

Runs came cheap in 1930. The Cardinals and the New York Yankees each scored more than a thousand runs for the season. At the other end of the spectrum, the last-place Philadelphia Phillies allowed 1,199.

Ironically, those same Phillies out-hit the pennant-winning Cardinals .315 to .314. The Major Leagues consisted of 16 teams in 1930, which translated to 128 slots for position players. Incredibly, 71 individual hitters hit over .300 that season.

Billy Terry of the New York Giants batted .401. With the exception of Ted Williams, who hit .406 in 1941, no player in baseball has hit .400 since. Terry achieved his mark by getting 254 hits in a 154-game season, which tied Lefty O'Doul's mark for the most hits in a season for the National League. Ichiro Suzuki of the American League's Seattle Mariners established the Major League record of 262 in 2004 during a 162-game season.

And how about Babe Herman, who finished second in the National League in batting? All Herman did was hit .393, making him the highest runner-up in a National League batting race in the 20th century.

In addition to setting the Major League record for RBIs, Hack Wilson set the National League record for home runs with 56, which stood until 1998 when performance-enhancing drugs became a part of the equation.

While Wilson's 190 RBIs set a new record, Lou Gehrig had 174, Chuck Klein had 170, and Al Simmons had 165.

Forgotten in the massive offensive onslaught were Joe Cronin's numbers. The Washington Senators shortstop had 203 hits while compiling a .346 batting average with 13 homers, 41 doubles, and 126 RBIs, accounting for one of the finest seasons ever accomplished by a shortstop. Yet he did not make the top 10 for any offensive category in 1930.

Pitching took a beating in 1930. Dazzy Vance and Lefty Grove seemed to hold some secret other pitchers were not privy to as Vance had a 2.61 ERA, while the next closest ERA in the National League belonged to Carl Hubbell at 3.87; and Grove had a 2.54 ERA to lead the American League with Cleveland's Wes Ferrell the next closest at 3.31.

The Phillies personified the state of pitching as a whole with a 6.71 team ERA; the overall National League mark was 4.97. And Guy Bush of the Cubs experienced a season like none other in his 17 years in the Major Leagues. The "Mississippi Mudcat" allowed 155 earned runs, which amounted to 45 more than he had ever allowed in a season. Bush finished his career with a 3.86 ERA, but he posted a 6.20 ERA in 1930, pitching in the same conditions in which his teammate, Wilson, lit up the scoreboard.

Aside from Grove's success, the rest of the Athletics staff had three starters with ERAs over 4.00. The runs surrendered by the Athletics staff were more than compensated for by the likes of Jimmie Foxx and Simmons, who combined for 73 home runs and 321 RBIs.

Not until the steroid-fueled years of the 1990s and early 2000s would any year come close to having the kind of offense that prevailed in 1930. And even with better chemistry, the offense during the steroid era still did not compare to what happened during the 1930 season.

Chapter Sixteen

After 1930

HACK WILSON LIVED LARGE FOLLOWING THE 1930 SEASON. EVEN though he did not break Babe Ruth's single-season home run record, he remained the king of Chicago. In addition to being king, Wilson had been the best player in baseball for a season.

Since 1911 there have been three different "official" Most Valuable Player awards.

First came the Chalmers Award that was in place from 1911 to 1914, and then the League Award ran from 1922 through 1929—both rewarded the top player in the league.

After a year in which no award was given in 1930, the Baseball Writers Association of America came up with the Most Valuable Player Award, which they began giving out in 1931.

Had there been a Most Valuable Player Award in 1930, Wilson would have won the award hands down. The fact that there was not an award for a year that Wilson would have won the honor seems to fit Wilson. Despite going toe-to-toe with Ruth, he never quite measured up. And by the time the award was back in place, what had been for Wilson was gone.

Though Wilson did not relish the idea of Hornsby becoming the manager of the Cubs, he never could have imagined what happened next. From all indications, Wilson believed he would continue to put up years like he had in 1930. Perhaps he had finally grown comfortable enough with who he was to believe that many seasons like 1930 were on the horizon.

Wilson carried a carefree spirit into the offseason following the 1930 season. Included were vaudeville performances in Chicago in which he was supposed to perform in a quartet along with Gabby Hartnett, Kiki Cuyler, and Cliff Heathcote. Wilson had his hand out for any possible endorsements, and there were plenty. Haberdasheries hired him to model men's clothes, which was ironic given that few men carried a build like Wilson's.

Ed Burns of the *Chicago Tribune* witnessed one of Wilson's on-stage performances and wrote the following:

> *After his first matinee Hack thought he could dance better than Terpsichore and Bo-Jangles Bill Robinson combined and that he possessed the voice of a nightingale, much sweeter than Caruso's ever was. As the act went on, Wilson's superiority complex increased to the point where the presence of his three pals irritated him and he wanted them to hide behind the piano while he was doing his stuff.*

Oddly, not until the *Sporting News* noted in January of 1931 that Wilson had driven in 190 runs did the fact that he had done so receive any notice. Even so, being RBI king barely registered when compared to being the long-ball king. Based on what Wilson had done in 1930, the idea that the slugger would eventually break Ruth's mark had legs and added to his popularity.

Based on the extraordinary offense that took place in 1930, most everybody in the majors agreed the game needed to be tweaked prior to the next season. In the crosshairs for the punch list of changes was a modification of the baseball.

All of the owners in baseball, save for the Yankees, voted to have the Spalding company change the baseball to a model with raised and longer stitching made of a coarser thread. Said stitching would help pitchers grip the ball, which in turn would help add snap to their breaking pitches and therefore make hitting those pitches more of a difficult proposition. In theory, the raised stitches would also cause more friction against the air, thereby adding additional break. The American and National Leagues used different balls, and the National League went a step further by having the horsehide covers of the balls thickened, a measure designed to deaden the ball.

In addition to the changes made to the baseball, some rules were altered. Beginning in 1931, balls that bounced before clearing the fence were declared ground-rule doubles instead of home runs. That same year the rules regarding the sacrifice fly were changed. Prior to 1931, a sacrifice fly was granted to the hitter any time he advanced a runner with a fly out, and thus, the batter was not charged with an official time at bat. Under the change, a sacrifice fly was awarded only when a fly ball scored a runner from third base.

While the game changed behind closed doors, Wilson spent the offseason cashing in on literally every opportunity that presented itself. In addition, he signed a new contract with the Cubs that paid him $33,000 in 1931, which was a nice bump, but left him $47,000 short of what Ruth was making. In hindsight, Wilson probably should have seen that several factors were producing a perfect storm of negatives that would hurt his performance in 1931. Never did he see the cruel winds blowing in his direction. When he boarded the train in February of 1931 for Catalina Island and spring training, the dreams of another banner season were intact. His performance had improved each year he was with the Cubs, so he figured he had nowhere to go but up.

Wilson received a wake-up call upon his arrival for spring training. Hornsby no longer had to work behind the scenes to undermine the manager; he was the manager and he had his own set of rules. Some of his rules could be viewed as stringent, others ridiculous, and most of the rules did not bode well for Wilson.

Prior to the beginning of the exhibition games, Hornsby had his team go through four-hour workouts without lunch. In addition, he kept weight charts for all of his players and he instituted a midnight curfew. Hornsby did not smoke or drink, so he expected his players to follow suit. And, save for the racing form, Hornsby did not read, so he banned newspapers from the clubhouse because he didn't want his players wasting their eyesight on words when those same peepers could be used to better see a baseball. He wanted his players to personify professionalism, which meant not being seen drinking in public or smoking a cigarette while in uniform. Of course, he did not look in the mirror to examine how attending the horse races could be viewed as unprofessional. In short, Hornsby's rule translated to an uptight and unhappy clubhouse.

Wilson got off to an especially slow start in 1931 when he hit .238 with no home runs and two RBIs in 42 at-bats in April. He did not hit his first home run until May 2 during a 6–3 loss to the Cardinals. Soon his mood began to change from the fun-loving slugger to a solemn slump-ridden figure. The previous year he had made everything look so effortless. Suddenly he hated playing for Hornsby, and he worried about his future for the simple reason he told reporters: "I'm being paid big money to hit and I'm not hitting."

Speculation about why Wilson's production had fallen so dramatically focused primarily on his eyesight. As with most of Wilson's failures, everybody figured that if his eyesight had declined it had been because he had not taken care of himself.

"I guess a lot of people think I was half stiff all the time I was playing," Wilson said. "That's not true. I played 11 years in the big leagues and I never ever took a drink before a game. Sure, afterwards. And sometimes I'd play with a bad hangover. But I never took a drink before a game."

Not having McCarthy in Wilson's corner building him up hurt the outfielder a great deal. Instead of Wilson having someone to help him move past his failures and insecurities, Hornsby brought

226

negativity and a disdain for Wilson and everything about him. And, according to Al Lopez, the less lively baseball affected Wilson more than it did a lot of hitters.

Wilson "hit the ball the other way," Lopez said. "Most of his home runs went to right field. Once the ball was changed, it seemed to hurt hitters who tried to hit for power the opposite way. Probably took about 10 to 15 feet away. That turned a lot of balls that were home runs in 1930 into fly outs in 1931."

Wilson hit .262 with 2 home runs and 11 RBIs in May. He performed better in June when he hit .276 with 7 home runs and 14 RBIs, but he began to unravel. He received a one-game suspension prior to the Cubs' June 27 game against the Braves in Boston after he violated the team's midnight curfew the night before.

Wilson slipped back to .269 with 2 home runs and 16 RBIs in July before hitting .241 with 2 home runs and 18 RBIs in August, the month when Wilson's and Hornsby's relationship finally reached a boiling point.

In the second game of a doubleheader against the Giants in New York, home plate umpire Beans Reardon ejected Wilson from the game for arguing with him about a called third strike. Even after he had been thrown out of the game, Wilson went to his position in center field, where he made different signals with his hands to express his displeasure with Reardon. Eventually, Wilson's teammates had to usher him from the outfield to the Cubs' bench. To punish Wilson for his antics, Hornsby boldly stated that Wilson would not play for the remainder of the season.

On September 4 with Wilson still under Hornsby's suspension, Hornsby got caught short on his bench and rather than starting Wilson, he started pitcher Bud Teachout in right field against the Reds in Cincinnati.

Hornsby escalated the punishment against Wilson on September 6 when he suspended him without pay for the remainder of the season due to his actions on the train when the team left Cincinnati after losing six straight to the last-place Reds. During that episode, Pat Malone had punched a pair of Chicago sportswriters with the drunken Wilson encouraging his friend to do so.

Three days later during a charity exhibition against the White Sox with a crowd of 34,865 watching at Comiskey Park, Chicago fans expressed their displeasure with Hornsby's handling of Wilson by showering him with lemons throughout the afternoon. Al Capone watched the game from the front row while sitting next to his bodyguard.

Wilson took most of the blame for the Cubs' failures in 1931. William Wrigley Jr. would not allow any of the blame to fall on Hornsby when the fans began to realize what they were missing by no longer having McCarthy as the team's manager.

"I have said before that Joe McCarthy became a bit too lenient last season," Wrigley said. "Some of the boys took advantage of it. They got into habits that can't be broken over night. Hornsby will stop them or there will be some huge slices in salaries. Wilson gets a monthly pay check in excess of $6,000, but he isn't earning it."

Even before the conclusion of August in 1931, discussions had begun about Wilson not fitting into the Cubs' plans for the next season and where he might get traded. He finished the 1931 season at .261 with 13 home runs and 61 RBIs, which ranks as the largest free fall in Major League history from one season to the next: .095 points less on his batting average, 43 fewer home runs, and 130 fewer RBIs.

Since neither the Cubs nor the White Sox won the pennant in their respective leagues in 1931, the Chicago City Series again took place. And once again the White Sox became champions of the city. During the series, a conversation between Gabby Hartnett and Capone was captured by a photograph, leading Commissioner Kenesaw Mountain Landis to make an edict forbidding players to fraternize with fans. Seventeen days after Hartnett and Capone talked, Capone was convicted of tax evasion on October 17. After Capone's conviction, he spent eight years in prisons in Atlanta and on Alcatraz Island.

The Cubs traded Wilson and Teachout to the Cardinals for Burleigh Grimes on December 9, 1931. Before Wilson could play for the Cardinals, they traded him to Brooklyn prior to the 1932 season. During the offseason after the 1931 season, J. Roy Stockton wrote a piece for the *Sporting News* entitled, "Wilson Buffeted by Cubs and Cards, Striving Hard for a Comeback," in which Wilson spoke about the 1931 season:

Naturally, after my good year of 1930, the fans were expecting me to do something every time I went to bat and even the spring training crowds razzed me pretty hard. That bothered me and I kept on getting the old razzberries all year. Some people said I was a batting flop because I was carousing around too much. That was all wrong. I went out occasionally, but not as much as I did the year before, when I was hitting all those home runs. You have to do something for recreation, but I was in condition to play every day. They told me at Chicago that I'd have to quit this and that, but I'm not signing any pledges. I have a wife and a boy and baseball is my livelihood and I'm not going to do anything that will prevent me from earning my living that way.

Being traded to Brooklyn essentially wrote Wilson's baseball epitaph. The odd dimensions of Ebbets Field did not suit Wilson's stroke, though he did revive his career in that 1932 season by hitting .297 with 23 home runs and 123 RBIs. But he did little in 1933 and 1934 when he had a combined 15 home runs with 81 RBIs over the course of the two seasons. He played briefly with the Phillies in August of 1934 and then his career was over.

The ratification of the 21st Amendment took place on December 5, 1933, and it repealed the 18th Amendment. Women served as a powerful faction in having the ban of alcohol lifted. The country was worse off, it seemed to most, when alcohol was illegal because hoodlums had gained far greater power due to the wealth they accrued from the illegal sale of alcohol. With the massive wealth gained by gangsters came corruption of government officials and a general lawlessness, which was personified in the city of Chicago and through Capone's machine.

Activist Pauline Sabin founded the Women's Organization for National Prohibition reform in 1929. By 1931, the organization had swelled to a membership of over 1.5 million, serving as a large voting contingent favoring the repeal of Prohibition. Other organizations recognized the need for Prohibition to be repealed, and the Democratic Party embraced the repeal of Prohibition when Franklin Roosevelt ran for President in 1932.

Once elected, President Roosevelt signed the Cullen-Harrison Act on March 22, 1933, which allowed 3.2 percent beer and wine to be sold, the logic being that at that low percentage of alcohol, getting inebriated would be a difficult prospect. Legal beer and wine sales began on April 7, 1933. State conventions then ratified the 21st Amendment and Prohibition laws were repealed, but to what degree remained somewhat contingent on preferences in local jurisdictions, as dictated by the voters' choice.

Though a conviction took place for the murder of Jake Lingle, most felt the wrong person had been punished and that the man who pulled the trigger was never found. Some felt that the Lingle killing brought the beginning of the end of gang activity in Chicago, but the truth of the matter was the repeal of Prohibition and the conviction of Capone simply changed the complexion of Chicago's underworld, which delved into other areas.

Whether Prohibition was in place or not, Wilson continued to drink with a vengeance after leaving the game. Once out of baseball, he did not adapt to life as an average Joe.

For a while he tried to make a living off his name in Chicago at an establishment on Rush Street where his job was to introduce the dancing girls and entertain the crowd with old baseball stories and jokes. Wilson would remain late into the night after the show lamenting to anyone who would listen about the sudden and cruel end to his career.

"I batted .307 for 10 years in the majors; I could draw 40,000 and more out there," Wilson said. "They loved me. Why did it have to end? God, it didn't have to end."

Eventually the sadness of having a fallen legend assume such a demeaning role prompted him to leave the city where he once had been king.

Wilson lost everything—including his wife to divorce and his son due to his father's behavior toward his mother—and he worked at menial jobs for low pay the rest of his life until he died at the age of 48 on November 23, 1948—approximately three months after Babe Ruth died on August 16, 1948. He was found in a morgue in Baltimore, a penniless man who had died of a lung ailment. The National League provided burial funds and his funeral was held in Martinsburg with more than 200 in attendance.

Wilson was inducted into the Hall of Fame in 1979 by the Veterans Committee.

~~~

When Hornsby took over as Cubs manager, it ultimately helped expedite the end of Wilson's career. But Hornsby would not last long as a Cub.

After the 1931 campaign, Hornsby's own status as manager came into question, particularly after Wrigley died. Bill Veeck had to deal with allegations Hornsby had been borrowing money from his players to cover the funds he lost gambling. Veeck also understood how miserable being a player under Hornsby was. Seeing that the Cubs had a good chance to win the pennant in 1932, Veeck fired Hornsby after 99 games even though the team had a 53-46 record.

A bitter Hornsby had his own ideas about why he had been fired. Of course in his mind he had done nothing wrong. He believed that when he used a rookie, Frank Demaree, as a pinch hitter, Veeck held it against him, holding the opinion that Hornsby should have hit himself. Regarding that situation, Hornsby said: "These second-guessing general managers. They get a young player, want you to use him, but then complain when you try to find out what he can do in a jam. Demaree didn't that time, but he will." Hornsby also believed that Charlie Grimm and Gabby Harnett had gone to the front office to try to have him fired.

A compelling message about what the Cubs players felt about Hornsby was delivered when the Cubs rallied and managed to win the 1932 National League pennant after Hornsby's dismissal. When shares were divvied up for reaching the World Series, the players left him out in the cold without so much as a fraction of a share.

Judge Kenesaw Mountain Landis called Hornsby into his office during the 1932 season to again address Hornsby's problems at the horse track. The belligerent Hornsby boldly told the commissioner of baseball that he saw no difference between betting at the horse track and playing the stock market, which sent a shot firing across the bow with Landis since he had invested some of Major League Baseball's money in Samuel Insull's utilities, which failed miserably.

Through it all, Hornsby continued to hit. At the age of 37, Hornsby found himself broke, continuing to suffer from a bad heel, divorced, and having few friends remaining in baseball when he went to the Cardinals as a pinch hitter/utility infielder in 1932. Despite all those troubles, Hornsby still managed to hit .326.

In 1933 he moved to the American League for the first time when he became the player-manager of the St. Louis Browns. His fourth official American League at-bat became the stuff of legends.

Hornsby coached third base, a custom many managers followed back in those days, and the Browns were playing the New York Yankees when Hornsby inserted himself into the game as a pinch hitter against Lefty Grove.

The great Yankees left-hander could not resist calling out to Hornsby: "So here's the great National League hitter, Mr. Hornsby."

Hornsby did not speak with his mouth but rather with his bat. He blasted the first pitch Grove threw onto the pavilion roof in right-center field at Sportsman's Park. Hornsby spoke after the home run telling Grove, "Yes, you @#$%, that *was* the great National League hitter, Mr. Hornsby."

Browns owner Phil Ball had Hornsby's back. He liked what the Rajah represented. Few circumstances would have prompted Ball to fire Hornsby. Unfortunately for Hornsby, Ball died and the new owner of the team, Donald L. Barnes, who had made his fortune as the head of a small-loan firm, brought aboard a new general manager, Bill DeWitt. Ultimately this led to Hornsby's end with the Browns. When DeWitt discovered Hornsby again going over the edge at the horse track, he reported his findings to Barnes, who confronted Hornsby with the information he had obtained from his general manager when Hornsby went to purchase stock in Barnes's small-loan company. Barnes asked Hornsby if he had acquired the money to purchase the stock from winning at the horse track. Hornsby did not lie to the owner, but their exchange escalated until Hornsby told Barnes: "I don't see where playing the horses is as bad as charging exorbitant interest rates to widows and orphans."

Barnes fired Hornsby. That was 1937 and Hornsby effectively had orchestrated his own exodus from the Major Leagues. The Rajah was inducted into the Hall of Fame in 1942, but he remained away from the majors, wandering around between minor league jobs in the Texas and Pacific Coast Leagues until he resurfaced again in 1952 when Bill Veeck Jr. hired him to manage the St. Louis Browns for a brief stint, then with the Cincinnati Reds for a two-year stint.

Hornsby died on January 5, 1963.

Once William Wrigley Jr. began listening to Hornsby, McCarthy knew he was gone. During the waiting period for the inevitable to happen, Warren Brown asked McCarthy if he would like to manage the Yankees. McCarthy told him he would. The Chicago sportswriter then arranged for a friend of his to let Yankees owner Col.

Jacob Ruppert know that McCarthy was available. Shortly after the meeting, Ruppert contacted Wrigley, who gave Ruppert permission to contact McCarthy. They met shortly after Wrigley announced that Hornsby would be the team's manager in 1931.

Thus, McCarthy became the manager of the Yankees. Ruppert gave him complete control of on-the-field decisions as well as trades. Ruppert also warned McCarthy about Babe Ruth. The Bambino had long wanted to become the manager of the Yankees and this desire to manage would likely translate to some dissension, particularly when some of the players favored the slugger. McCarthy didn't flinch.

Ruth remained with the Yankees through 1934 and McCarthy never really won him over to his side. However, he did earn the respect and devotion of the other players.

In McCarthy's first year with the Yankees they finished second, but he guided them to the American League pennant in 1932 and they swept the Cubs in the World Series. McCarthy then endured three straight second-place finishes. In another era, McCarthy might have been fired, but the Yankees had patience because they liked the way he managed the team. He rewarded their patience by guiding the team to four consecutive World Series championships from 1936 through 1939.

Unlike John McGraw's small ball that came in the era before the advent of the long ball, McCarthy liked employing players who could hit the baseball and letting them swing for the fences. Nowhere did playing power baseball fit better than it did with the Yankees in the late 1930s. By the time the 1941 World Series had run its course, the Yankees under McCarthy had collected their sixth World Series in six trips to the Fall Classic.

Some managers do their best at getting a top effort from an over-achieving team. Others can't win without talent. And then there are the managers who know what to do when they have the talent. McCarthy fit that bill. While he had shown great acumen for building a team while with the Cubs, he demonstrated a true ability to manage when he had the talent while with the Yankees. If McCarthy had the players he wasn't going to lose. He understood how to push the right buttons for the best players and how to get them to perform up to their abilities. McCarthy's knack was reflected in the manner with which the Yankees went about their business. Rarely did they have a closely contested pennant race, and once they reached the World Series they normally had their way with the National League team. Talented players respected McCarthy for the way he managed on a daily basis and the way he paid attention to details. The great Joe DiMaggio would say of McCarthy: "Never a day went by when you didn't learn something from McCarthy."

McCarthy resigned his post with the Yankees in May of 1946, and he became the manager of the Red Sox in 1948. After two years with Boston, he retired 59 games into the 1950 season and never managed again.

Prior to Wilson signing his contract with Brooklyn for the 1932 season, the team held a ceremony to commemorate the event. McCarthy attended. In a bittersweet moment, Wilson told McCarthy he wished he could play for him, to which his former manager told him he wished the same.

Shortly after Wilson died in 1948, McCarthy and others who were with Wilson during his Cubs days contributed to have a monument built to honor him. The finished product stood 10 feet tall and was 30 inches at its base. Included was an insignia of a baseball and crossed bats with the following inscription: "One of baseball's immortals, Lewis R. (Hack) Wilson rests here."

When the statue was completed in September of 1949, McCarthy left the Red Sox to attend a ceremony at the Rosedale Cemetery in Martinsburg, West Virginia. Also attending the ceremony were Kiki Cuyler, John Schulte, and Charlie Grimm. McCarthy spoke at the ceremony and said the following:

"To me, along with the sorrow I experience in thinking of Hack, so comes the pleasing memory of happy days with him. This monument we unveil to this memory recalls great accomplishments in baseball. His record speaks for itself, and it will be long remembered by millions of youngsters and the men he played with."

McCarthy paused after his speech and shook his head before a smile spread across his face: "He was a marvelous little fella'."

McCarthy's legacy remembers him as one of the best managers in Major League history. In 24 seasons he compiled a record of 2,125-1,333, and he won seven World Championships with the Yankees. In 1957, McCarthy was elected to the Hall of Fame. He died on January 13, 1978.

CHAPTER SEVENTEEN

The Missing RBI

HACK WILSON'S RECORD RBI SEASON STOOD AT 190 FOR 69 YEARS
before a missing RBI was discovered.

Cliff Kachline, who served as the Baseball Hall of Fame's historian, received a letter dated November 17, 1977, from Larry Wigge, a staff writer for the *Sporting News*. In addition to Wigge's letter, Kachline found another letter in the envelope.

Kachline had worked at the *Sporting News* for 24 years as part of the publication's editorial staff. Wigge's letter noted that the box scores that ran in the *Sporting News* in 1930 did not have RBI totals, so they did not have a way to answer the following handwritten letter from James Braswell, a Chicago resident at the time, who wrote suggesting that if they checked Hack Wilson's work from July 24 through August 5, 1930 they would discover Wilson had knocked in at least one run in 11 consecutive games. And given that contention, Braswell went on to suggest that Wilson should have joined Mel Ott in the *Sporting News' Baseball Record Book* as the co-holder of the National League record for consecutive games with an RBI.

Kachline ran a quick check and then wrote a letter to Braswell noting that Wilson's day-by-day record for 1930 credited him with RBIs in only 10 of the 11 games from the period in question. But Kachline further noted that the box score from an Associated Press account of the game credited Wilson with an RBI for the game that took place on July 28.

Soon thereafter, Kachline sent another letter to Braswell, and sent a carbon copy of his letter to Wigge. In his letter, Kachline reported that according to *Chicago Tribune* and *Chicago Herald-Examiner* accounts of the second game of the July 28, 1930, doubleheader between the Cubs and Reds at Wrigley Field, Wilson had singled home Kiki Cuyler from second base in the third inning and eventually scored on a single by Charlie Grimm. While the newspaper accounts indicated that Wilson and Grimm should have both been credited with RBIs, the official records showed Grimm with two RBIs and Wilson with none. Therefore, Kachline surmised, Wilson should have had a streak of 11 consecutive games with an RBI.

In addition to working at the Hall of Fame and having worked at the *Sporting News*, Kachline was a founding member of the Society for American Baseball Research (SABR), an organization that often looks to the past to address statistical inaccuracies such as the one involving Wilson's phantom RBI.

He decided the matter needed to be addressed by the Baseball Records Committee, which came into being in 1975 to try to solve such discrepancies. Kachline presented a report to the committee on December 7, 1977, and the committee delayed any action based on inconclusive evidence, along with the fact they had more pressing matters at the time, and further research needed to be performed.

Paul MacFarlane of the *Sporting News* joined Kachline to work on the Wilson project and proposed writing a story on the subject. However, the editor of the *Sporting News* turned him down, citing that the publication's policy toward correcting records was to first present the evidence to the Official Rules Committee. Because of the importance of statistics to baseball, they had to be positive the numbers were correct.

The Wilson project remained dormant for many years until 1998 when Kachline went public with his pursuit to mint the missing RBI, at which point the Elias Sports Bureau, baseball's official statistician, did not agree with Kachline.

The need to make sure the RBI mark indeed was accurate became dire in 1998 when Juan Gonzalez of the Texas Rangers arrived at the All-Star break with 101 RBIs. Kachline told Ken Daley of the *Dallas Morning News*:

> *With the major league record being 190 in a season, it seems awfully important to verify whether it's 190 or 191. And we have verified, without any doubt whatsoever, that it's 191. It should be officially corrected before there's a consummation of this season, because Gonzalez conceivably has a chance [to break the record].*

Elias held steadfast in their belief that Wilson should not be credited with another RBI unless new information came forth. Their position could be understood. Faulty record keeping often defined games in the 1930s. So they could not simply embrace such an historical change without some substantial proof; to do otherwise might set a precedent that would dictate future inquiries about alleged past inaccuracies.

To Major League Baseball's credit, they reviewed the matter further, getting former *Chicago Tribune* baseball writer Jerome Holtzman involved. Holtzman, who had accepted a post as baseball's historian, scrutinized play-by-play accounts of the game and box scores from Wilson's 1930 season. Elias and the commissioner's office also continued to review Wilson's totals, which led to a change being officially made on June 22, 1999. On that day Wilson's record expanded to 191 RBIs for one season and his career RBI total moved to 2,062.

Commissioner Bud Selig made the following statement: "There is no doubt that Hack Wilson's RBI total should be 191. I'm sensitive to the historical significance that accompanies the correction of such a prestigious record, especially after so many years have passed, but it is important to get it right."

Despite the change, Wilson's plaque in Cooperstown remained unchanged and the description of his accomplishments begins: "Established major league record of 190 runs batted in and National League high of 56 homers in 1930."

Chapter Eighteen

Perspective on 191 RBIs

In the top of the ninth inning in a July 23, 2007, game between the New York Yankees and Kansas City Royals, Alex Rodriguez lined a single to center field off Royals right-hander Ryan Braun to score Melky Cabrera and give A-Rod his 100th run batted in of the season.

A 100 RBI season is one of those magical plateaus for any hitter; most would do anything to reach the lofty number just once in their careers, and yet, there A-Rod sat with triple digits after just 98 games. But consider this: while a hundred RBIs after 98 games is impressive, A-Rod needed 91 more in the Yankees' final 64 games to tie Major League Baseball's RBI record. He finished with 156 for the 2007 season, falling a significant 35 short of the record.

Hack Wilson's 191 RBIs in 1930 is one mark that may well stand the test of time. Several current and former Major Leaguers talked about the prospect of the record ever being broken.

Frank "The Big Hurt" Thomas, who played in Chicago for most of his 19-year Major League career and had a career-high 143 RBIs in 2000, doesn't believe the record will ever be broken.

"Nah, not in today's game," Thomas said. "Today's game has changed. You've got relievers. Sometimes you'll face three or four different pitchers in a nine-inning game. You didn't see that back in the '30s. Most of the time the starting pitchers started the game and they finished what they started. Today's game has changed and the relievers are a big part of the pitching success against hitters."

Ron Santo spent 14 of his 15 Major League seasons with the Cubs and had a career-high 129 RBIs in 1969; he agreed with Thomas.

"I can't see it [being broken] at all," Santo said. "There have been a couple of guys who have had a hundred RBIs at the All-Star break, and still couldn't do it. I don't think anybody's going to do it. There are days you come to the plate and you don't have somebody on. In order to do that, you're going to have to hit a lot of home runs to get a lot of RBIs. When you look at it, Billy [Williams], Ernie [Banks], and me, we all drove in a hundred runs. I just can't see it happening. One-hundred ninety is unbelievable."

Josh Hamilton of the Rangers had 130 RBIs in 2008, but wasn't in tune to the RBI record, so the number caught him off guard.

"That's crazy," Hamilton said. "I look at what the guys in front of me have done to get on base and you wonder what his guys were doing. That's an incredible number. Has anybody gotten close to it?"

Lou Gehrig remains the player who came closest to reaching Wilson's mark. In 1931 the "Iron Horse" of the Yankees followed his 174 RBI season of 1930 with 184 RBIs. Consider, too, that Gehrig, and not Wilson, might have established an even higher mark than 191 in 1930 had he not broken the pinky on his right hand with three weeks left in the season. After the final game, he went to St. Vincent's Hospital where doctors operated on his finger. In addition, they cleaned up bone chips in his left elbow. After having 35, 43, and 49 RBIs in May, June, and July, Gehrig had just 40 RBIs in total for the final two months of the season. Unless something drastic changes in baseball, Gehrig's 1931 season will likely remain the closest anybody ever gets to reaching Wilson's mark. In large part, this can be attributed to the fact that Major League hitters possessed a different mindset during Wilson's era. While they had embraced the idea of swinging for the fences, they did so with an eye toward caution where the strikeout was concerned. To swing, miss, and head back to the dugout with one's head down felt like the equivalent of a date with the guillotine. Toward the end of the 20th century, that mindset had changed dramatically.

Hitters moved to an approach that saw them never get cheated on a swing even if they faced a two-strike count. During the notorious period Major League Baseball experienced in the late 1990s and early 2000s, many of those swings were fueled by performance-enhancing substances. The steroid years might have brought the best opportunity for anybody to break Wilson's mark. Slugging went through the roof, as did RBIs, and the schedule included 162 games, or eight more than the 154-game slate when Wilson set the mark. So why didn't the record fall during the steroid period?

Prior to 1990, players had hit 50 or more home runs just 17 times. Players surpassed the 50 home run plateau 24 times after the 1989 season. Logic would seem to suggest that an increased number of home runs would generate more runs scored, which, in turn, would equate to more RBIs. But Manny Ramirez's 165 RBIs in 1999 was the closest anybody came to breaking the record during the era.

To understand why that logic did not translate into reality, one must first examine the table-setters for today's sluggers. Will anybody have a group like Wilson had hitting in front of him? The group's numbers were staggering. Wilson found himself surrounded by perhaps the greatest-ever collection of right-handed hitters on one club, which obviously played to his favor. On the down side, opposing managers limited the number of left-handers they threw against the Cubs that season.

Woody English and Footsie Blair hit in either the top or second spot in the order, followed by Kiki Cuyler in the third spot and Riggs Stephenson or Gabby Hartnett in the fifth spot behind Wilson.

English had a .430 on-base percentage, hit .335—accruing 214 hits—en route to scoring 152 runs. Cuyler hit .355 that season with 13 home runs, 17 triples, 50 doubles, and he scored 155 runs. That he drove in 134 RBIs can be seen as a tribute to Wilson, as opposing pitchers chose to pitch to Cuyler on many occasions rather than pitching to Wilson. Meanwhile, Stephenson hit .367 with an on-base percentage of .421 and Hartnett hit .339 with 37 home runs and had a .404 on-base percentage. In other words, opposing pitchers faced a dilemma: pitch to Wilson or put him on base and have to pitch to Stephenson or Hartnett: hardly a pleasant decision.

Blair fell far behind the others at the top of the order, hitting just .273 with a .306 on-base percentage. Some might speculate about what Wilson would have done had Rogers Hornsby played in more than 42 games that season. Based on the Rajah's track record, conventional wisdom suggests that Wilson would have had even more chances to hit with runners on base with Hornsby hitting in front of him. However, while Hornsby would have reached base a lot more than Blair, he would have countered the additional times he would be on base for Wilson by driving in the runners on base before Wilson had the opportunity to do so. The previous season, Hornsby hit .380 while batting third in the order—in front of Wilson, putting him on base 317 times on hits, walks, and hit-by-pitcher. But he also drove in 149 in 1929. Or exactly what happened to Stephenson, who had just 68 RBIs in 1930 despite hitting .367. Years later, when asked how he could have just 68 RBIs when he hit fifth for much of the season and hit .367, Stephenson would normally be prompted to chuckle, which he did when *Baseball Digest* asked him about the disparity in 1979.

"I batted fifth, behind Wilson," Stephenson said. "People ask me why, with my high batting average, I only drove in sixty-eight runs. Well, there weren't many on base after Hack got through."

Also remember, not only were the players in front of Wilson getting on base with great regularity, but so were the hitters following him in the order. The on-base percentage for the entire team was .378 and the team batting average was .309.

Modern teams have seen table setters who have enhanced the possibility of increased RBI totals. One unique team that comes to mind is the 1985 St. Louis Cardinals. At the top of the lineup they had speedsters Vince Coleman and Willie McGee. Coleman had a .320 on-base percentage and McGee .384, and they were followed in the batting order by Tommy Herr, a hard-nosed second baseman with modest power. Nevertheless, Herr finished with an incredible total of 110 RBIs while hitting just eight home runs.

That Cardinals' lineup also had a thumper in Jack Clark, who had 22 home runs and 87 RBIs that season. Despite the group of table setters up in front of them, neither Herr nor Clark even sniffed Wilson's mark. Why not? Several factors can be cited.

For starters: relief pitching.

As Thomas pointed out, many pitchers back in Wilson's day took the mound and threw the first pitch of the game and did not leave the mound until the final pitch had been thrown. Generally, any pitcher is tougher the first time through the batting order than the second, and the progression worsens each succeeding time through. While Wilson might have been hitting a third, fourth, or even fifth time against the same pitcher in any given game, modern hitters might see the same pitcher three times during a game before they start looking at a parade of relief pitchers. And given the abundance of statistics regarding match-ups between hitters and pitchers, most hitters will be looking at a pitcher who either has a history of success against that hitter or a pitcher whose splits indicate that he is better against a right-hander or left-hander due to the pitches he throws, which means most match-ups will be in favor of the pitchers. Those pitcher-batter contests normally take place from the sixth through eighth innings before hitters then must face another modern beast: the closer.

A closer's sole purpose is to start the ninth inning when his team is ahead in the ballgame and get the final—and most diffi-cult—outs of the game. In Wilson's day, no such beast as a Mariano Rivera or Dennis Eckersley existed to enter the game and silence any potential rallies.

Today's hitters are looking at a different variety of pitchers, which limits their chances of making contact with the ball, but when they do manage to put the ball in play, they face additional problems not faced by players in Wilson's day.

First, there is the positioning of the fielders. Managers study hitting patterns for every hitter in the opposing lineup to identify the areas where most of the balls they hit are directed and they adjust the defense accordingly. Some of these defensive placements are subtle, but they effectively manage to limit a hitter's success by taking away the spots where their hits normally land. Facing more drastic limitations are the modern left-handed power hitters who pull the ball; they are particularly susceptible to defensive placements. In any given at-bat they can step to the plate and be looking at fielders shifted all the way to the second-base side of the field to force a choice: try to pull the ball into a smaller area dense with fielders or alter the swing and try to hit the ball to the opposite field.

The players trying to field the balls hit by modern hitters are faster and more athletic, giving them greater range while enabling them to further limit a ball from landing safely on the grass. On top of that, this new breed of player cut from a more athletic form is armed with what amounts to a jai alai cesta when compared to the gloves worn during Wilson's day.

All of these factors add up to fewer runners on base when a big RBI man comes to the plate, which translates to fewer opportunities to drive in runs during a game.

Hypotheses aside, what Wilson did in 1930 and how he did it must be forever remembered and appreciated. Of his 56 home runs, 23 came with nobody on base, 25 came with one runner on base, and three with two on. He did not hit a grand slam that season. When added up, Wilson's home runs accounted for 97 RBIs, which meant he drove home another 94 without clearing the fences.

Billy Herman played his rookie season with the Cubs in 1931 and saw Wilson during the season many referred to as Hack's "great hangover." Nevertheless, Herman would say years later that the modern pitching "wouldn't bother Hack much."

"He had something I don't see today—ability to hit any ball he could reach to any field with equal power," Herman said. "Everything's pull hitting nowadays—down the foul lines the short way to fences pulled in as close as 250 feet. Hack's shots went 380 to 400 feet, on the average. And he sprayed them so the outfield never could get set."

Comparing different players from different eras has forever proved a difficult proposition, though baseball lends itself to such comparisons because of the numbers and the seasons those numbers represented. A story recounted many times in the past tells of Cubs slugger Dave Kingman's brilliant idea to make more money. The 6'6", 210-pound slugger, who played for the Cubs from 1978 through 1980, asked Cubs general manager Bob Kennedy if he could get a bonus written into his contract rewarding his breaking the club RBI record, to which Kennedy replied with a straight face: "Absolutely." Kingman's highest RBI total for a single season came in 1984 with Oakland when he had 118.

Will anybody ever break Hack Wilson's record? Woody English addressed that prospect in a March 1978 article written for *Baseball Digest* by Bob Dolgan of the *Cleveland Plain Dealer.*

"We don't have to worry about the [Wilson's RBI record getting broken]," English said. "Nobody will ever break that one. Even guys like Babe Ruth and Lou Gehrig couldn't."

Could Hack Wilson time travel, plunk down in a modern Major League game and accomplish the same things he accomplished in 1930? We'll never know. What is known is that Wilson's career is over, and whether or not anybody disputes how he compiled his numbers or when he compiled them, Hack's 191 remains a number that appears out of reach.

ACKNOWLEDGMENTS

GROWING UP IN TAMPA, FLORIDA, I LOOKED FORWARD TO SPRING when Major League teams would come to the area to get ready for the coming season. The Cincinnati Reds trained in Tampa and played their games at Al Lopez Field, named for the Hall of Fame catcher and manager. So you can imagine what a thrill I experienced to become a friend of "The Senor" as an adult working as a sportswriter for the *Tampa Tribune*.

Al often let me into his world, telling me stories about his time in the Major Leagues. I could listen to him all day talking about the players I'd known only as black and white photos in the books amid my ever-expanding collection of baseball tomes. During one such conversation, Hack Wilson's name came up, which led to a lot of banter about the RBI record. Of course, Al actually saw Wilson drive home many of the runs while he played against Wilson as a catcher for the Brooklyn Robins in 1930. From that conversation, the idea began to germinate about doing a book on Wilson's record-setting season. I would go on to interview Al at a later date about numerous players he played against, including Wilson. In addition, through Al I got to know Tony Cuccinello, his dear friend, who also played in the Major Leagues and against Wilson during the 1930 season. I considered both men great friends and I'm thankful for their friendship and insights.

This project could not have come to fruition without Tris Coburn and Frank Scatoni. Their efforts helped me to refine the scope of the work and ultimately find a publisher, so thanks guys.

And to Keith Wallman, my editor at Lyons Press, I can't thank you enough for the quality edit you performed on the book. Not only did you correct mistakes, but you enhanced the copy.

Finally, thanks to Patti, my wife, and my kids, Carly and Kel. I love you all.

Notes

Chapter One
1. ... still feel respectable." —*Chicago Tribune*, March 8, 1979.
8. ... hands in Philadelphia." —*Life* magazine, July 29, 1948.
9. ... right with me." —Donald Honig, *The Man in the Dugout*.
9. ... his unconditional release." —Fred Lieb, *Connie Mack*.
10. ... opening pitcher for the World Series." —Red Smith, *To Absent Friends*.
10. ... sucker we're going to see in this Series." —Ibid.
12. ... we didn't score." —Rogers Hornsby and Bill Surface, *My War with Baseball*.
12. ... but it will be the ball." Robert S. Boone and Gerald Grunska, *Hack*.
12. ... under a blanket." —Ibid.
13. ... sinister intentions. —*Chicago Tribune*, October 10, 1929.
13. ... from now on." —Ibid.
13. ... even three games." —Ibid.
15. ... that's what we're doing." —*New York Times*, October 13, 1929.
16. ... from pitcher to catcher?" — Peter Golenbock, *Wrigleyville*.
17. ... and that's fatal." —*Life* magazine, July 29, 1948.
17. ... let it go at that." —Associated Press, October 13, 1929.
17. ... ever seen on a ball field." —Ibid.
17. ... there in center field." —Ibid.
17. ... either to the sun." —Ibid.
17. ... and you get hits." —Ibid.
19. ... dazed as he stepped outside." —Clifton Blue Parker, *Fouled Away*.
19. ... them next year." —Ibid.
20. ... only been right." —*Chicago Tribune*, October 14, 1929.
20. ... any ball hit to Wilson." —Rogers Hornsby and Bill Surface, *My War with Baseball*.
22. ... had done with Ehmke." —Glenn Stout, *The Cubs: The Complete Story of Chicago Cubs Baseball*.
23. ... a World Series is not a season." —*Chicago Tribune*, October 14, 1929.
23. ... tea and cookies today." —Donald Honig, *The Man in the Dugout*.
24. ... great winter all the same." —Robert S. Boone and Gerald Grunska, *Hack*.
25. ... You can't figure 'em." —Ibid.
25. ... and prescribed treatment." —Ibid.

Chapter Two
30. ... seek an athletic career." —*Chicago Tribune*, September 24, 1929.
35. ... heart for Jack Scott." —Ibid.

35. ... that let in two runs." —*New York Times*, September 28, 1923.
39. ... bullpen and he hit it." —*New York Times*, June 10, 1924.
44. ...The Cubs then drafted me." —Robert S. Boone and Gerald Grunska, *Hack*.
45. ... the next five years." —Donald Honig, *The Man in the Dugout*.
47. ... yes. But drunk, no." —William F. McNeil, *Gabby Hartnett: The Life and Times of the Cubs' Greatest Catcher*.
47. ... pick up all tabs." —*Chicago Tribune*, March 8, 1979.
48. ... such as Caliban." —*Sports Illustrated*, April 11, 1977.
48. ... delayed 12 minutes." —*Chicago Tribune*, June 22, 1928.
48. ... required three stitches." —*Chicago Tribune*, February 12, 1930.
49. ... in needling opponents." —John Snyder, *Cubs Journal*.
49. ... broke up the fracas." —Donald Honig, *The Man in the Dugout*.
49. ... word and mean it." —Robert S. Boone and Gerald Grunska, *Hack*.
50. ... I can tell you." —Donald Honig, *The Man in the Dugout*.
50. ... himself more properly." —United News, July 13, 1929.

Chapter Three
53. ... take a look at yourself." —*New York Times*, January 14, 1978.
54. ... a blind spider." —*Louisville Courier-Journal*, July 24, 1925.
55. ... quarter million dollars." —*Chicago Herald Examiner*, October 13, 1925.
56. ... Southern term for "master." —*Baseball Digest*, August 2005.
57. ... do the club any good." —*Chicago Tribune*, June 8, 1926.
59. ... a man that far." —*New York Times*, January 14, 1978.
59. ... had the nerve to do that." —*New York Times*, January 14, 1978.
61. ... don't you think?" —*Baseball Digest*, November 1971.
61. ... go out riding tonight." —*Baseball Digest*, June 1996.
61. ... down a little." —*Baseball Digest*, March 1978.
63. ... into the Major Leagues." —Clifton Blue Parker, *Fouled Away*.
65. ... asking me in Boston." —*Baseball Digest*, April 1948.

Chapter Four
68. ... retiring at 11:30 p.m." — *Chicago Tribune*, September 24, 1930
68. ... be a great player, too." —Glenn Stout, *The Cubs: The Complete Story of Chicago Cubs Baseball*.
70. ... No way." —*Sports Illustrated*, October 9, 1978.
71. ... tell you how to pitch?" —Ibid.
72. ... a chance to swing." Bob Broeg, *Super Stars of Baseball*.
72. ... upset the apple cart." —Interview with Al Lopez, June 1992.
73. ... want it done my way." —Bob Broeg, *Super Stars of Baseball*.
75. ... that kind of offer." —Ibid.
75. ... play second base." —*Chicago Tribune*, September 20, 1929.
76. ... in my whole life." —*Sporting News*, January 1, 1933.

76. ... shall we make it, Al?" —Bob Broeg, *Super Stars of Baseball*.
77. ... joined the Ku Klux Klan." —Fred Lieb, *Baseball as I Have Known It*
77. ... that was his downfall." —National Pastime 13 [1993], p 82.

Chapter Five
83. ... any place but in the sun." —Robert S. Boone and Gerald Grunska, *Hack*.
84. ... grudge stuff." —*Chicago Tribune*, December 14, 1929.
84. ... are a worthless lot." —Ibid.
86. ... count this time." —*Chicago Tribune*, December 15, 1929.
87. ... 'Papa' embroidered on them." —*Chicago Tribune*, December 17, 1929.
89. ... already been licked." —Ibid.
89. ... come through again." —*Chicago Tribune*, December 23, 1929.

Chapter Six
95. ... that could be made." —David Martinez, *The Book of Baseball Literacy* (Second Edition)
95. ... and in resiliency." —*New York Times*, July 19, 1925.
98. ... because of this act." —*New York Times*, August 19, 1920.
100. ... hold and swing." —*New York Times*, July 19, 1925.

Chapter Seven
106. ... misjudge his soup." —Daniel Okrent and Steve Wulf, *Baseball Anecdotes*.
107. ... what to do with." —*Sports Illustrated*, April 11, 1977.
107. ... be no signing." —*New York Times*, January 8, 1930.
109. ... every three months." —*New York Times*, February 4, 1930.
110. ... on the line." —*New York Times*, March 9, 1930.

Chapter Eight
125. ... other is a plumber." —*Baseball Digest*, December 2005.

Chapter Nine
137. ... facts must be faced." —*Chicago Tribune*, April 25, 1930.
143. ... heart out of them." —Charles C. Alexander, *Breaking the Slump: Baseball in the Depression Era*.

Chapter Ten
151. ... us to the other." — Phillip Fox, *Adler Planetarium and Astronomical Museum, An Account of the Optical Planetarium and a Brief Guide to the Museum*.
153. ... But hurt? Oh boy!" —Clifton Blue Parker, *Fouled Away*.
154. ... to protect himself." —Alan H. Levy, *Joe McCarthy, Architect of the Yankee Dynasty*.

156. ... forgot to dodge." —*Baseball Digest*, May, 1959.

Chapter Eleven
None

Chapter Twelve
173. ... of modern times." —*Minneapolis Tribune*, July 1, 1930.
178. ... any of these enterprises." —Charles C. Alexander, *Rogers Hornsby, A Biography*.
179. ... then the ice." —Bill Veeck, *Veeck as in Wreck*.
182. ... weren't going to say anything." Robert S. Boone and Gerald Grunska, *Hack*.

Chapter Thirteen
185. ... my several lodges." —*Chicago Tribune*, August 3, 1930.
188. ... drank the previous night." —*Baseball Digest*, October, 1974.
191. ... in this very inning." —*Chicago Tribune*, August 27, 1930.

Chapter Fourteen
201. ... treated me right." —*Chicago Tribune*, September 7, 1930.
201. ... manager can expect." —Ibid.
201. ... to embarrass him." —Ibid.
202. ... in one season." —*Chicago Tribune*, September 18, 1930.
212. ... try a golden goose." —*Sporting News*, October 2, 1930.
213. ... didn't deserve that." —*Chicago Tribune*, September 24, 1930.
213. ... balked at orders." —Ibid.
215. ... in my estimation." —*Chicago Tribune*, September 26, 1930.
217. ... of the former record." —*Chicago Tribune*, September 29, 1930.
218. ... entered the National League." —Clifton Blue Parker, *Fouled Away*.

Chapter Fifteen
None

Chapter Sixteen
226. ... and I'm not hitting." —*Chicago Tribune*, August 16, 1931.
226. ... took a drink before a game." —*Baseball Digest*, October 1974.
227. ... into fly outs in 1931." —Interview with Al Lopez, June 1992.
228. ... but he isn't earning it." —*Chicago Tribune*, July 1, 1931.
231. ... God, it didn't have to end." —*Chicago Tribune*, October 28, 1979.
232. ... time, but he will." —Bob Broeg, *Super Stars of Baseball*.
232. ... hitter, Mr. Hornsby." —Ibid.

233. ... that *was* the great National League hitter, Mr. Hornsby." —Bob Broeg, *Super Stars of Baseball.*
236. ... marvelous little fella'." —*Charleston* (West Virginia) *Gazette,* September 28, 1949.

Chapter Seventeen
None

Chapter Eighteen
244. ... after Hack got through." —*Baseball Digest,* February 1979.
247. ... outfield never could get set." —*Baseball Digest,* May 1959.

Bibliography

Books

Alexander, Charles. *Breaking the Slump, Baseball in the Depression Era.* New York: Columbia University Press, 2002.

Alexander, Charles. *John McGraw.* Lincoln: University of Nebraska Press, 1995.

Alexander, Charles. *Rogers Hornsby, A Biography.* New York: Henry Holt and Company, Inc., 1995.

Boone, Robert S., and Gerald Grunska. *Hack.* Highland Park, Ill.: Highland Press, 1978.

Broeg, Bob. *Super Stars of Baseball.* St. Louis, Mo.: *Sporting News,* 1971.

Conner, Anthony J. *Baseball for the Love of It: Hall-of-Famers Tell It Like It Was.* New York: Macmillan, 1982.

Creamer, Robert W. *Babe: The Legend Comes to Life.* New York: Simon and Schuster, 1984.

Debs, Victor. *Still Standing After All These Years: Twelve of Baseball's Longest Standing Records.* Jefferson, NC: McFarland, 1997.

Doxsie, Don. *Iron Man McGinnity: A Baseball Biography.* Jefferson, NC: McFarland, 2009.

Enders, Eric. *The Fall Classic: The Definitive History of the World Series.* New York: Sterling, 2007.

Golenbock, Peter. *Wrigleyville* (3rd Edition). New York: St. Martin's Griffin, 1999.

Honig, Donald. *The Man in the Dugout.* Lincoln: University of Nebraska Press, 1977.

Hornsby, Rogers and Bill Surface. *My War with Baseball.* New York: Coward-McCann, 1962.

James, Bill. *The New Bill James Historical Baseball Abstract.* New York: Free Press, 2001.

Jordan, David M. *The Athletics of Philadelphia: Connie Mack's White Elephants, 1901–1954.* Jefferson, NC: McFarland, 1999.

Kavanagh, Jack. *Ol' Pete: The Grover Cleveland Alexander Story.* South Bend, IN: Diamond Communications, 1996.

Koppett, Leonard. *The Men in the Dugouts: Baseball's Top Managers and How They Got That Way.* Philadelphia: Temple University Press, 2000.

Leventhal, Josh. *The World Series: An Illustrated Encyclopedia of the Fall Classic.* New York: Black Dog & Leventhal Publishers, 2001.

Levy, Alan H. *Joe McCarthy, Architect of the Yankee Dynasty.* Jefferson, NC: McFarland, 2005.

Lieb, Fred. *Baseball as I Have Known It.* New York: Tempo-Grosset and Dunlap, 1977.

Lieb, Fred. *Connie Mack, Grand Old Man of Baseball.* New York: G.P. Putnam, 1944.

Macht, Norman L. *Connie Mack.* Lincoln: University of Nebraska Press, 2007.

Mack, Connie. *My 66 Years in Baseball.* Philadelphia: Universal House, 1952.

Martinez, David H. *The Book of Baseball Literacy* (Second Edition). Lincoln: Authors Choice Press, 2000.

McNeil, William F. *Gabby Hartnett, The Life and Times of the Cubs' Greatest Catcher.* Jefferson, NC: McFarland, 2004.

Parker, Clifton Blue, *Fouled Away.* Jefferson, NC: McFarland, 2000.

Ritter, Lawrence S. *The Glory of Their Times.* New York: William Morrow, 1996.

Smith, Red. *To Absent Friends.* New York: New American Library, 1982.

Snyder, John. *Cubs Journal.* Cincinnati: Emmis Books, 2005.

Sowell, Mike. *The Pitch That Killed: The Story of Carl Mays, Ray Chapman, and the Pennant Race of 1920.* New York: Macmillan, 1989.

Stout, Glenn. *The Cubs: The Complete History of Chicago Cubs Baseball.* New York: Houghton Mifflin, 2007.

Veeck, Bill and Ed Linn. *Veeck as in Wreck.* Chicago: University of Chicago Press, 2001.

Voigt, David Quentin. *American Baseball, Vol. II, From Commissioners to Continental Expansion.* University Park: Penn State University Press, 1983.

Articles

Blaisdell, Lowell. "Legends As an Expression of Baseball Memory." *Journal of Sports History,* Vol. 19, Winter 1992, 227–43.

Breit, Harvey. "Mister Baseball Starts His Second Career." *New York Times Magazine,* May 11, 1952, 12–17.

Brown, Warren. "Down Memory Lane." *Baseball Digest,* November 1971, 90.

Cannon, Jimmy. "Lessons From McCarthy." *Baseball Digest,* June 1969, 62.

Cobb, Ty. "They Don't Play Baseball Any More." *Life,* March 17, 1952, 137–53.

Considine, Bob. "Mr. Mack." *Life,* August 9, 1948, 93-105.

Dolgan, Bob. "Teammates Recall Hack Wilson." *Baseball Digest,* March 1978, 64.

Drooz, Al. "…But Memories of Hack Wilson Fade Away." *Baseball Digest,* October 1974, 56.

Gershman, Michael. "Wooden Weapons." *Sports Heritage,* July-August 1987, 25–32.

Holway, John B. "Hack Wilson Belted Homers, Hecklers With Equal Gusto." *Baseball Digest,* June, 1996, 78.

Kachline, Clifford. "Hack Wilson's 191st RBI: A Persistent Itch Finally Scratched." *Baseball Research Journal,* January 2001, 114.
Kram, Mark. "Why Ain't I in the Hall?" *Sports Illustrated,* April 11, 1977, 88–90.
Lardner, John. "Mr. McCarthy Continues." *Baseball Digest,* February, 1946, 46.
Partin, Clyde. "Lewis Robert 'Hack' Wilson 1900–1948," paper presented at the North American Society for Sport History, May 23–26, 1986, in Atlanta, Ga.
Rothe, Emil. "The Day Hack Wilson Set His RBI Mark." *Baseball Digest,* June, 1973, 80.
Rumil, Ed. "He Hoops It Up for the Red Sox Now." *Baseball Digest,* March 1948, 14.
Shutt, Timothy Baker. "Year of the Booming Bat." *Sports History,* September 1987, 26-33.
Sporting News, October 2, 1930.
Sporting News, January 1, 1933.
Steadman, John. "King Hack Wilson." *Baseball Digest,* February 1990, 65.
Stull, Dorothy. "Conversation Piece: Rogers Hornsby." *Sports Illustrated,* September 10, 1956, 32-34, 64.
Stump, Al. "Better Then or Now?" *Baseball Digest,* May 1959, 61.
Vass, George. "Hall of Famers Who Got Away." *Baseball Digest,* December 1979, 40.
Verducci, Tom. "Feasting On Rib-eyes." *Sports Illustrated,* June 15, 1998, 38-43.
Wilks, Ed. "The Year When Hack Wilson Put It All Together." *Baseball Digest,* January 1972, 56.
Wilson, Lewis. "How I Became Sunny Boy." *Baseball Digest,* October 1959, 17.

Newspapers
Atlanta Constitution
Chicago Sun-Times
Chicago Tribune
Martinsburg Journal
New York Sun
New York Times
Seamheads.com
Virginia Pilot

Interviews
Tony Cuccinello, August 1991.
Al Lopez, June 1992.
Frank Thomas, 2008.
Ron Santo, 2008 (interview by Carrie Muskat).
Josh Hamilton, 2008 (interview by T. R. Sullivan).

INDEX

ABOUT THE AUTHOR

Bill Chastain began his journalism career as a Tampa-based freelance writer, writing stories for publications such as *Nation's Business, SPORT Magazine, Baseball Digest,* the *Sporting News, Tampa Bay Business Journal,* and *Inside Sports,* before working as a reporter for the *St. Petersburg Times* and the *St. Petersburg Evening Independent.* Chastain went to the *Tampa Tribune* in 1990 and worked for 12 years as a columnist and sports reporter, during which time he also served as a correspondent for *Sports Illustrated.*

Chastain worked as an adjunct professor at the University of South Florida, teaching magazine journalism, and has gained a high profile in the Tampa Bay area through radio and TV appearances and various speaking engagements. Currently he works for MLB .com covering Major League Baseball's Tampa Bay Rays.

Chastain is the author of *The Steve Spurrier Story: From Heisman to Head Ball Coach,* a biography of the former University of Florida and Washington Redskins football coach; *The Streak,* a baseball novel; *Payne at Pinehurst: The Greatest U.S. Open Ever,* a narrative about the 1999 U.S. Open played at Pinehurst and won by the late Payne Stewart; *Steel Dynasty: The Team That Changed the NFL,* about the Steelers dynasty coached by Chuck Noll; *Purpose and Passion: Bobby Pruett and the Marshall Years;* and *Peachtree Corvette Club,* a novel. Chastain lives in Tampa, Florida.